MW01174856

So this is the world
& here I am in it

The Writer as Critic Series, exclusive to NeWest Press
Smaro Kamboureli, Series Editor
$24.95 CDN • $19.95 US

IX: *Apocrypha: Further Journeys* by Stan Dragland
ISBN 10: 1-896300-63-4 • ISBN 13: 978-1-896300-63-4
*Writers' Alliance of Newfoundland & Labrador Rogers Cable Non-Fiction Award 2005

VIII: *Lyric / Anti-lyric: Essays on Contemporary Poetry* by Douglas Barbour
ISBN 10: 1-896300-50-2 • ISBN 13: 978-1-896300-50-4

VII: *Faking It: Poetics and Hybridity* by Fred Wah
ISBN 10: 1-896300-07-3 • ISBN 13: 978-1-896300-07-8
*Gabrielle Roy Prize 2000

VI: *Readings from the Labyrinth* by Daphne Marlatt
ISBN 10: 1-896300-34-0 • ISBN 13: 978-1-896300-34-4

V: *Nothing But Brush Strokes: Selected Prose* by Phyllis Webb
ISBN 10: 0-920897-89-4 • ISBN 13: 978-0-920897-89-8

IV: *Canadian Literary Power* by Frank Davey
ISBN 10: 0-920897-57-6 • ISBN 13: 978-0-920897-57-7

III: *In Visible Ink: Crypto-Frictions* by Aritha van Herk
ISBN 10: 0-920897-07-X • ISBN 13: 978-0-920897-07-2

II: *Signature Event Cantext* by Stephen Scobie
ISBN 10: 0-920897-68-1 • ISBN 13: 978-0-920897-68-3

So this is the world & here I am in it

DI BRANDT

THE WRITER AS CRITIC: X
Series Editor: Smaro Kamboureli

Copyright © Di Brandt 2007

All rights reserved. The use of any part of this publication reproduced, transmitted in any form or by any means, electronic, mechanical, recording or otherwise, or stored in a retrieval system, without the prior consent of the publisher is an infringement of the copyright law. In the case of photocopying or other reprographic copying of the material, a license must be obtained from Access Copyright before proceeding.

Library and Archives Canada Cataloguing in Publication

Brandt, Di

So this is the world & here I am in it / Di Brandt.

(Writer as critic ; v. X)
Includes bibliographical references.
ISBN-13: 978-1-897126-09-7
ISBN-10: 1-897126-09-3

I. Title. II. Series.

PS8553.R2953S6 2006   C814'.54   C2006-905286-7

Editor for the Board: Smaro Kamboureli
Cover and interior design: Katherine Melnyk
Cover image: Aganetha Dyck, "Lady in Waiting." Photo by Sheila Spence, 1995.

 Canada Council for the Arts   Conseil des Arts du Canada   Canadian Heritage   Patrimoine canadien   edmonton arts council

NeWest Press acknowledges the support of the Canada Council for the Arts and the Alberta Foundation for the Arts, and the Edmonton Arts Council for our publishing program. We also acknowledge the financial support of the Government of Canada through the Book Publishing Industry Development Program (BPIDP) for our publishing activities.

NeWest Press
201–8540–109 Street
Edmonton, Alberta T6G 1E6
(780) 432-9427
www.newestpress.com

1 2 3 4 5 10 09 08 07

PRINTED AND BOUND IN CANADA

for Eunice

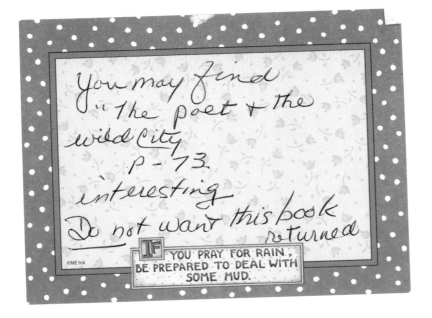

You may find
"The poet & the
wild city
p - 73.
interesting
Do not want this book
returned

IF YOU PRAY FOR RAIN,
BE PREPARED TO DEAL WITH
SOME MUD.
©ME Ink

Among the Keres, "context" and "matrix" are equivalent terms, and both refer to approximately the same thing as knowing your derivation and place. Failure to know your mother, that is, your position and its attendant traditions, history, and place in the scheme of things, is failure to remember your significance, your reality, your right relationship to earth and society. It is the same as being lost—isolated, abandoned, self-estranged, and alienated from your own life.

Paula Gunn Allen, "Who is Your Mother?" *The Sacred Hoop*

Once you recognize that you were robbed, then you have a place to begin.

Maria Campbell, *The Book of Jessica*

it wasn't about being Mennonite, or Indian, or Jew:
it was about you, you.

di brandt, *mother, not mother*

She is the sound of the mad dreams of some of this world's people who still think that the mountains are fed by her story and cause the hilly grass to grow and the waters of the spring to crash back to the sea.

Martín Prechtel, *The Disobedience of the Daughter of the Sun*

Table of Contents

Illustrations

This land that I love, this wide, wide prairie

It is impossible for me to write the land. This land that I love, this wide, wide prairie, this horizon, this sky, this great blue overhead, big enough to contain every dream, every longing. How it held me throughout childhood, this great blue, overhead, this wide wide prairie, how it kept me alive, its wild scent of milkweed, thistle, chamomile, lamb's quarters, pigweed, clover, yarrow, sage, yellow buttercups, purple aster, goldenrod, shepherd's purse, wafting on the hot wind, hot clods of dirt under our bare feet, black, sun soaked, radiating heat, great waves of heat standing in the air, the horizon shimmering, flies buzzing endlessly, wasps, bees, cicadas under the maple trees, dripping with sap, the caragana hedges brushing the air lazily, heavy, golden with blossoms, the delirious scent of lilacs in bloom, hot pink begonias, marigolds, sweet peas, spider queens, wild yellow roses, crimson zinnias, baby's breath, the cool fresh smell of spruce, jack pine, elms gracefully arching overhead, asparagus, cucumber, radishes, onions, peas, beans, corn, raspberries, strawberries, chokecherries, gooseberries, blackberries, yellow currants, red currants, Japanese cherries, cantaloupe, watermelon. It was heaven, the prairie was, the gift of its bounty accepted easily by us, her children, running barefoot all summer, through the garden, the fields, feet hating the constriction of shoes in the fall, the return to school desks and books and sweaty silence. The hot dry smell of wheat during harvest, the sexy smell of our own skin, bellies, thighs. The call of crows, killdeer, sparrows, kingbirds, barnswallows, robins, orioles, nuthatches, woodpeckers, blue jays, mourning doves, the surprise of toads, little frogs, earthworms after rain. The bellow of cows, the cool west nuzzle of calves' noses, the grunt and snuffle of huge pink sows wallowing in dirt, the squeal of newborn piglets, soft newborn kittens in the barn. How I loved you, how I love you, how I love you.

This stolen land, Métis land, Cree land, buffalo land. When did I first understand this, the dark underside of property, colonization, ownership, the shady dealings that brought us here, to this earthly paradise? Our thousand acres of prime black farm dirt, waving with wheat, barley, flax, oats, corn, alfalfa, and later, sugar beets, buckwheat, yellow rapeseed, corn. Our many fields patched together painstaking, passionately, laboriously by our father, with devoted help from our mother, field by field, bank loan by bank loan, from a single field and two-room shack in the 1940s, shortly after the war, into a large, modern farm in the sixties and seventies, debt-free, fully mechanized, flourishing. Was it the time our mother searched through our winter drawers for underwear and stockings, to give to the long-skirted, kerchiefed, brown-skinned woman who walked across the fields from her teepee camp a few miles away to our door, hands outstretched? Who was she, we pestered our mother, where did she come from? Why does she need to ask us for things? Was it when I first read about our Canadian history in grade six, where I first heard about the Hudson's Bay Company and the founding of Rupert's Land, vast land holdings across the prairies in what had previously been First Nations and Métis territories? The sale of Rupert's Land to the newly established Canadian government in 1869, we found out, was followed by the arrival of numerous immigrant groups to take up farming in what had previously been uncultivated grasslands. These had not been fair negotiations; there were numerous resistances to land treaties forced upon First Nations and Métis peoples after the unscrupulous slaughter and disappearance of the buffalo, their main livelihood, culminating in the great Riel Rebellion of 1886. And later, in Mennonite history class, I heard about our own arrival as a people, a group of a thousand land-poor peasants from Ukraine, by ship and then Red River wagon, to what became known as the West Reserve, near the United States border, in the newly formed province of Manitoba, in 1875. So we would have been part of the agricultural project of the newly formed Canadian government, and one of the reasons for the Métis rebellion. Was it then I began to doubt the purity of our fathers' pacifist stance refusing to fight in the war, choosing to go to CO camp in northern Manitoba to cut timber instead, or even, in some cases, enduring imprisonment, refusing to defend the land with their bodies, their hands, while at the same time clearly benefiting from the territorial struggles that created Canada? And yet there was betrayal involved for them, too: the Governor General had promised them "exemption from any military service" as a condition of their immigration to Canada (Zacharias 30).

It was something else, something unspoken, invisible yet tangible in the air, in the vibrations of the rich black prairie soil under our feet, a memory, lingering in weeds, in grassy ditches, on the edges of fields, a wildness, a freedom, faint trace of thundering herds of buffalo and men on horses, whooping joyfully, dangerously reigning them in for the kill, unbroken prairie, sweet scented, rustling, chirping, singing, untamed, unsubdued, stretching to the wide horizon, women and children sitting around a campfire, the smell of woodsmoke in the air, the incessant beating of drums. There was no getting hold of this memory, this ghost, this whiff of another world, another way of life, no way to see it, or understand it, and yet it was there, in the wind, calling to us, plaintive, grieving, just beyond the straight defined edges of our farms, just outside the firm rational orderliness of our disciplined lives. I spent many hours during adolescence following its scent, alone, escaping the house and yard, tracing its outline, its beckoning shadow in the clouds, in bushes, in forgotten bits of prairie near creeks or bogs, in our twenty acres of pasture out back behind the yard, still unbroken grassland, buzzing with crickets and grasshoppers and flies, redolent with wildflowers and cowpies and sage.

There was another memory, too, hidden in my blood, my bones, that sang out to me sometimes in that place of newly broken prairie, an older memory, of a time when the women of my culture had voices and power and freedom, and their own forms of worship, across the sea, out on the green hills under the moon, in the Flemish lowlands of northern Europe, a sturdy peasant life, deeply rooted, before the persecutions, the Inquisition, the Burning Times, the drowning times, the hanging times, before we became transients, exiles, hounded from one country to the next, seeking refuge from wrathful authorities who hated our adult baptisms, our democratic communities, our refusal to bow down to priests and kings. Before the violence of the persecutions got internalized in our psyches and we began inflicting them on each other, the same violent subjugations of body and spirit the Inquisitors visited upon us. Only we did it secretly, in our homes, we did it to our young children, so no one would see us, we did it to our blossoming young men and women, with ritual beatings and humiliations, so they would have no voice, no will, no say of their own. Our women were kept bound with rules of humility and obedience, as servants to the masters, their husbands who owned all the land, owned everything, and went to church with heads held high, proud in their democratic brotherhood, proud in their tyrannical lives at home.

The first time I went to an Aboriginal moon ceremony near Winnipeg, a few years ago, at night, in the bush, with a group of women, led by Anishinabe elder Myra Laramee, I had a strong sense of recognition coursing through me: I remember this, I remember this, my body sang. I remember when we gathered, my women ancestors, around fires like this one, free-spirited, surrounded by trees, not so many centuries ago, before we were made to tremble under the wrath of God, the vengeful One, and his long-armed, heavy-handed henchmen, our bishops and fathers. I remember when worship meant laughter and dancing and lovemaking under the moon, carelessly, instead of sternly remembering the torture of innocence, and fearing the night, and obeying our husbands, and sitting still in church.

This man's land, owned and plowed and harvested by men. And the women kept as servants and slaves. When did I first understand this, that the women had no place, no voice of their own in the Mennonite farm village economy, even though they worked as hard as the men, keeping huge gardens, and weeding and canning all summer long, and cooking and sewing and cleaning year round? Even though, according to traditional Mennonite land inheritance customs, all the children inherited equally; even though the seed land for our farm was our mother's bridal inheritance. Was it the time my father ostentatiously brought out the black farm book, where he kept his accounts and his field notes, after dinner, and announced it was time for our brother to begin learning about how the farm was run, and my sister Rosie and I crowded round, full of curiosity, and he sent us to help our mother do the dishes instead? Was it then I began to hear the hypocrisy of our fathers' endless talk of religious community and anti-hierarchy and brotherhood? Was it the time we joined a 4H sugar beet club, and our dad said, no, only boys can grow sugar beets, and he sent us to pull weeds in our brother's acre all summer instead? (I always loved the weeds more than the cultivated plants, they were prettier, wilder, they smelled nicer, I admired the way they kept coming back, insisting on their right, their place on the prairie.) And at harvest time our brother had a record yield and made a lot of money, several hundred dollars, and when we complained about the unfairness of it, our dad ordered our brother to pay us for our labour and he gave us each a dollar. (It still sticks in my throat.) Was it the many times we watched our mother swallow her disappointment, her disagreement, her own wishes, her needs, in deference to our father? And later, there were calves, entire fields, a series of new motorcycles and trips across the country, a half share in a new pickup truck for our brother, and for us, five cents a pound for picking raspberries and strawberries all morning in the summer heat, if there were customers for them, which came on a good day to 35 cents in our pockets. And strict rules about how we could spend it and where we might go. And eventually, a half share in the entire farm for our brother. And for us, disapproval, endless disapproval, for our women's bodies and dreams, going off to the city to find our own lives, with no parental support, our mother's eloquent, unspoken dreams of freedom and adventure raging in our blood, unacknowledged.

When the Governor General Lord Dufferin visited the Mennonite settlements on the Manitoba Reserve in 1877, two years after their arrival en masse from Ukraine, he found, as historian William Schroeder tells it, a beautifully decorated arbour in which three young Mennonite girls in lace kerchiefs were serving hot lemon seasoned tea, surrounded by flower bouquets wrapped in poetic lines of welcome, in German, hung on little pine trees. After listening to the Mennonite Bishop's welcoming speech, His Excellency addressed the gathering of a thousand or so new immigrants thus:

> Fellow citizens of the Dominion, and fellow subjects of Her Majesty: I have come here today in the name of the Queen of England to bid you welcome to Canadian soil. . . . You have left your own land in obedience to a conscientious scruple. . . . You have come to a land where you will find the people with whom you associate engaged indeed in a great struggle, and contending with foes whom it requires their best energies to encounter, but those foes are not your fellow men, nor will you be called upon in the struggle to stain your hands with human blood—a task which is so abhorrent to your religious feelings. The war to which we invite you as recruits and comrades is *a war waged against the brute forces of nature*; but those forces will welcome our domination, and reward our attack by placing their treasures at our disposal. It is a war of ambition, for we intend to annex territory after territory—but neither blazing villages nor devastated fields

will mark our ruthless track; our battalions will march across
the illimitable plains which stretch before us as sunshine
steals athwart the ocean; the rolling prairie will blossom in
our wake, and corn and peace and plenty will spring where
we have trod. (104-5)[1]

Schroeder does not specify how the Mennonites received His Excellency
the Lord Dufferin's speech, so liberally sprinkled with military metaphors. I
imagine they grimaced and recoiled from this language, reminiscent as it must
have been of recent persecutions suffered at the hands of the Russian military,
and other military persecutions before that. Still, the weird, contradictory
combination of warfare and husbandry, conquest and cultivation of land, the
convenient blanking out of its recently displaced inhabitants and devastation
of First Nations cultures, the split attitude toward the prairie he articulated is
a deadly accurate description of Mennonite farming practice in Manitoba as
I knew it, growing up in Reinland.

How come, I remember asking my dad, if the wheat is poisoned by the
red stuff you've sprayed on it before seeding, to kill bugs, poisoned enough so
we can't taste handfuls of it anymore as it gets poured into the seeder troughs,
how come it won't poison us later when it grows new plants, too? Every year
(while the US and USSR were building bombs), there were new pesticides, new
herbicides, bigger machines, fancier equipment to disseminate them more
quickly, efficiently; every year the chemicals became more poisonous, as the
weeds became hardier to withstand them, as the pesticide companies and seed
companies grew larger to sustain and control this burgeoning market. My
father scoffed at safety measures against pesticides. He remembered spraying
DDT all over his bare arms to ward off flies, before it was banned. And
look at me, he'd chortle, healthy as an ox. He was annoyed at new spraying
restrictions as they arose. He died of cancer at age sixty-one.

My brother quit farming at the age of forty-seven and left the community
in desperation, due to environmental illness, almost certainly caused by
exposure to pesticides. And that was the end of Elm Ridge Farm, my father's
thousand acre dream, which we sacrificed so much of our lives for, his carefully
stitched together playing field, so unsolid after all, scattered back into the
hands of strangers. The end of our family's many centuries old way of life.
Here is how Harvey, my brother, described his symptoms shortly thereafter,

in a letter from Calgary, Alberta, where he has been extensively treated by a doctor specializing in chemical sensitivities through the past decade:

> My weakened body has begun to react to fumes besides farm chemicals like automobile exhaust, commercial cleaners, fabric dyes, glues, ink, paint, perfumes, and scented personal care products. My body reacts instantly when exposed to these. Different fumes will cause different symptoms to occur. Fatigue and exhaustion are usually the end result. I have done very little driving during the past year due to fatigue and loss of muscle control. Driving is also affected by loss of vision due to cataracts in the lenses of both my eyes. (Letter to the author, May 15, 1996)

In a little more than a hundred years, we, the immigrant settlers of this beautiful land, have managed to poison the land and our food sources and our own bodies so drastically as to jeopardize the future of all life in this country. The birch trees in the Pembina Hills close to our farm village, which we used to visit every fall to admire their flaming orange colours before the onset of winter, are dying. The rivers are being choked with reeds and fungi, because of fertilizer run-off in the water systems. Many people in south central Manitoba, in the heart of Mennonite farmland, are dying of cancer, MS, pneumonia, leukemia, all of them victims of damaged immune systems and, indisputably, environmental pollution. There are very few birds now, very few frogs, toads, gophers, foxes, deer, very few wildflowers and prairie grasses left. It is the same in other farming communities across the nation, and elsewhere in this province. It is the same in other provinces and countries across the globe.

In all those years of listening to preachers preach to us, every Sunday, in the Mennonite village churches, endlessly exhorting us to repentance, to a more ethical life, not once did I hear a single one of them talk about the land, except to pronounce gleefully that we "shall have dominion over it," a special permission, a decree from God, though, on the other hand, paradoxically, we should not go to war to defend it. Not once, in all those lists of sins— fornication and lust and desire and whatnot that we were endlessly warned against—not once did I hear one of them talk about an ethical practice of

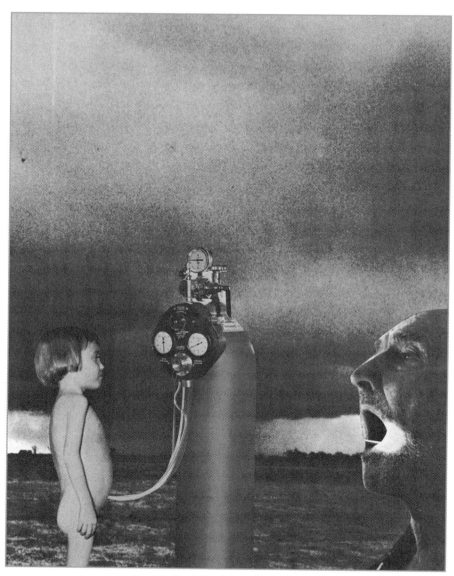

Fig. 1 Lydia Chiussi, "Euphonia," 1996.

land ownership, or address the politics of gender and race, the economics of chemicalization, the dangers of pesticides and herbicides and fertilizers, or the implications of genetic manipulation of seeds and livestock, for the land and the creatures in it, and for our own bodies. Quite the contrary: much of Christian doctrine, as we were taught it, was precisely about turning our gaze away from the beauty and call of the living natural world to a symbolic invisible one located somewhere vaguely in the sky. When I became a vegetarian at age twenty and began cooking organically, my father said, "You're trying to sabotage my farm."

Like almost all farmers in the modern era, he was a victim of economic exploitation by multinational corporate interests, my friend Owain Jones pointed out, which are profit rather than health driven, and proliferate false propaganda about the environmental risks of chemicalization. We were walking along the beach of the Moray Firth, in northern Scotland, on the edge of the North Sea, where we were attending an environmentalists' conference. Owain's passionate outburst—his father was a Welsh farmer, and his family story is similar to mine even though he's a son, not a daughter, and was not brought up in a separatist, migrant culture, and lives on another continent—startled me into empathy for my father, who worked so hard to provide for us, who so loved his farm. Empathy for my mother, who had so much imagination and feeling, and so little decision-making power. Empathy for my people, the Mennonites, who didn't realize they were being swindled by the promise of riches into corporate practices they wouldn't have approved of if they'd understood them. Empathy for the citizens of Canada who have worked close to the land, in good faith, and been implicated in so much exploitation by the corporate powers who were organizing giant, and as it turns out, potentially lethal, takeovers, without declaring themselves. Empathy for the First Nations and Métis peoples of Turtle Island who signed treaties, albeit under duress, with strangers who practised duplicity, that put their inheritance and the future of this great land in jeopardy. It has been the same, and worse, in other countries around the globe.

This is why I weep, sitting on a wooden verandah in Winnipeg not far from the Forks, where the Red and the Assiniboine Rivers meet, on a beautiful tree-lined street canopied by great green elms, on this beautiful July evening, in this prairie landscape that is still heaven, still paradise on earth, despite the volatile weather, the bugs, the mosquitoes, the endangered earth and air, because I remember, somewhere my body still remembers, when it wasn't so, when this beautiful land was unconquered, unsubdued, unbroken, when the people of this land tried to live in harmony with its shifts and rhythms instead of in violent conquest over it, when the creeks and ditches were filled with frogs and meadowlarks and red-winged blackbirds and butterflies and wild clover and bees, instead of sprayed grass, when the fields were grazing grounds for wild herds of buffalo and antelope and deer, instead of straight hard rows of chemically altered grain.

There is regret in me, regret I feel deeply, sharply, here in my belly, sometimes, so I can hardly breathe, for this slow dying prairie, how she lost her stupendous wildness, forever, around the time my great-grandparents came to settle the dispossessed First Nations territories, to break them, to plant their rich farms and gardens, that I am so grateful for, so sad about. It is why I cannot write *the land*, because I am torn inside over it, my implication in its demise as lawful, unlawful, heir to it, dispossessed, in exile from it, my helplessness in the face of such massive destruction, my ongoing love for the prairie, how her beauty still catches my throat, her power, majesty, so much bigger than we are. There is still time to turn it around, to save the land, undo its massive poisoning, the scent of prairie on the hot wind, calling out to me, my love, *eck lev dee*, *ni-ma-ta-ten*, I'm so sorry, *ki-sa-ki-hi-tin*, I love you.

Listening to Christine:
Telepathy, ambivalence and the future in
Mavis Gallant's *The Pegnitz Junction*

How are we to understand Christine, the twenty-one-year-old protagonist of Gallant's celebrated novella, *The Pegnitz Junction*, a young woman with highly unusual telepathic powers, accompanying her thirty-one-year-old lover Herbert and his child little Bert from a week-long rendezvous in Paris, back home through the stunned post-war German landscape, through the Pegnitz Junction? We don't know very much about her, except that she has a second lover back home, a young theology student, her fiancé, that she has told a lot of lies to her relatives to manage this rendezvous in Paris, that they will come to meet her at the station when she gets home, and that she lightens her hair with camomile instead of commercial bleach, "because of some vague promise she had given her late grandmother when she was fourteen" (4). So she is a woman surrounded by family, then, rooted in family, and yet here she is, drifting between lovers, between the slightly pompous, slightly ineffectual Herbert, a professional engineer and a pacifist, whose wife left him without warning, abandoning their child to him, and the theology student, at the moment buried in books, preparing for exams (which he failed the first time), reading Bonhoeffer, a younger and perhaps less impressive contender, though surely more approved of by her relatives.

Remarkable in this story is the way Christine receives "information" from the surrounding world, not at all like Herbert, with his scrupulously correct facts, meticulously collected and neatly, logically presented, in a manner quite oblivious to the feelings or imagination of either their subject or the listener. Christine's information, on the other hand, comes to her erratically, intuitively, empathically, though without much effort on her part, in the form of "fine silver crystals forming a pattern, dancing, separating, dissolving in a glittering trail along the window" (23). Her information is not scientific, it does not add up to an organized set of data, with strategies or conclusions. Rather it comes as bits of people's inner voices, replaying the detailed, trivial, mundane recollections of their lives, as they sit mulling through old thoughts, in the train or out waiting in the station next to her. It is not particularly useful information to her. She has no way of connecting it with anything. It comes to her randomly and unbidden, out of context. Nor does she share this information with anyone. Unlike Herbert who likes to state his facts to other people, impressing them with his efficiency and knowledge, Christine merely observes these random bits and pieces of people's lives. She seems curious and often mesmerized by the information, interrupting her conversation with Herbert and little Bert to listen in on her neighbour's inner monologues, and in this way she has some choice, some power over the information, though unlike Herbert, who would have authoritative and dismissive responses ready for each one if he heard them, she reserves judgment on it.

Later in the novella the information seems to be coming in all jumbled, like "dirty cinders" or "mud," instead of crystals (85). Christine despairs of making sense of it, no longer enjoying it, feeling it to be more "interference" than information, since it may as easily, she thinks, represent "old and tarnished stuff which had come to her by error" (85) than any sort of illumination. This is so even when it is information about Herbert, her lover, whose memories of the ex-wife who ran away are not efficacious to either of them, she realizes, but merely annoying. We too are no longer mesmerized by all these bits of stories scattered across the German landscape like garbage, the debris of people's lives, what's left over after the shaping events of their collective and individual histories have occurred. Like Christine, we see that what's happened has happened, and though people persist in circling round and round over their past pleasures, and particularly their past grievances, there is nothing to be done about them. Nothing changes, nothing can be changed. And information about it, whether in the form of people's particular responses to small crises such as the train being late and the conductor's rude behaviour, or whether in the form of inner reminiscence, is merely that: information, without knowledge or wisdom or release attached.

Gallant commented to Geoff Hancock in 1978 that the novella represents a kind of "personal research" into the origins of fascism in Nazi Germany, not in the large historical sense of investigating its causes in political structures and movements, but rather, a close-up look at "its small possibilities in people" (Hancock 41). Most readers, it would seem, have understood these "small possibilities" for fascism, as we see them spelled out in the small-minded, fearful and antagonistic gestures of Gallant's parade of characters through the novella, to be normative in the text, so that Christine's moment of disillusionment represents little more than confirmation of a more general psychic paralysis. Neil Besner, for example, describes the German stories as "articulating a specifically German psychology of inertia and bewilderment, enacting postwar German culture's dazed introspection into its own recent history," though he hastens to add that "the 'Fascism' Gallant recreates in these stories is both more generally Western and more particularly human than a specifically German political, cultural, or emotional aberration" (67). George Woodcock sees the collected stories in *The Pegnitz Junction* as representing "the emerging world of modern Germany which the Nazi age has cut off like a black curtain from the traditional past" (83). Janice Kulyk Keefer identifies Gallant's narrative style in the novella and companion stories with the postmodern sense of alienation from history and cultural memory: "chaos and order leak into one another, creating an 'interference' that prevents the novella's recording consciousness from ever relating any one thing she hears to any other" (159).

Each of these critics accepts Christine's moment of despair about the usefulness of information about the past as representing an overall pessimism in the novella about the present state of Western culture, after its dismally violent record through two world wars with their unthinkable atrocities and paralyzing after-effects. Unlike Margaret Laurence, say, who in a moment of illumination and reflection has her character Morag Gunn in *The Diviners*, an ocean removed from the war and its numbing effect, exclaim: "*A popular misconception is that we can't change the past—everyone is constantly changing their own past, recalling it, revising it. What really happened? A meaningless question. But one I keep trying to answer, knowing there is no answer*" (49). By the end of the novel Morag has formulated a kind of dictum regarding her revisionary strategy, one that acknowledges both responsibility to "what really happened" and the large creative possibilities inherent in rearranging our individual and collective histories, in order to move forward: "*Look ahead into the past, and back into the future, until the silence*" (370). For Gallant, in *The Pegnitz Junction*, observing the frightened, belligerent, small-minded postwar German citizenry trying desperately to salvage some sort of personal dignity in the face of so much shame, so much unthinkable pain from what one small cultural group leader calls "the Adolf-time" (70), such extravagant rewriting of history is clearly, at least for this moment, this time of stunned recollection, with its necessary denials and petty avoidances, impossible.

But then there's Christine. Her telepathic powers are more than a clever narrative device on Gallant's part to move us through a pastiche of vignettes about German citizens on trains. Though they are certainly that too—I remember very well the first time I read this novella and the impression it made on me, the impact of the surreal German landscape and its people mediated through Christine's precise, clear gaze. Is she a visionary? Is she schizophrenic? Is she a modern-day mystic developing extra-sensory perception like Doris Lessing's Linda Colby and Martha Quest in *The Four-Gated City*, in response to the increasingly complex technologization of our world, and as a hedge against electronic failure? Here's Gallant's comment about her:

> She is not inventing or making up stories. Everything that the young woman sees when she looks out the train window, she really does see. A kind of magic, if you like. To my mind, a short circuit. She really does know all these stories. She really does know what has happened to everyone. Someone wondered if she was schizophrenic. No. There is a German expression, 'I can hear him thinking.' I've always liked that. I could hear him thinking. Because one does very often. (Hancock 65)

If there is hope in this narrative, surely it rests here, in the extraordinary capacity of this character, a young woman of twenty-one, on the cusp of her life, wavering between the possibilities of conventional family life and marriage, and the unpredictable challenges of staying with Herbert and taking the place of his runaway wife, little Bert's absent mother. Her ability to receive intimate information about people in the form of "silvery crystals" (23), as well as simply accurate perceptions about people, signals this one citizen's ability to transcend the petty egotism of the rest with intelligence, imagination and genuine empathy for the other. Such empathy, as philosopher Emmanuel Levinas has observed, is a minimal requirement for an ethical state (82-5). In this sense, Christine's knowledge challenges us to similarly open ourselves to information about people in the world around us, and as readers, to pay closer attention to her experience. Christine's empathy, most often, does not take the form of affection for the people she meets and recognizes; it is not, for the most part, empathy in the sense of identification or fellow feeling, but rather a rare ability to *see through* people's disguises and bluffs to what they're really about. This ability extends not only to strangers but also, significantly, to her lover, Herbert, with his authoritarian and hypocritical foibles and mannerisms. Her increasing disillusionment with the "information" she receives on the train ride from Paris to home suggests her increasing recognition of her countrymen's and -women's spiritual paralysis, and perhaps also, sadly, her own increasing absorption in it.

There are two significant exceptions to this trend. The first is her encounter with Sigi, the sorrowful man she meets at the unnamed frontier station on the way to Pegnitz, who is looking across the barbed wire barrier to the villages on the other side, remembering his family's near escape from Nazi persecution somewhere close to this location, in a daring midnight run across a dark field, into the waiting arms of co-conspirators. Christine's encounter with Sigi is deeply moving in this narrative, both in the depth of her recognition of his terrible war-time experience, in the midst of this deaf and dumb and unfeeling crowd, and in the accurate, intuitive response she makes to his reminiscences at this unnamed and desolate frontier spot, even though they do not speak to each other in words:

> She saw that he knew she knew everything; the expression on his face was one of infinite sorrow.
>
> What are you doing here? she tried to ask as they nearly met. Why spend a vacation in a dead landscape? Why aren't you with all those others in Majorca and Bulgaria? . . . Decide what the rest of your life is to be. Whatever you are now you might be forever, give or take a few conversions and lapses from faith. Besides, she said, as they silently passed each other, you know this was not the place. It must have been to the north. (60)

Gallant chooses not to depict the war and its atrocities as melodrama; she absolutely resists the kind of impersonal exhibitionism and righteous moralizing we often see both survivors and witnesses tempted by in the media and in Hollywood, even now, a half-century later. Gallant talked in her interview with Hancock about what it was like for her, as a young journalist in Montreal, to witness the first concentration camp photographs arriving in 1945:

> You can't imagine the first time seeing them. I kept saying, 'We're dreaming. This isn't real. We're in a nightmare.' . . . Now, imagine being twenty-two, being the intensely left-wing political romantic I was, passionately anti-fascist, having believed that a new civilization was going to grow out of the ruins of the war—out of victory over fascism— and having to write *the explanation* of something I did not understand. (40)

It is easy to imagine Gallant's personal identification with the twenty-one-year-old Christine, with her open eyes and intuitive spirit, as witness to the war and its effects, and to see here in her intimate and yet distant encounter with Sigi next to the barbed wire frontier still manned by police guards with guns and dogs, reflections of Gallant's own face to face encounter with the dilemma of its survivors.

I am challenging, then, Gallant's early unsympathetic reviewers, John Hofsess and William Pritchard, for example, who saw her as "evad[ing] responsibility for saying or caring very much about her characters and their situation [in the name of aestheticism]" (Hofsess 4), and "never confronting her philosophical paradoxes [and accepting] the irrational without a fight" (Pritchard 21). I am also questioning insightful, sympathetic later critics such as Besner and Ronald Hatch, who nevertheless concur in emphasizing the hopelessness of this narrative: "None of the characters is able to see the past as creating the present" (Hatch 102), and "Recent history is a nightmare from which the characters cannot awaken" (Besner 70). Interestingly, the question survivors must ask themselves, as Gallant depicts it here, is the same question witnesses and those who participated more directly in the war must ask: how to go on from here? In this sense the novella resists (re)drawing official battle lines; each person is first of all human, each person is responsible for his or her own subjectivity, even though each participates also in the larger group with its affinities and culpabilities.

The other exception to Christine's increasing absorption into the cultural malaise around her is her response to little Bert, who strikes her at the beginning of the novella as an annoying child, with his high-pitched voice, his emotional neediness and jammy hands. She is equally annoyed with Herbert's overprotective and often hypocritical parenting. "She would never marry Herbert," she thinks as they board the train in Paris, "—never. Not unless he placed the child in the strictest of boarding schools, for little Bert's own sake" (13). And yet, as the narrative progresses, it is Christine who increasingly takes over the parenting of little Bert, making up funny little stories for him and protecting him from getting lost on the trains, though often interrupted by the unimaginative Herbert, who fails to appreciate her playfulness with him. "Whatever happens," she says to him suddenly, fiercely, near the end of the novella, "we must not become separated. We must never leave each other. You must stop calling me 'the lady' when you speak to your father. Try to learn to say 'Christine'" (79-80).

As Besner insightfully points out, Gallant reverses an earlier "tableau" here to signal a character's emotional growth. As Christine leans against little Bert at the Pegnitz station, feeling "his comforting breath on her arm" (80), we cannot help but recall how earlier on the Paris train, the child stood next to her, "breathing unpleasantly on her bare arm, commanding her to read about Bruno" (12). For Besner, this reversal "communicates little Bert's metamorphosis into a child from a 'little (Herr)Bert' for Christine, and it also conveys Christine's need for human contact" (91). What strikes me most, however, in this scene and the moments leading up to it, is Christine's own gradual metamorphosis into a maternal figure, into a mother for little Bert. In a novella abounding with absent, runaway, imprisoned, dead mothers and petty-minded, mean-spirited grandmothers, this is no small thing. In fact, if we look at *The Pegnitz Junction* in maternal narrative terms, what we see here is quite an amazing reconstruction of the deeply important bond between child and woman from a surprising source.

Think about Christine as the young, uncommitted, deeply ambivalent, two-timing lover of two men, the self-righteous engineer and the failing theology student. Think about her as the deceitful, lying daughter of a devout family, who has to tell a web of lies to steal a week of "emancipation" (5) with Herbert and little Bert in Paris. Think about her as the self-absorbed two-bit fashion model, self-conscious, judgmental, inexperienced, barely past school age, who can see quickly through people's pretences as indeed children and young people can, and yet not know what to do about any of it. "She was at one of those turnings in a young life where no one can lead, no one can help, but where someone for the sake of love might follow," writes Gallant (4). And yet it is Christine, not Herbert with his single-minded vision, his inability to "be captivated in the same way by two people at once" (4), who becomes the moral centre of the story, insofar as there is one. It is she who approaches most clearly the position of sympathetic parent to the affection-hungry little Bert and his beloved adopted sponge and alter ego, Bruno. It is she who learns, for the sake of love, to follow her instinct, her gut feeling, despite Herbert's constant reproaches and interferences, and despite the stupefying cultural message written large all around her, to not care, not pay attention, not notice. It is she who engages imaginatively, and therefore ethically, with the child, who needs her.

If Alice Miller is right in her claim that the psychic roots of Nazism lie precisely here in the broken interchange between children and their parents, between dependent child and caretaking adult, so that children grow up not having their feelings validated and therefore deeply vulnerable to the authoritarian and sadistic claims of a cruel, eloquent, totalitarian leader who promises spiritual and political liberation (65-74), then we must attach great significance to Christine's maternal gesture in this moment. Perhaps it is not accidental that the interior voice she hears most often on the train is Frau Joseph Schneider's, the nasty-minded American immigrant widow who has come back to tend her unloved dead husband's grave so she can collect the $800 allocated for that purpose in his will. Frau Schneider's monologues are filled with invective and petty old grievances gone sour in the mouth, and yet, I recall, she made the greatest impression on me of anyone in the novella (after Christine) the first time I read it, mainly because of her astounding catalogue of food, where she lists all the meals and dishes she cooked for other people over a lifetime of domestic work. We do not see much emotional mothering coming from her, either in the present or in her mental life review, but what we do see is the tremendous amount of nurturing and dedication involved in simply cooking for people, day in, day out, over many years. We also see the extraordinary bounty of the earth, with its rich variety of vegetables and fruits and grains and meats, enough to feed the world, if we can figure out how to tend and manage it equitably and well.

Near the beginning of the novella, it occurs to Christine that she is expected to behave "like a mother" to little Bert, that in fact she has been brought on this trip to see whether or not the two of them can get along. Feeling caught in a triangle of admonishments from Herbert about the child, she considers how she "might blackmail little Bert if ever she married Herbert" (10). She is immediately ashamed of this thought, recognizing it as "an inherited method, straight from her late grandmother's velvet parlor" (19). In fact, most of the mothers and grandmothers we see on this train ride through Germany do blackmail their children, making them look and feel older than their elders. One thinks of the little gang of sweaty girls on their way home from camp, and how deflated their "bossy" leader, the "little gangster," looks as she gets off the train, only to receive admonishment from her mother for her tardiness, in the name of the waiting grandmother nearby, with her ostentatious humility and endless selfishness (22). Clearly the kind of parenting Gallant has in mind as a solution to the moral paralysis of postwar Europe is not of the humble martyr kind, with its inevitable reversals and betrayals. Christine's recognition of her own grandmother as "blackmailer" (20) and her resistance to Herbert's authoritarian overprotectiveness of little Bert, on the one hand, and lack of imaginative empathy, on the other, begs another model of parenting that might take into account the child's emotional experience, his own inner truth.

There is very little of this latter kind of healthy parenting in *The Pegnitz Junction*, but we catch a glimpse of it in the final moment of the novella, where Christine affectionately turns to little Bert, and insists on telling him the story, finally, without interruption or interference from Herbert or anyone's inner voices. The story, the one she's been trying to invent for him all the way from Paris, is about Bruno, the adopted sponge who soaks up so much love and attention, and his many siblings. "Bruno had five brothers, all named Georg," she begins. "But Georg was pronounced five different ways in the family, so there was no confusion. They were called the Goysh, the Yursh, the Shorsh" (88). Christine's insistence on imaginative, metaphorical language, squarely against Herbert's repeated emphasis on reasonableness, and her playful proliferation of individual nicknames for the generic brothers with their single identity, suggests the rebirth of creativity in this broken landscape. Besner makes a similar point in his reading of this scene: "The fact that Christine's last word is a story about brotherhood and community, told to a child, indicates at least the hope for a new direction, out of the destructive and repetitive cycles suggested throughout" (92). Christine's resistance to interference and information without meaning, further, signifies that she is no longer "passive in life," but ready to take charge, to assume responsibility, to set off in "some wild direction" (4) as she has wanted to do for some time.

What does Christine have that the other characters in the novella don't have? Is it not her very ambivalence, her inability to choose between the two lovers that Herbert so chides her for on the train, her unwillingness to accept definitively either of less than satisfactory life options, that gives Christine her moral edge? Is this not where her courage lies, to resist the emotional paralysis around her, to lie and cheat, if necessary, her way into "emancipation," freedom, and so, willy nilly, to create new possibilities? Theologian Christine Keller has called such inability and unwillingness in oppressed subjects to choose between negative options "constructive ambivalence," describing it as "not a matter of lukewarm indecision but of a rather precise contrast of affirmation and negation, resembling the Taoist logic [of] neither/nor *and* both/and" (24).

Anthropologist Lewis Hyde identifies ambivalence, along with the urge to lie, cheat and steal, as qualities of the trickster, a central figure in all traditional cosmologies. The trickster, according to Hyde, possesses not only amoral appetite, cunning and folly, qualities we are familiar with in the Western tradition through the ritualized figure of the clown, but also, transformative powers that belong, generally speaking, in the realms of prophecy and shamanic transformation: "Where 'truth' does not satisfy appetite, an artus-worker will find the weak joints in supposed essences and open them up. In trickster's world, appetite is a pore-seeking power, and thus the appetites prophesy. Their prophecy reveals the hidden joints holding an old world together, the hidden pores leading out. If you don't believe it, try keeping Hermes away from your cattle; try keeping Monkey out of the orchard when the fruit gets ripe" (292). In these ways, Hyde explains, the trickster reveals the available plenitude of the world, hidden to us because of our routine structures of order which filter out the muddy ambiguities existing everywhere, the "DNA junk" between lettered codes, in wait for us to discover and refashion them anew. The rediscovery of the world's plenitude therefore includes not only sensuous pleasure but also linguistic multiplicities: "Motley-in-motion can be refigured as the babel of tongues, and its mental reflection as the polyglot mind" (299).

Think of Gallant's depiction of Christine, listening to the random messages being thought all around her on the train, as we read Hyde's strikingly similar description of the trickster's motley recognitions: "The prophetic trickster points toward what is actually happening: the muddiness, the ambiguity, the noise. They are part of the real, not something to be filtered out. Many messages arrive simultaneously, each in a different tongue. Inexhaustible meaning, inexhaustible language, inexhaustible world, it's all the same" (300). Is this not how the hapless, undecided Christine is able to respond to little Bert, because she is willing to follow, in the midst of her directionless bewilderment, her own free-spirited curiosity and desire, so that she sees him not as a reflection or mini-version of herself, the way Herbert sees him, but as an other, a separate being, with his own needs, his own pulsing, independent life spirit, though firmly in her care? "[As] if he were someone she loved but was not afraid of losing" (Gallant 87), she thinks, as they sit waiting for the train at the Pegnitz Junction, telling stories.

That crazy wacky Hoda in Winnipeg: A brief anatomy of an honest attempt at a pithy statement about Adele Wiseman's *Crackpot*

Hoda the hooker, Hoda the fat whore, Hoda the neighbourhood misfit who turns her social misfortune energetically and enterprisingly into profit and laughter, Hoda the confused teen mother who gives birth in the middle of the night in terrified isolation to an unanticipated boy child, to be abandoned immediately after on the steps of the Winnipeg Jewish Orphanage with only an enigmatic note suggesting princely origins, "Good old Mamma Hoda" (274), who holds onto her ardent private grief, and mothers a generation of sons into sexual adulthood, in whose generous rolling flesh we find the democratic mixture of the seed of both Jews and gentiles, so that her child has at least ten unidentified fathers and no mother, or rather three adoptive ones, including herself, Hoda the designated offspring of "the poorest, most unfortunate, witless creatures" (21) in the Russian Jewish village of her ancestors, married with hasty ceremony in the graveyard according to an old legend to ward off the plague and the threat of pogroms, Hoda the chosen one, both spit upon and admired, born of desperation and representing hope and new beginnings, Hoda the immigrant daughter, promise of a new life in the New World, first-generation Canadian, Hoda, whose own dream of a rescuing prince, son or lover, vaguely derived from a blending of Messianic, ancient classical heroic and British colonial myths, culminates in a nightmare of *CONDOMS, PRURIENCE, INCESTRY*, in a grotesque parody of Winnipeg's motto, Commerce Prudence Industry:

Who is this Hoda? Or rather, how is this Hoda, this implausible, grotesque, lusty, larger-than-life promiscuous female survivor of plagues, pogroms, police brutality, neglect, and abuse, and nevertheless an inheritor of and believer in grand dreams, and dispenser of huge portions of love and pleasure, how is this Hoda *us*? If Hoda signifies Winnipeg, both the place, the landscape, the city, and its citizens, "stirring the muddy waters in the brimming pot together" (304) at century's end, as prophesied in Hoda's mixed up dream at the end of the novel, what kind of Winnipeg is it that Adele Wisewoman (as Birk Sproxton has informally dubbed her), or Wildwoman (as I want to call her) gives us in this crazy, crazy novel? And to what end? Wiseman once admitted she wanted to be known as "Manitoba's foremost insensitive, indelicate, pushy, loud, offensive lady writer" (1970, 101). In the story of Hoda, the brashy North End loudmouth intimidated by no one, she gets her wish.

Character- and plot-wise, *Crackpot* is surely the most ambitious, outrageous novel ever written about, or set in, Winnipeg. Wiseman has set herself the impossible task of depicting *sympathetically* this promiscuous, business-minded, socially challenged fat woman, who barehandedly knocks down city police during a riot otherwise known as the Winnipeg Strike, and not only copulates with nearly every man and pubescent boy in the city including her own son, but in spite of and even because of it all, ends up a respected, almost respectable, and certainly loved member of the community. Wiseman goes further. She would have us believe in Hoda's essential innocence. She would have us believe an old bizarre legend about the doomed offspring of village idiots, how they can through the blessing of the community become, paradoxically and unreasonably, its salvation. She would have us identify with Hoda and her complicated, tragic but triumphant life. She would have us identify with every mother's son who comes to sink his loneliness in her gaping flesh, gasping his eager too quick love.

This is about as far away as you can get from, say, Carol Shields' late century Winnipeg in *The Republic of Love*, where the women are polite, demure, prudent, and professionally successful; where despite the shakiness and unpredictability of contemporary marriage conventions, reasonable women like Fay MacLeod vow, after one or two unhappy encounters, never to have casual sex again, to hold out for romance and marriage instead. And they get it, in fairly traditional terms, complete with balloons, clouds, roses, extravagant love letters and promises of till death do us part. Characters may harbour temporary feelings of insecurity and unhappiness with respect to intimate relationships and even their work, but are nonetheless securely independent, socially and economically. Together, they make up the civilized web of intricate interconnections that constitutes Shields' urbane vision of the contemporary cosmopolitan post-AIDS city. She calls it Winnipeg in this novel, but it could be any city in the so-called developed world, with a few minor variations in street names and details in weather conversation—what landscape has been reduced to in the generic post-industrial scene, Shields' oeuvre.

On the other hand, Hoda, unusual and striking as she is, bears a surprising resemblance to a number of women in recent Manitoba fictions: Prin, for example, Morag Gunn's obese, inept, well-meaning adoptive mother in *The Diviners*; Tomson Highway's Black Lady Halked of *Dry Lips Oughta Move to Kapuskasing*, promiscuous drunken mother of the hapless alcohol-damaged Dickie Bird, who gives birth to him in a bar in a grotesque parody of Christ's birth in a sheepfold; Armin Wiebe's fat good-natured Oata Needarp, in *The Salvation of Yasch Siemens*; and Shields' own Mercy Goodwill in *The Stone Diaries*, from another time, roughly contemporaneous to Hoda's, whose private indulgence in sensuous eating has made her obese enough to hide a full-term pregnancy even from herself, and whose girl child is orphaned, like Hoda's little Pipick, through Mercy's untimely death during her sudden, unexpected childbirthing. And there are other such large mother figures in contemporary prairie writing, such as Hiromi Goto's inarticulate mumbling masturbatory bronco-riding grandmother, Obachan, a.k.a. "The Purple Mask," in *Chorus of Mushrooms*. Add your own to the list.

What's up with that, as Ian Ross, a.k.a. Joe From Winnipeg, might ask. The great Canadian mother as white whale, Moby Jane of the Prairies, Good Old Manitoba Mama. Here is evidence of the self-proclaimed multicultural stance typical of Canadian prairie thinking, so different from the revolutionary "melting pot" American fantasy, forever obsessed with abandoning home and lighting out to the frontier, the open road, or escaping lawlessly to sea. More traditionalist and domesticated, but also, interestingly, in Thomas King's words, "slightly wild, more out of hand, disorderly, even chaotic" (1993, 312), freedom from the mother/land, from home, after all not necessarily signifying freedom from such institutional dynamics as expansionism and corporate control of local resources and the New World Order. The white whale à la prairie depicted here not as booty, as raw material, as quest object, but as maternal body, struggling for consciousness, agency, voice. The mother story birthing itself out of the traditional blank in great gasps of pain and labour. The industrially generated orphan plot rewriting itself as culturally specific abandonment of both child and mother, as tragic rift between them. The immigrant settler narrative writing itself from exile and forgetting into remembering, recreating the mother-child connection, a sense of history and tradition, of home. The prairie landscape not as wilderness to be exploited but as sustaining body, as living breathing (adoptive/biological) mother. Hello: "I love you."

But why promiscuous? Why incestuous? In an interview with Roslyn Belkin, Wiseman explained she wanted to explore narratively the "best possible reason for the worst possible deed" (151), as in Hoda's supreme act of love in resisting her maternal impulses toward the boy David, after recognizing him as her lost son, when he comes to pay tribute to the neighbourhood prostitute like every other pubescent boy. Instead of embarrassing or rejecting him, she takes his money (sent to him secretly from her own savings), and lets him "make love" (241) to her instead. In Francis Kaye's reading of the novel's morality, it is "not that good can come out of evil, but that good can, miraculously, endure evil. And telling the story somehow enables the endurance" (88-89). But what is good and what is evil in this upside-down, carnivalesque world? In the last few pages the aging Hoda becomes respectably monogamous, having found a man whose emotional suffering in the Nazi camps matches hers in depth and horror, a man who loves her. But that significant shift in her social status due mainly to age and circumstance does little to mitigate Wiseman's unrestrained celebration of illicit sexuality throughout the novel, nor to undo its unrelenting dark vision of human experience. There is no censure of the many husbands and boys who visit Hoda to get their rocks off for pay; in fact, they are portrayed with much greater sympathy than their indignant prudish stay-at-home wives. Nor is there any criticism for Danile, Hoda's foolish blind father whose steadfast refusal (or is it simply inability) to look reality in the eye, or to contribute in any substantial way to his own keep, catapults the young Hoda into her life of prostitution.

The only targets of moral criticism are the downtown pimps who beat their whores, and child molesters: Yankl the butcher, for example, who initiated young Hoda into her livelihood by demanding fellatio behind the meat counter for supper scraps. And Limprig, the Orphanage director who was found to be, alas, too fond of his young female charges, and is moved to the Home for the Aged as punishment. The latter instance becomes significant in Hoda's own life. Having heard the story told impassively by her Uncle Nate, she is unmoved by it until "Daddy got so upset, and was so disgusted, and cried out in Yiddish against human baseness" (199), and then, writes

Wiseman, "something came to life in her, shards of an irrevocable Hoda, buried all these years in her own flesh, searing through her to a lost wholeness . . . The instant of illumination was like an electrocution . . . *You don't do that to children*" (200). The realization does not take her out of her sordid, varied life in the moment. The restoration is internal. Yet it marks the significant turning point in her life toward social restitution.

Above the local Jewish community that is Wiseman's focus hover the oppressive spirits of Western capitalism, nationalistic government and anti-Semitism, which contribute to and in many ways cause the narrow-mindedness and suffering of the community. These oblique but ubiquitous institutional presences are confronted briefly in such incidents as Hoda's accidental participation in the Strike, and her schoolgirl suffering at the hands of the anti-Semitic, prudish teacher Miss Bolthrumsop (dubbed "Bottoms Up" by the students). The most dramatic of these incidents is Hoda's triumphant jumbled speech at the Public Health office next to City Hall, where she proclaims loudly to the gathered citizens in the waiting room that Winnipeg's motto should be replaced in light of free-wheeling entrepreneurs like her friend Hymie's, international bootlegger and millionaire, with "a picture of a big, naked arse, and underneath it just two words, 'RISK IT!'" (217).

Hoda's outsider status, then, to not only mainstream Winnipeg and Canada, but also her own local Jewish neighbourhood, is what enables her to conduct a life of economic and psychological independence and lively social interaction with a large community, in contrast to the neighbouring wives with their narrow minds and lives. Reading this novel together with *The Diviners*, which came out the same year by Wiseman's best friend Margaret Laurence, one can't help noticing similarities: both novels are on the side of sexual and economic freedom for women; neither is particularly impressed by the conventions of marriage; neither tries to recuperate the "family" at the end of the story, though both narratives turn on the irrevocable bond between mothers and their children. Both insist on an authentic emotional life for women, no matter what its cost; both value tradition in the form of old legends and memories of the past, while promoting cross-cultural tolerance and understanding. In both cases, the plot is open-ended, with little sense of comfort or closure for either the children, who leave to make their own way in the world, or their mothers, who celebrate and grieve their going. (Hélène Cixous said that the mother story is not a quest but a giveaway; it begins in plenitude and is inscribed by loss. Its understanding of love is not acquisition, or holding power over, but letting go, letting go, letting go [1981, 53]).

Still, there are important differences. Laurence writes in the realist mode, with subtle layerings of legend and biblical allusion through her characters' names and story-telling. Wiseman writes in the carnivalesque mode, with its deliberate flouting of convention and authority, in the name of the amoral earthy body and its needs. From the point of view of the body, what means promiscuous? What means incestuous? Both are simply manifestations of the ubiquitous power of the sexual urge, which drives every living being to copulate and procreate. As with Native trickster myths, the appropriate response to carnival is laughter rather than judgment, since by its parodic performance of social conventions, morality is shown to be artificially and arbitrarily constructed, and therefore (re)negotiable. Carnivalesque writing grossly exaggerates events and characters to make its point; Hoda in this sense is, as Ellen Gordon observes, herself one long "ironic conceit" (73 n.7). It's important, too, to keep in mind the communal aspect of carnivalesque writing: isolating a single character's actions for judgment is contrary to the intersubjective nature of human relations and responsibility. Carnival plays on the sensibility of "shame"—the neighbours are watching, and you too have been caught coming out of the dirty shed in the backyard, we're in this together—rather than the more isolationist, righteous, finger-pointing dynamic of guilt. This of course makes any attempt at simple moral interpretation of the novel problematic.

Magdalene Redekop, in her quirky and brilliant study of Alice Munro's fiction, *Mothers and Other Clowns*, identifies Munro's mother figures as "mock mothers," or clowns, whose foolish performance "challenges old symbols of maternity" (120), such as the Virgin/Whore binary that has kept women in Western culture bound to impossibly elevated images of motherhood. Redekop identifies the figure of Mother Folly, who presided over medieval fool festivals, as an important predecessor, citing William Willeford's description of her:

> The momentary abrogation of the Pope's authority in the joke
> of the fool festival allows the representation of the feminine
> within the cult, the Virgin and the Bride of Christ, to be
> opened to kinds of femininity that are excluded from that

representation. Within the cult, selfless maternal compassion is represented, but jealous rage is not; chastity is represented, but whorishness is not . . . During the fool festival the walls of the pure feminine vessel admit for a moment the coarse and seemingly chaotic vitality of the Mother Nature to whom the fool belongs. (Cited in Redekop 121)

Redekop reads Munro's use of maternal clowns deconstructively: that is, not as a ritual catharsis of potentially subversive cultural elements as in the medieval rite, but as a narrative recipe for women's liberation from traditional Western stereotypes, a collapse of the old divine comedy.

It is provocative to set Willeford's medieval Christian allusion next to the kabbalistic legend referred to by Wiseman in the novel's epigraph, credited to a text by sixteenth-century Jewish mystic Isaac Luria:

He stored the Divine Light in a Vessel, but the Vessel, unable to contain the Holy Radiance, burst, and its shards, permeated with sparks of the Divine, scattered throughout the Universe. (Cited in Sherman 3)

Kenneth Sherman has traced the structural significance of the Lurian legend in *Crackpot*, delineating its three crucial phases and the way they are played out in the novel: the "self-limitation or exile of God"; the "breaking of the vessel"; and the "harmonious correction and mending of the flaw" (33). Sherman argues for a happy ending: "The broken vessel has been mended, and a vision of universal inter-action, sexual as well as spiritual, is promised to all" (11), essentially through the redemptive agency of Lazar, Hoda's late-blooming lover, who offers both love and a link with her own history as a Jew, with his stories of survival in a German death camp.

All this may be so, but I'm with Redekop in wanting to interpret this novel's ending as revisionary rather than merely restorative—unless we think of restoration in the widest possible sense, reaching all the way back to prehistorical matriarchal modes, whose unrestrained celebration of maternity remains available to us through sculptural images of the grossly exaggerated pregnant female body, such as the Venus von Willendorf's.

Since Lazar first appears in the text fifteen pages before it ends, he can only

Fig. 2 Venus von Willendorf, c. 25,000 years old.
Naturhistorisches Museum, Vienna, Austria.

function as *deus ex machina* with regard to agency. While his appearance is a powerful reminder of Jewish experience on the other side of the Atlantic—a history Hoda and her family have luckily escaped in its fullest impact, though not in its ongoing resonances by emigrating to Canada—his presence provides little answer to the maternally centered, chaotic narrative that is Hoda's life. Hoda, after all, long ago gave up the hope of a rescuing prince who would offer her fame and fortune. Even her own son, pompously named David Ben Zion, whose mysterious origins invest him with a princely and even messianic aura in the community, and who, according to the legend that haunts his own and his mother's birth, signifies hope and the promise of a better future for Jews, disappears without ceremony near the end of the novel. This after having been taken down from saintliness by his own swaggering nickname for himself, "Prince David Pipick Ben Zion MacFuck, the fastest trigger in the West!" (236): an epithet that the narrator ruefully tells us "turned out to be true" (236) during his first visit to Hoda after much neighbourhood boasting among the boys.

Nor is there oedipal, biblical, or any other kind of punishment in this narrative for the shocking act of mother-son incest. As with Moll Flanders, another lusty fictional character whose sexual escapades made her a successful immigrant to the New World several centuries ago, unwitting mother-child incest is one of the inherent risks of mothers separated from their children, by reasons of necessity or accident, at birth. What happens to genealogical anxiety if women copulate and procreate and go on living outside of marriage—as indeed they do, Laurence and Wiseman both declare, where marriage and the conventional "family" are found to be inadequate in protecting and nourishing the feminine? Let it go, say these novels, live with it. Nothing is certain anyway. Even if you know who your kid is, look what can happen. You can't control the future. You can't control people. You can't control the wayward, unpredictable reproductive process. Don't even try.

But do use condoms, says Wiseman. Don't sleep with a man whose child you couldn't bear to bear, says Laurence, in a more prudent vein. Take care of the needy among you, so that the desperation of mothers forced to abandon (or abort) their children may be avoided. And love love love your children, no matter what. They're what we've got, our link with the future, our true loves, what we've been given, accidental or chosen, whoever, wherever they are. That deep, irrational bond between parents and children, biologically and adoptively, individually and communally, is after all, these novels passionately argue, what makes us human.

What about Wiseman's seemingly casual endorsement of mother-son incest in this context, though? Although deeply and universally understood as the founding principle of human sociality and kinship structures, observes Elizabeth Barnes, the incest taboo seems to be up for redefinition whenever societies are experiencing major cultural shifts (1-13). Oedipus, for example, as Evelyn Reed has argued, found himself caught between two irreconcilable systems, an older matriarchal system that privileged mothers and their brothers (and denigrated husbands as tolerated outsiders) and the emergent patriarchal system that privileged fathers and their sons (at the expense of mothers). He literally didn't "know" who his kinsmen were (457). In the English developmental novel, which documented the rise of industrialism and the cultivation of individuality, primarily through the destruction of traditional extended family systems, exploitation of the working classes, and enslavement of African peoples, incest often assumed the reverse side of the fear of racial and class contamination (Yoshikawa 358-376). In pre-Nazi Germany, the term *Blutschande*, which originally signified pollution of the bloodline by sexual contact among relatives, gradually came to signify pollution of the bloodline by violating the outer boundaries of the German race as well. Fear of incest and cross-racial contamination, meanwhile, was projected by the dominant white population onto its eroticized and racialized other. In nineteenth-century English and American literature, Jews were frequently typecast as incestuous, and Blacks as sexually voracious (Yoshikawa 361). In light of this history, Wiseman's emphatic celebration of racial impurity and the impossibility of defining or controlling genealogical bloodlines through the control of maternal reproduction carries great political import. Not only does she reverse the paternalistic logic of Oedipus and the Oresteia by re-enacting the mother-son incest that was its founding moment and then condoning it, but she also revalorizes the persecuted matrilineal ethnicities that lingered covertly throughout this same history, flouting the racist and matriphobic legacy of Europe and North America by simultaneously flaunting and denying the charge of inbreeding and social disorder in the ghettoized Jewish community. "For you I will be/the incestuous Jew," she is singing in this novel, much as Leonard Cohen does in "The Genius" (Cohen 78-79), putting on the guises of anti-Semitism the better to escape it. These are trickster moves, in

Lewis Hyde's sense of the term, altering the prevailing social myths through sly subversion from within, slipping the traps of exclusion through parody and cunning (Hyde 17-38).

On the other hand, Wiseman in no way condones the sexual abuse of children. Yankl's sexual violation of the young Hoda behind the butcher's counter for meat scraps is less threatening to the purity of the family bloodline than her own lovemaking with her son David in the prostitute's shack. Yet Wiseman emphatically denounces the former and condones the latter, clearly drawing a line between acts of violence and acts of love and generosity, their spirit and intention easily trumping legal and biological ramifications. Hoda's motive in providing sexual services to her son is, after all, generously and wholesomely inclined; she does it to prevent her son's public embarrassment, standing in line with his buddies to visit the neighbourhood whore. That is, she swallows up his potential ignominy by simultaneously enacting her clearly defined maternal function of nurturing her son, and giving it up, by accepting her designation as illegitimate, communally owned prostitute in its stead. Or to put it another way, she gives up the name of the mother in order to be a mother: a conundrum many women under patriarchy have faced and variously negotiated.[1] As Marie MacLean points out in her aptly titled study, *The Name of the Mother*, the lack of their own names under the Law of the Father enabled mothers to negotiate fluid identities throughout patriarchal history. These negotiations often partook of the carnivalesque through inversions of proprieties from which these mothers were excluded, but also envisioned social utopias beyond the order of the Law (1-11). The history of Jews in Christian Europe, many of whom practised their laws and rituals in secret to prevent persecution, follows a similar parabola of covert identifications, carnivalesque inversions and trickster escapes.

There is another level of subversion as well. Peter Stallybrass and Allon White make much of the "grotesque" body, "protuberant, fat, disproportionate, open at its orifices" (183) in their investigations of the carnivalesque, as a necessary correction to the purified classical body with its discreet foreclosure of physicality in a pretense of autonomy over animality. Carnival, they write, "denies with a laugh the ludicrous pose of autonomy adopted by the subject within the hierarchical arrangements of the symbolic at the same moment as it re-opens the body-boundary" (183-184). They have in mind the boundary between body and mind, but the reopening of the body-boundary can also be understood as a recognition of the border blur between body and surrounding environment. This is how Hoda becomes not only figurative, but literally representative, of not only earthiness but also earthliness, the human body as microcosm of Winnipeg, the prairie, the earth itself. If one of the projects of Christianity and modern capitalism, its heir, was to annihilate traditionalist local knowledges in Europe and around the globe that "kept local peoples synchronized with the rhythms of place"—as it had previously been the project of Judaism in the Middle East (Keller 147)—then Wiseman's recuperation of the intimate metaphorical and literal connection between human body and earth-body is a grand revisionary gesture indeed.

Interestingly, despite her more literal identification of the maternal subject with earth, and land, and the mineral/plant/animal body, Wiseman's conception of "place" is considerably more urban than Laurence's. The cities of *The Diviners*, Winnipeg, Toronto, London and, briefly, Vancouver, are barely sketched, compared with the rich landscape of the Wachakwa Valley near Manawaka, where Morag grows up, and the river and frogs and geese and herons near McConnell's Landing, where she spends her middle age. Wiseman's Winnipeg, by contrast, is a detailed city of streets and back alleys and verandahs and woodsheds and public buildings, a city with policemen and welfare workers and factories and public health. Hoda's Jewish neighbourhood may seem village-like in its customs and close-knit relations, but she herself roams far beyond it into gentile territory, participating in socialist meetings and even getting involved in the Strike. The prairie landscape, on the other hand, makes its appearance only in the occasional brief reference to birdsong or a flowering hedge. Even Shields has more prairie in her cosmopolitan, generic Winnipeg, albeit mostly in the form of "weather," what landscape has been reduced to in the electronic media.

Wiseman's caustic essay, "A Brief Anatomy of an Honest Attempt at a Pithy Statement about The Impact of the Manitoba Environment on my Development as an Artist," contains more prairie landscape than the whole of *Crackpot*. (Thank you, Adele, for the pithy title.) Here's a typical passage, subtitled *"Manitoba, I Hate You"*:

> By the scars of old mosquito bites shall you know him, and by his voice crying out in the wilderness of distant places, aye, even as far away as Toronto, boasting that he

comes from the best place of all to come from, and wild horses wouldn't drag him back to that narrow, provincial, materialistic, intolerant atmosphere (from Toronto!), that unbearable landscape, that unliveable climate.

Besides, he's making a better living elsewhere. And so say all his friends, all ex-Manitobans too, curiously enough.

Axiom: You can leave Manitoba, but you can't leave it behind." (1970, 102)

When Wiseman does get serious for a moment about her topic, she addresses it allegorically:

Logically or no, there are things which I feel about myself as a writer which feel just like the feel of the look of the prairie. Certain qualities have analogous visual shapes for me. I see the landscape of my youth in a certain predilection for epic themes and structures, a certain relentlessness, a stubborn disinclination to compromise, to cooperate even, to accept any other terms than my own. It is difficult to temporize or to evade or to hide when you live in my prairie feelscape . . . The North Winnipeg I grew up in was the very incubator of conflicting absolutes. I relate my tendency to go for broke, to try to make an equation for the secret of the universe every time I sit down to the typewriter, to my continuing need to make some kind of total sense of the complex environment of the Winnipeg I knew, the Noah's ark of my childhood, the Tower of Babel of my adolescence. I could go on and admit that I owe a certain marked windiness of style to overexposure at an impressionable age, to the winds of Portage and Main in winter, but I will do no such thing. One should at least be able to call one's flatulence one's own. (105)

It is a truism in Canadian literary studies that most Canadian fiction, even though most writers and most Canadians live in cities, has been predominantly rural based, though that profile is changing now. But we have always had a fine contingent of urban Jewish writers. So many of them have written about cities that the old saying must surely be revised: Mordecai Richler, Leonard Cohen, A.M. Klein, Jack Ludwig, Miriam Waddington, Henry Kreisel, Rick Salutin, Libby Scheier, Ann Decter, Phyllis Gottlieb, Rhea Tregebov, Kenneth Sherman, Carol Matas, Meira Cook, Laurie Block, to name just a few. It is Jewish writers who have shown us how to write *the city* in Canada.

For Wiseman, decidedly urban Canadian, cultural activism in *Crackpot* signifies socialism, defending the cause of workers against capitalist interests, a cause that dates back for Hoda to stories of the old country and her uncle Shem Berl fighting against the Czar. Hoda, practical as she is, believes in both the rights of workers and free enterprise, and operates her own "small business" with a judicious mixture of the two. For Laurence, on the other hand, having escaped the city for a more idyllic rural setting, the moral question is not who controls industry, but whether we should even have it at all, and on what terms. Sitting in her study overlooking her neglected garden, Morag Gunn worries about the increasingly poisoned environment. She feels first guilty about her failure as a back-to-the-land "new pioneer," but gradually comes to celebrate the weeds overtaking the land. Perhaps we have gardened too much, suggests Laurence. The wild no longer threatens us with its vastness, its uncultivatedness, but rather with its possible disappearance altogether under our zealous care.

Ironically, Wiseman has more to say about multiculturalism in Canada than Laurence as well, even though it is never her stated theme, as it is for Laurence. For Hoda, a North End Winnipeg Jew, cross-cultural awareness is simply a fact of life, permeating every centimetre of her experience. For Morag Gunn, growing up Scots Presbyterian in a Scots Presbyterian town, awareness of other cultural traditions and affiliations is hard come by, and its necessity for Morag (and us all) is one of Laurence's main arguments. Significantly, it is Morag's poverty, growing up on the wrong side of the tracks, that enables her to identify with Jules, the Métis boy. Through witnessing his sense of cultural displacement, she remembers her own Scots heritage of displacement from the Highlands. (Perhaps Neil ten Kortenaar is right in criticizing the novel for making too much of the analogy between the Highlanders' and the Métis people's removal from their respective ancestral lands, and not enough of the historical opposition of the Métis to the arrival of the Selkirk Settlers, whose successful immigration spells out ongoing oppression for them [11-35], though Laurence can be commended for tackling settler guilt on this point more vividly and directly than any other non-Aboriginal writer in Canada to date.) For Hoda, whose world is more communally defined, poverty per se is not isolating. Hoda's desperation is caused by the community to which she was born, which is therefore responsible for her experience. One of the best jokes of the novel is the way Hoda manages to claim her family inheritance from stingy Uncle Nate, who has donated his money ostentatiously to the Jewish Orphanage instead of helping out his relatives, through her son David's stay there. Wiseman's plea for cross-cultural tolerance cuts both ways. While she defends Jewish communal life against the pressures and prejudices of the dominant culture, she also argues for opening the community's narrow boundaries to the surrounding world. Her argument for understanding Jewish life in Winnipeg thus extends easily to other minority groups caught in similar positions in Canada.

The Diviners ends with Pique's song album, inherited from her Métis father Jules, proclaiming the survival and triumph of Métis identity in Canada, despite the pressures put on Métis culture historically, and ongoingly, by immigrant settlers. We are all Métis, the novel proclaims, in the sense that we are all, as Canadians, heirs to at least two distinct cultural traditions, foreign and indigenous. Pique's song, "The mountain and the valley hold my name," weaves an intimate connection between people and landscape, in the hope of establishing a sense of home for immigrant culture in Canada, while at the same time renewing the First Nations' sense of home in their own land: a utopian fantasy, perhaps, but is it not a necessary one, if we are to heal the wounds of our traumatically intertwined histories?

Crackpot ends with Hoda's magnanimous vision of a magic circle encompassing all she knows: "Soon, she promised extravagantly, in the ardour of her vision, they would all be stirring the muddy waters in the brimming pot together" (304). In this sense, David the unlucky chosen son, does become the novel's future promise, and its answer; in his blood flow pieces of his many fathers, and in his upbringing are reflected the affections of his several mothers. We are all hybrids, we're all in this together, this novel claims. The phrase "muddy waters" constitutes an oblique nod to the history of First Nations, for whom the forks of the Assiniboine and Red Rivers at the heart of downtown Winnipeg was a historic meeting place.

As Laurence reminds us in her Introduction to the New Canadian Library edition of *Crackpot*, the Cree name Winnipeg means "muddy waters" (8). It is perhaps not a large enough nod in a settler novel describing cross-cultural relations in Canada, but I do think Wiseman's vision opens dialogue with Aboriginal and Métis cultures in other important ways, in its understanding of the communal nature of human society and irreverent celebration of the mother and the earthy muddy human body.

Canada as melting pot, after all, or perhaps, rather, cooking pot, with distinct chunky flavours. Our lives may add up to mere parodies of our ideals, but through them runs the ubiquitous presence of those who brought us here, and those who were already here, in this epic, stubborn, relentless land, our many traditions, our inescapably hungry bodies, and the foolish, eager hopes of our mothers and fathers, our inadequate ancestors who, in spite of their mistakes, and struggles, and tragic displacements, loved us.

"Why do you lie there just shaking with laughter?" Revisiting Dorothy Livesay's *The Husband*

Dorothy and I were drinking coffee in The Green House in the library tunnel at the University of Manitoba. It was the summer of 1991. The cafeteria was closed. We were trying to content ourselves with foul-tasting instant dispenser brew. Dorothy was passing through town on literary business. I was researching a project in the Elizabeth Dafoe Library. Coffee with Dee was a cultural event: she was a keen-eyed matriarch of the Canadian literary scene, full of strong opinions and news. That day she was worried about the experimental writing being done by contemporary women writers such as Daphne Marlatt and Gail Scott. Though she had been highly experimental throughout her own life and work, she mistrusted the theoretical shift toward poststructuralism and deconstruction that swept the North American academy in the mid '80s. She also tended to be harder on women's writing than on men's, perhaps in part because she cared about it more. These were writers whose work I admired, so we were immediately in disagreement.

Changing the subject, I mentioned her novella, *The Husband*, which I had recently read and liked. Still, I ventured, I have a question for you about the ending. I was convinced by everything except the part at the end where Celia, the narrator, sends away her sweet young secret lover and goes back to her unattractive, depressive, aging husband. I don't understand why she did that after feeling so creatively energized by the love affair. I expected a sharp reply but, to my surprise, Dorothy sighed. Your question confirms for me what I felt all the time, she said. The editors convinced me to change the ending, to make it less dramatic and more conventional, more conciliatory toward the husband. I didn't want to, but they thought it would sell better that way. But it hasn't really done that well, and I wonder how many other people feel as you do. (In fact the novella received mixed reviews.)

I was amazed. Was this the same Dorothy whose feisty poems took on the world, unflinchingly facing down factory owners and literary critics and motorcycle gangs, singlehandedly rewriting the code of what's permissible to say about women's sexuality in Canadian print? Of course I didn't know then this novella's history, how it had taken Dorothy more than twenty years to find a publisher for it. Indeed, I had little sense then of the kind of stamina it had taken for Livesay to create her astounding oeuvre altogether, going so persistently and courageously against the grain of the acceptable mainstream with the slimmest of institutional support throughout her long prestigious career.

The Husband was written in 1967, the year Livesay won the Governor General's Award for Poetry for *The Unquiet Bed,* during a writer-in-residency at the University of New Brunswick. It was published in 1990. Several versions of the manuscript were collected among Livesay's papers at the University of Manitoba Libraries' Department of Archives and Special Collections, along with a wealth of other unpublished works.[1] Several publishers have since recognized the merit of many of these works and brought forth new publications, including, most significantly, *Archive for our Times: Previously Uncollected and Unpublished Poems of Dorothy Livesay*, edited by Dean Irvine (1998).

Why did she leave so much high quality writing unpublished? Livesay may have felt *The Husband* was too experimental in both style and subject matter to be acceptable to a Canadian audience at the time of its writing. There is evidence that the manuscript was submitted to Ryerson Press in 1967 and rejected (Banting 179), which is surprising given the success of *The Unquiet Bed* published by Ryerson that same year. As with much of her unpublished work, one has the sense that she spent much more time and energy writing than organizing submissions to editors. Livesay's prefatory "Author's Notes" in the book refers delicately to the twenty-three year hiatus between the writing of the manuscript and its publication, alluding to the distance she often must have felt between the cosmopolitan outlook of her writing and the guarded Canadian milieu: "This [motif of an older woman having an intense love affair with a younger man] had been an acceptable theme in European literature, especially in France, but I believe that in the sixties and seventies it had not yet been explored in Canada. Happily, by 1990, my contribution will have seen the light of day" (n.p.).

The novella is epistolary in structure, consisting of a series of letters written by Celia, a middle-aged housewife and sometimes artist, married to an aging and retired husband named Hugo, who recently suffered a debilitating stroke and is recovering slowly, and without grace. The couple has come from Toronto to Fredericton for a few months in order to be close to Hugo's brother and sister-in-law, George and Lily, and the university community they are part of, and presumably, to reconnect with the landscape of Hugo's childhood during his convalescence. "You have to hand it to an author who can reveal the plot in her foreword and still have you tapdancing through a book to see how it turns out," comments Christina Montgomery in her review of the novella for *The Vancouver Sun* (D20).

Celia's letters are addressed to various people close to her, her stepson David, her sister Maudie, and her former art teacher Max, whom she likes to call "cher Maître." There are also occasional "Notations," private observations sent to no one. The novella documents a fall and winter in the life of Celia and Hugo, during which, feeling displaced in the provincial Maritime town and desperate for spiritual companionship while nursing her morose invalid husband, Celia falls into an emotionally satisfying romantic liaison with a young English boarder named John. After several months of erotic and intellectual companionship between them, Hugo suffers a bad fall, looking for his wife in the night (in fact she was upstairs in her bed, alone, but had left a light on by accident in the living room downstairs), and ends up in hospital with a broken leg.

At this point, stunned by the accident, Celia realizes her first loyalty and duty is to her husband, despite convincing earlier evasions of the same in conversations with both John and Maudie. "I see more clearly now that my loyalty is to Hugo," she confides to Maudie, "because he needs me the most. It is mainly because of me that he has kept going, kept from wishing himself dead. . . . There's no way 'round it, is there? You cannot put your own desires first" (76). She firmly and abruptly dismisses John—for his own sake, as she puts it, not hers: "You must be free to find your own mate, your own age" (77). It is a statement surely fraught with ironies, given the highly problematic age discrepancy in her own marriage.

The novella ends with a hasty—and this is where I find it most unconvincing and unsatisfying—brief gesture of reconciliation between Celia and Hugo. We are asked to believe that the fall has somehow improved this depressed man's spirits, that having to nurse a broken leg as well as a paralyzed one is (mysteriously) uplifting! "Hugo seems much more philosophical—almost his normal, pre-stroke self" (78). Celia, for her part, is suddenly, inexplicably, willing to abandon her own urgent interests, in order to devote herself to "cleaning, cooking, reading to Hugo; or listening to radio or TV, with him" (79). This after nearly a hundred pages of high tension over the lack of enough room to pursue her own desires sexually and artistically in this marriage. Even her plans for painting are, as she tells Maudie, "in blackout," and she hardly has time to write letters now. We might read this outcome as desperate or tragic—as indeed Barbara Gowdy does in her perceptive review of the novella, calling the home Celia must return to a "prison" (C17)—except that the final letters are liberally sprinkled with words like "happiness" and "joy," and the novella ends on what is surely meant to be a symbolic, hopeful note: "Hugo had got the fire going" (82).

I am interested in this novella for many reasons, despite its failed ending. Generically, it is a delicate experiment in telling a complex story through simple but intensely poetic language that somehow belies its slim length: it is a novel written by a poet. The epistolary structure, always difficult to manage plot-wise, here becomes the occasion for a series of opinion pieces by Celia that are part-essay, part-exclamation. Yet, in their profoundly dialogic nature, they achieve the kind of intersubjective communal sensibility we associate with oral and dramatic works. The narrative moves along quickly without a lot of external events happening, driven by Celia's intense inner experiences. It is preceded, unusually, by a list of "The Cast," in which only Celia is designated by profession: "The Artist." The rest of the characters, in an interesting reversal of social conventions vis-à-vis gender, are named only by their social relation to her: "Her Elder Sister," "Her Husband," "Her Boarder." That is to say, it is a profoundly cross-generic, hybrid and slyly experimental text that offers illuminating insights into the limits and possibilities of both genre and gender.

The character of Celia is startling to readers accustomed to Livesay's assured poetic and public voice. Livesay has taken care here to underline the constraints of women who are conventionally married and find themselves in restrictive social situations. Celia is more keenly aware of these constraints than some wives might be, having had a tumultuous relationship with a young "wild" lover, Michael, in her youth, and having grown up, as she recalls to Maudie, "rootless" and "bohemian," in strong contrast to the genteel landed folks she finds herself surrounded by in Fredericton (110). It is fascinating, and wrenching, to see the spiritual contortions Celia undergoes trying to play the patient, dutiful servant wife to the morose depressive Hugo, while desperately—one might argue heroically—trying to keep her own adventurous passionate artistic spirit alive.

It is tempting, of course, to speculate about the autobiographical nature of *The Husband*. The "First Draft" manuscript is unapologetically listed under "Autobiographical Fiction" in the Archives catalogue (*The Papers of Dorothy Livesay*, iii). Pamela Banting confidently asserts in the accompanying archival note that the novella "derives from Livesay's love relationship with a younger man during the 1960s" (*Papers* 179). As far as I can see, this claim is speculative. But we do hear in Celia's intense frustrations, her repeated self-questioning and frequent apologies, particularly to her sister Maudie, a version of the kind of frustration Livesay herself must have felt, and has expressed in her memoirs, living for years in an emotionally unsatisfying marriage, and prevented for many years from earning her own living due to arcane hiring laws, preventing married women from full-time employment outside the home (Stevens 48-54). On the other hand, Celia's character is much less self-assured than the Dorothy Livesay we are accustomed to encountering in her essays and poems.

Kristjana Gunnars, in an archival note on Livesay's bibliographical clippings, observes that almost all newspaper profiles on her work described her "as either someone's daughter, someone's wife, a housewife, and later as someone's mother and grandmother. Seldom is the writer spoken of as a writer only." Livesay, comments Gunnars, "has always faced some form of conflict between her self-image and her strongly held convictions. Her press and journal coverage goes a long way in explaining this conflict" (22). Celia's highly conflicted self-identification as dutiful wife, on the one hand, and expressive artist, on the other, can be read as a version of Livesay's own long-time struggle to be both a woman and a free spirit in Canada in a time when these categories were considered to be mutually exclusive.

Perhaps, as Celia observes to John, the French and the Italians are "much more reasonable about these matters" than Canadians, accepting triangles as a normal part of the marriage arrangement. Certainly the notoriety around the Clinton-Lewinsky affair in the mid '90s suggests that North Americans in general are not comfortable with a narrative involving adultery, even in the much more conventional configuration of older married man and single young woman, however many people are actually indulging in versions of marital unfaithfulness secretly. In Hollywood, adultery most often still ends in death for one or other of the adulterers, most often the woman. (Adrian Lynes' *Fatal Attraction* and Woody Allen's *Crimes and Misdemeanors* come to mind.) Perhaps we are simply more duplicitous about these things than the Europeans: I know of many women who do carry on extramarital affairs, either secretly, or with the knowledge of their partners, in a '60s-inspired "free love" or discreetly "open marriage" arrangement, even though such ideas have fallen into strong public disfavour since the discovery of AIDS and the backlash against feminism in the '80s and '90s. Some would admit they are having secret affairs to rejuvenate themselves in unsatisfactory marriages or long-time relationships, juggling the personal satisfactions of secret affairs with the public obligations and privileges of marriage with a certain degree of discomfort. Some use heterosexual marriage as a screen to carry out clandestine lesbian affairs, feeling for various family or public professional reasons that coming out is too costly; others discover an affair to be an unconsciously intentional dramatic action that propels them outside of a relationship or marriage, into happier circumstances and arrangements. In this matter, as so often in her career, Livesay was in the vanguard of arguing for women's independence and freedom, both professionally and erotically, though not without a sense of accompanying social responsibility, caring for those one has committed to caring for, not taking advantage of the young, and so on. The novella does not end with death for the heroine, as it surely would have a hundred years ago (even in France), and likely still would in mainstream America, but with a restoration of domestic peace and harmony for the married couple, and increase in emotional fulfillment for all three people involved.

The Husband holds many additional delights. The cosmopolitan, literate Celia indulges in keen observations about the social niceties of New Brunswick society, steeped, as she experiences it, in provincialism. One of the novella's prominent themes—one might argue its major theme—is a multi-faceted discussion about aesthetics. There is the lively ongoing conversation with John, the young lover, about the relative merits of objectivism and expressionism. He, as the "poet," is a mouthpiece for a pared down modernist imagism; his collection of poems is called *Still Lives: a precise delineation of the object seen*, a poetics to which Celia, painter and narrator, adds Livesavian socialist consciousness and passion: "I fear the artists in this area," she writes to Max, "although experimental and original, have not come to terms with such subject matter. Could it be that emotion is lacking? The feel for the pleasure of work, that you'd find in Russia or China?" (33) There are numerous engaging discussions between Celia and John along these lines. Celia is interested in Huxley's observation in *The Doors of Perception* that, in Livesay's paraphrase, *"at most times and most places men have attached more importance to the inscape than to objective existence, have felt that what they saw with their eyes shut possessed a spiritually higher significance than what they saw with their eyes open"* (52). She rejects, however, Huxley's explanation for this traditional obsession with "inscape," and derogatory attitude to the "outer world," as articulated in the following passage: *"Familiarity breeds contempt. And how to survive is a problem ranging in urgency from the chronically tedious to the excruciating. The outer world that we wake up to every morning of our lives is the place where, willy-nilly, we must try to make our living. In the inner world there is neither work nor monotony"* (52). Celia is careful to distinguish between the mystic's sense of escape from the phenomenological world of the senses, as described by Huxley, and her own celebration of cosmic mystery, which incorporates a full-bodied appreciation of the robust physical world. Neither does she accept a wholly materialist objectivist approach to the outer world, in which nature is seen as a dispirited assembly of discrete matter, available for dissection and analysis without regard to its ecological integrity. In this popular contemporary paradigm, subjectivity becomes, of necessity, narcissistic and even pathological, "a mental world," in Celia's words, "more squalid and more tightly closed than even the world of conscious personality" (53). It is a condition exacerbated by the emphasis of modern psychoanalysis on the self, isolated from the outer world of the political and the phenomenological. For Celia, by contrast, inscape and outer world are spiritually, psychically and physically connected to each other; their relationship is best apprehended through emotional and erotic engagement with the beloved, through intense close-up encounters with the regenerative beauties of nature, and through the powerful medium of art, which takes us, magically, to the "impersonal" heart of things: "Colours suddenly relate to each other . . . and to forms. It is inexplicably 'right'" (53).

Livesay's deep connection with nature, a prevalent theme in her poetry, finds eloquent expression in Celia's lyrical description of the rural landscape around Fredericton, mediated through eroticism and art. Here is one such passage:

> Sunday turned out to be lovely—crisp and cool. Not enough rain had fallen to carry off the leaves, but just enough frost had nipped them. John drove me, in his light green Volkswagen, along the river and then up behind it into hilly farm country. He had found an old farm on a little creek, with an abandoned field in front—some old apple trees, surrounded by sloping banks, flaming with hardwood. There were aspens, maples, oaks, as well as small bushes of wild grapevine, a deep blood red. And red berries of the thorn tree, somber spikes of sumac. I didn't know where to begin! First I sketched the house—all tumble-down, from inside, sun falling on the tipsy floor through a window; and beyond, that fiery forest. This perhaps will be the most dramatic picture. Then I wandered down near the banks of a creek, all soft with pine needles and fallen leaves—splashed colour. (52)

Diana Relke has pointed out that a prominent aspect of Livesay's political project is her attempt at poetic mediation between the natural world and the human community, which in the modern world exist, as Livesay sees them, in a state of mutual alienation (148). In order to accomplish this monumental task, Livesay seeks to "explode the illusion that culture can possess nature; we may invade it and occupy it but this does not mean that we know it on its own terms" (Relke 149). But for Livesay the wildness and free-spiritedness of nature are not awe-inspiring or sublime in the Romantic sense, nor found far away on steep mountaintops. These qualities are rather intimately interwoven into the human domestic context; we too possess free-spirited natural wildness, her writing suggests. It is what animates our sense of beauty, eros and pleasure. It is the essence of our life spirit, and is best expressed in the language of metaphor, the language of intimate relationship, as well as appreciation of strangeness, otherness, the language of poetry, of praise, gratitude and love.

What was the unconventional and less conciliatory original ending of the novella? How much would it change our reading of this text? This question took me eventually to the University of Manitoba Archives, where I was astonished by several things, beginning with how little the manuscript was changed from the First Draft, except for the ending. This made identification of the editors' interventions a relatively easy task. More astonishing by far was the discovery of how radical these interventions were, not in terms of the number of pages involved, which are relatively few, but in terms of altering the text's meaning. The publishers and editors at Ragweed at this time (in the late '90s) were Laurie Brinklow and Louise Fleming. When I asked Ms. Fleming by telephone whose idea the revisions were, she said, "It was a collective decision." To what extent the editors were influenced by Desmond Pacey's earlier critical comments on the manuscript, expressing what were evidently similar views, is something I can only guess at. It was Pacey, then Vice-President at the University of New Brunswick, who facilitated her writer-in-residency there in 1967; Livesay presumably requested his commentary on the manuscript at that time. It appears among Livesay's papers in an undated four-page letter (Box 95, Folder 1).

The original ending is dramatically different from the published one. The archive includes five very similar versions of the manuscript, most of them subtitled "First Draft."[2] In my reading of the novella here, I have chosen to work with the manuscript version in Folder 1, which I call First Draft A. In First Draft A, then, Celia and Hugo carry on extensive conversations during their reconciliation after Hugo's accident, both in the hospital and later after he comes home, which establish several key points. First, they read together and discuss a passage written by "Colette's husband," presumably a chapter from Colette's third husband Maurice Goudeket's memoir, *Close to Colette*, which addresses, among other things, the question of disparity in ages between marriage partners. The reading and discussion has been Hugo's suggestion. Afterward, he comments on the husband's devotion to Colette's writing career and haltingly apologizes to Celia for not offering her more similar support in her artistic endeavours: "I've been thinking . . if you had had more of a break . . from the demands of the family - my family, that you took on?" (79)

His question brings tears to Celia's eyes. "He had never before admitted anything like that," she observes. "Why Hugo," she replies, "I didn't think you cared." "I care," he responds, stroking her hair. It is the first sign of renewed tenderness between them, though we have been prepared for this moment by the image of Hugo's eyes lighting up whenever Celia comes into the room in the hospital.

Celia is more deeply implicated in Hugo's fall in First Draft A than in the book, and there are two differing accounts of what happened. In Draft A, described in a letter addressed "To David," Celia, in bed, hears her husband getting up in the night and starting down the hall (they sleep in separate rooms). Following him to the stairs she sees that he doesn't have his cane, and cries out "Hugo!" whereupon he slips and falls halfway down the stairs. In the second account, addressed "To Maudie," she is woken by the crash of Hugo falling and rushes to the stairs (71).

I assume Livesay intended the second account to be a glossed-over version of what really happened, since Celia is clearly on the defensive in this letter to her sister, who is after all privy to her affair. It is, however, the first and only time we perceive the narrator as unreliable, which introduces some ambiguity in terms of authorial intention. In both accounts Celia feels a certain guilt for Hugo's accidental injury, which is absent in the book, and this guilt precipitates her return to him—though it doesn't stop her from experiencing heightened passion for John and enjoying several more erotic encounters with him.

In fact, the separation from John is presented as a much more passionate and wrenching event for Celia in the manuscript than in the book. Compare the rather cold-hearted goodbye note to John in the published version— "Please! It is finished, John. Not only for my peace of mind, not only for Hugo's need—but because of you, also. There is no future for you, with me. . . . In time you will see reason" (77)—with this emotional declaration from First Draft A:

> To John:
> Now it is hitting me hard! I am in chains—more so than ever before. I cannot get out at all. I cannot see you.
> Thank you for phoning. At that hour, it is safe. He hears nothing.
> O my dear. Every meeting with your voice, even, arouses me again. It seems unbelievable that I cannot touch you,

also. So I begin to see that the situation is impossible. I want you too much. (77)

There is a lighthearted moment in the hospital in First Draft A, where Celia surprises Hugo "sitting up, not in—but beside the bed!" There are chrysanthemums on the table, the radio is playing, Hugo is smiling. Celia expresses her delight, only to hear a voice behind her saying, "It was not such a difficult job, after all." The voice, it turns out, belongs to "a very young, trim nurse, with straight short reddish hair under her cap." As she and Hugo tease each other, Celia feels a kind of twinge, "to think it was not I who could give him back his élan, but a young girl." So there is a hint at establishing a dynamic of reciprocity in their relationship here; this episode is followed by tender gestures between Celia and Hugo, evidence of their love for each other returning.

There are several other changes from manuscript to book, such as the regrettable deletion of some erotically charged, slightly naughty conversations between Celia and John. I cannot resist quoting one of them here in its entirety, given its spirited levity, so necessary to a text shot through with many kinds of grief:

—Why do you lie there just shaking with laughter?
—Because you're so ridiculous.
—I'm not ridiculous.
—Not, 'a subject for ridicule,' but *ridere*, to laugh. You're a
    laugh, my dicky.
—Tweet! . . . If I'm dicky, you're batty.
—The eminent Mr. Batty.
—Because you're batty to take no with dicky.
—Take care, or I'll beat you up—with my bat.
—No. But seriously, John!
—Yes?
—Are you paying attention?
—I am all ears—see!
—Well then: why do you love me?
—Because you are so ridiculous.
—And I love you for the opposite reason!

—What's that?

—You're so serious!

—Am I really?

—Yes. And gentle.

—M-m-m. Doesn't sound very masculine.

—But you are a man, as well. You take control. And that's really why I love you!

—I wouldn't be surprised . . . No one has ever found out before, how to handle you . . Is that it?

—I guess so.

—You little shrew, you.

—My parents didn't believe in corporal punishment!

—Well, I don't hold with those new-fangled, modern methods—Come here, you! Now I will beat you up. I will! I will! (First Draft A, 67)

There is also the revision of several letter headings from "Unsent Letter" or "Notations. Unsent Letter" to simply "Notations." This was one of Pacey's ideas: "I find the device of an unsent letter rather bothersome," he noted in his commentary on the manuscript. "Would a better way be to intersperse journal or diary entries with the letters? A woman might put into a diary what she would not put into letter" (Critical Comments, 3rd p.). Yet several reviewers of the book commented on the breakdown of the epistolary structure in the Notations. Personally, I find the notion of the unsent letter much more poignant in the context of Celia's consistent efforts at communication and their frequent frustration. I also disagree with another comment of Pacey's, which Livesay and her editors happily did not take up: "Could anyone report dialogue in such detail?" Pacey clearly has not spent a lot of time with women, whose oral memory for conversation is often astounding! And what about the vivid sense of memory that is after all the basis for all autobiographies and memoirs? Here again, happily, not all of Pacey's other suggestions have been taken. He takes exception, for example, to Livesay's critique of Maritime educational practices: "You begin," he complains, "from a prejudice (how acquired?) that NB is old-fashioned and behind the times," and goes on to boast, "I was the first matriculation examiner in Canada to break away from the old formal grammar questions" (3rd p.). Nevertheless, Livesay's scathing description of Maritime public schools as rigid and stifling, and even the university as a place where "young people are walking about in chains . . . longing to shake them off" appears unchanged in the book (51)—raising a question about the extent of Pacey's influence on Livesay or the publishers.

By far the most dramatic difference between the original manuscript and the book involves the surprise outcome of the affair with John. Shortly after Hugo returns from the hospital, he and Celia have a long heartfelt conversation in which Hugo reveals himself to be both sensitive and articulate. It becomes clear that he knew about the affair, and he gently offers her her freedom, if it is what she wants. Celia, touched, breaks into affectionate sobs and then delivers this bombshell: she's pregnant! (There is a short episode earlier in the manuscript, also edited from the book, where Celia and John briefly discuss birth control; she expresses the—as it turns out erroneous—opinion that at her time of life, age forty-five, when she has begun skipping the occasional period, she probably doesn't need it anymore.) Hugo responds, surprisingly, with a deep sigh. "That's what I should have given you, Celia." Since no one else knows who the child's father is, though we suspect that Maudie at least will surmise it, they decide to keep the child and settle in to their altered and renewed relationship.

Pacey, in his critical notes on the manuscript (according to pagination he is reading First Draft B), questions this highly dramatic outcome to the novella: "Is it a good idea to have her get pregnant? I can't see that it adds anything, and it risks a soap opera touch" (4th p.). As a woman, frankly, I can't help chuckling at this remark: it seems this outcome adds rather too much than not enough for Pacey's comfort, a baby and a large generous and apologetic gesture from Hugo! After all, the risk of pregnancy is a central element of women's sexuality, and unintentional pregnancies are common. As for Celia's dramatic lack of precautions throughout this whole episode, both in terms of birth control and protecting her marriage, any woman who has been through the extended and unpredictable hormonal ups and downs of the perimenopausal moment will find both the sudden desire for an illicit lover and increased risk of pregnancy during the body's last gasp of fertility and suddenly arrhythmic cycle easily credible! In this way, the novella's theme might indeed be said to be a meditation on women's experience of menopause, with Celia continuously bemoaning her age and loss of stereotypic youthful beauty, and John continuously contradicting her with hefty compliments, the largest being the gift of their mutually conceived child. How many Canadian fictions about menopause are there? Hardly any. Think of Morag Gunn's discreet sobriety and dark lack of a sense of the future at age forty-seven in *The Diviners*. In this deafening silence, Livesay, with typical panache, plunges ahead with exuberance and abandon.

Perhaps Livesay's original outcome for the affair is soap operatic—but aren't pregnancies, especially surprise ones, melodramatic by definition; isn't menopause, for that matter, for those who've been there, one long emotionally and hormonally volatile melodrama? Whether or no, it explains everything that's missing in the book: how Celia could bear to return to her husband; how the affair literally renewed her relationship with Hugo by providing her with a child, and him with the possibility of making amends for his former self-centredness; how each of them gives up something huge and important for the sake of their renewed relationship, she her lover, he the role of patriarch; how their separate and shared pain and generosity toward each other in this vulnerable, truthful moment actually brings about the desired transformation in their relationship. If readers wonder how Hugo can bear to accept the parenting of another man's child, it is after all not very different from what Celia has been doing for many years, parenting his sons from another marriage. Besides, he's in a fairly desperate situation, aging and in ill health, though we assume the renewal of their marriage will defer his anticipated death for some time.

This is a strikingly different ending from the unsatisfactory published version, which sets aside emotional fulfilment and the utopian dream of desire to reaffirm traditional marital conventions, centred on the taming and subduing of the wife's creative energies to sustain the husband's lacking sense of self: "Of course, I see it more clearly now that my loyalty is to Hugo—because he needs me the most. It is mainly because of me that he has kept going, kept from wishing himself dead. . . . So, there's no way 'round it, is there? You cannot put your own desires first" (76). These two endings diverge so dramatically from one another that I am moved to ask why the editors/publishers would have chosen to alter it in the way they did. Was it for commercial reasons, as Dorothy implied in her conversation with me? Was it because they lacked courage and chose a less challenging (though also much less satisfying) outcome? Was it because, as usual, Dorothy's emotional range and vision far exceeded the acceptable norm? Whatever the editors' investment in the narrative was, it seems clear that the revised ending contradicts the whole imaginative thrust of the novella. Returning home to dutifully cook, clean and read to her emotionally crippled and dependent husband, with her romantic secret untold and putting her own interests aside, may be an improved fate for Celia over the Victorian spectacle of lost drowned poisoned suicidal adulterous women, but it smacks, as Barbara Gowdy says, "of prison" (C17).

What about the fate of the young lover John? In the published version, he too is a loser, sent away by Celia for his own good, despite his offer of marriage. He gets over Celia's rejection of him, as she predicts in her goodbye note to him, very quickly indeed. Celia's goodbye note is dated November 20 and his conciliatory acceptance note arrives before December 12, the date of her reply, "Your letter has made everything all right"—just in time, we assume, for a clean family Christmas. Livesay makes a gesture near the end of the novella to address the question of male desire and eroticism more consciously than she has done throughout. In a letter to Max, Celia asks, "Why, since Blake, do there exist nudes of women only? Never a man in sight?" She contemplates briefly drawing Hugo nude in his wheelchair, then interjects, "No, of course not. Hugo would never permit it." Nevertheless "there are students on campus who are glad to earn fee money by posing as models. And for me, as a woman artist," Celia reflects, "this could be a real challenge" (80). Celia's interest in young men's desire is here problematically sublimated into professional artistic interest—problematically because creativity for her, until now, has been connected with being in love: how much will her art suffer as a result of her denial of desire in favour of duty? Is she rising from self-absorption to a higher notion of "impersonal" art? Or is the whole cycle about to begin all over again? In the unpublished version, on the other hand, John's desire remains more intact, and Celia's imminent career trajectory less precarious, in that he chooses to end the relationship and relinquish his claim on the child in order to follow a professional career elsewhere, having benefited hugely from Celia's emotional, erotic and artistic mentoring. Her womanly and maternal influence will hopefully save him from a life of objectivist emotional disengagement and therefore a fate like Hugo's. We do not assume that he recovers his emotional equilibrium, as in the published version, after their tearful, if mutually chosen, separation after three weeks! Hugo, on the other hand, is released into extravagant generosity toward Celia and the new child, a gesture that renews him spiritually and psychically, as opposed to, in the published version, petulantly leaning on her support for his survival.

The original ending, then, is more convincing and emotionally satisfying; it is also more consonant with Livesay's larger project, throughout her writing life, of liberating women's, and also men's, sexual and creative desire from conventions that have negatively bound us, notions of crippling self-sacrifice and emotional co-dependence, for example. Family and social life should not come at the expense of imaginative and erotic desire, but should rather be part of its creative expression, alongside a range of other activities, including artistic and public life. Such a harmonious resolution of potentially conflicting personal dynamics, even in Livesay's optimistic, strong-hearted, wide-angle vision, is not easily achieved, as *The Husband* and much of her poetry attest. Nevertheless, it is what the poet deeply believes in and fervently hopes for, and in the name of that vision, I challenge the publishers to re-issue the novella with its original ending (and naughty bits!) intact.

The happiest reader in the world:
David Arnason's joyfully revisionary stories

There are so many David Arnasons. There's the chainsmoking bibliophile Arnason with the photographic memory who founded the *Journal of Canadian Studies* and can recite (and has) on demand every book that was published in Canada between, say, 1900 and 1999. Or any given passage from Shakespeare or Tennyson or Milton, for that matter. Or Poe. There's the pink-cheeked ex-smoking raconteur Arnason who hosts wonderful parties and cooks a mean feast and organizes exciting international conferences and tells sly witty tender stories. There's the large generous entrepreneurial Arnason who founded Turnstone Press and the St. John's annual Literary Conference at the University of Manitoba, and was centrally involved in the public success of Artspace and the Manitoba Arts Council and later Anansi Press, and nurtured an entire generation of Manitoba writers and literary critics into being, not just by being around and influencing them, but by attending readings by fledgling new writers and actively hounding them for manuscripts, to their terror and eternal gratitude (as I can testify from personal experience).

There's the pioneering Icelandic Arnason with a fisherman's heritage and stubborn Interlake and prairie optimism who proudly celebrates his roots (or is it fins), and local community. This is the Arnason who sat for the huge Viking sculpture at Gimli (or so I always thought), that same Arnason often ranging far abroad and practising a kind of large-hearted international cosmopolitanism, alongside committed regionalism.

There's the white-haired slightly wild-looking scholar Arnason who keeps abreast of every critical trend and injects broad insight, enthusiasm, good-humoured irony and intellectual rigour into every academic encounter. There's the talented keen-eyed administrator who oversees departments and dissertation defences and arts councils and editorial boards with intelligence and fairness and panache. There's the wide-ranging restlessly talented writer Arnason who has tried his hand at and garnered international attention

Fig. 3 Gimli's 1967 centennial project: The Viking Statue, by Giorgio Barone.
Photo: G.N.L. Jonasson

for poetry, short fiction, novels, drama, documentary nonfiction, literary criticism, television and film. There's the shy Arnason who blushes easily and stumbles in the presence of women, and yet negotiates the various challenges of feminism with fairness and a clumsy grace. It is the larger-than-life combination of these many Arnasons that prompted the *Winnipeg Free Press* to dub him Manitoba's nominal "Dean of Arts" a few years ago. It is the ongoing presence of these many Arnasons that has distinguished and shaped the Manitoba literary landscape through several decades. Thank you, thank you, David Arnason.

These are too many Arnasons to talk about in any kind of detail all at once. The David Arnason I've chosen to write about here is the author of short stories, published in such collections as *Fifty Stories and a Piece of Advice*, *The Circus Performers' Bar* and *The Happiest Man in the World*. In other words, the pre-fractured-prairie-fairy-tale, post-contemporary-long-poem short story writer Arnason. It is his stories that have moved me most, of his large oeuvre. It was the stories that grabbed me, sitting on my verandah on Jessie Avenue sometime in the mid '80s, enjoying the brief gorgeous Winnipeg summer, snatching some reading time from my busy household filled with young children and dogs and cats and fish and gerbils and lizards and rabbits. I was busy, I was distracted. I was juggling a dozen freelance writing and editing and teaching jobs, squeezed in between the full-time demands of postgraduate studies in Canadian literature at the University of Manitoba. I was feeling overworked and undersupported, undervalued, as a woman graduate student with young children (though this is not a veiled reference to Arnason, who had not been my professor at that time—I'm wishing he had). I remember what I was experiencing in those years was a kind of dismay at the heartlessness that seemed to characterize much of postmodern theory, which seemed reflected back in the less than supportive world around me; for example, Paul de Man's emphasis on the extreme self-referentiality of texts, which was very influential in the North American academy then, or the kind of hysterical aesthetics and panic culture celebrated by theorists like Arthur Kroker, so radically different a rhetoric from the language of love and grief I had been brought up in the Mennonite villages of my childhood, and seemed to fit my mothering life much more adequately as well.

I was reading David Arnason's story, "Mary Yvette."[1] Ah, I thought, you see, there it is, that ironic, nearly cynical edge, which allows one to admit everything and be responsible, in the end, for nothing, in the manner of Robert Kroetsch's Sad Phoenician, say, who was casting his long shadow on all our prairie literary thinking in those days. It's a story told by a father, reflecting on his strained relationship with his daughter, Mary, who has renamed herself Yvette. "Somewhere along the way, between her yellow stuffed rabbit and a night of rage that I'd sooner not remember, we decided to open our love to hurt. We have chosen to let others in. She brings to me now a succession of lovers I despise, weak and worthless men who betray and damage her, and so we are both hurt" (*The Circus Performers' Bar*, 57). The father in the story goes on to declare, in clear understated prose, his paternal bewilderment and rage at having lost his two true loves, the young girl he married who has become a "distant woman who lives at the edges of my life" (57), and the daughter who once adored him, whom he thought he could protect, now absorbed by her own complicated life.

It is a story that knows itself in advance. This father understands the complex triangulations of father/mother/daughter. He acknowledges up front his paternal guilt, his failure to protect this sweet, once innocent, daughter from the world and, more importantly, from himself. He recognizes his irrational jealousy of her lovers, his impossible grief at her inevitable abandonment of him, as her first love, as she grows into adulthood. This is Lear, but in a sophisticated late-twentieth-century incarnation, self aware, ironic, half apologetic, knowing already the agony of the heath, thanks to Shakespeare and centuries of reflection upon his terrible lessons, and thus able to avoid it in the postmodern manner: tragedy foreshortened by reflexivity into a kind of bittersweet laughter. His narrator's voice is finely balanced between blame and self-pity, resignation and lashing out, irrational jealousy and self-conscious regret at his own "male inadequacy" (59), a phrase he reserves for the young no-good contenders for the daughter's affections, but with the smallest of challenges, would be willing to admit, goodhumouredly, is a description of himself, too.

It is a small story, no more than five pages long, but it packs a punch. It zeroes in with deadly accuracy on the troubled father-daughter nexus, which cultural theorist Lynda Boose has called the founding relationship of the family. Boose complains that we have given too little weight to the emotional economics of the traditional patriarchal exchange system, in which the daughter represented the exchange object, the mother its producer (whose role ceased after that) and the father its guarantor and broker, as owner and protector of the family unit. The meaning of all those old stories of angry, selfish fathers who block their daughters' exchange rather than disinterestedly handing them over or, at the other extreme, absent fathers who abandon their daughters emotionally and often literally instead of protecting them only in order to lose them, writes Boose, signifies a deep ambivalence in the father's role as simultaneously protector and broker, without a real partner: a sort of structured heartbreak at the centre of the patriarchal system and its devalued or absent (and dead) mothers, which is replicated over and over in the psychological dynamics of individual families (19-74).

Well, and we all know what Freud did with that conundrum, how he averted his eyes from the father's split affection, his broken-heartedness and desperate attempts to avoid loss and betrayal in a system that supposedly privileges him, often going so far as to violate the incest taboo that guarantees his power. Cheating the buyer in advance, but also, by that same act, confirming the very thing he wishes to deny, that the patriarchal promise is a lie, that he cannot, does not, own what he cherishes. Carolyn Heilbrun speculates that Freud himself may have indulged in this form of protest against the emotional cost of patriarchal privilege in his relationship with his daughter Anna (419). A man with an astounding capacity for emotional empathy and courageous excavation and insight, Freud was nonetheless unable to face the structural contradictions of patriarchy, its steep curve of internal pain. He imagined that by ascribing incestuous desire to the daughters instead of the fathers (or mothers) he might give them the task of resolving patriarchal grief: if not resolving then enduring, if not enduring then at worst carrying this "best kept secret," as Florence Rush calls it in her book by that title, to the grave with them.

Freud might have read Lear with greater care: how the great wheel of suffering turns back on the man who gives all his fatherly responsibility away to his daughters. How his split heart, his raging between demonic gestures of possessiveness and abandonment, too much love and too little, at the moment when he should graciously bestow upon the daughters their own lives, turns them against each other when he should give them lovingly to the world, and tears the kingdom to pieces. How the king, at the greatest height of his magisterial powers, reaches down into his heart and finds it, to his own great surprise and shock, bankrupt, bereft, empty. How there is no place to go after that except down into madness, the wilderness to which he has consigned every experience, every gesture, of vulnerability and tenderness. How he finds the face of love there on the heath, among the weeds, but only after it's too late, homeless, imprisoned, tortured, crucified.

Arnason's narrator knows all this. He understands how not to get caught in the patriarchal trap of psychic emptiness in the moment of power. Deconstruction and a couple of centuries of revolutions have given us, at least, this: we no longer believe in kings, and therefore cannot be disappointed when mere men fail to live up to that impossible fantasy we had of them. And we have all learned the lessons of a century of psychoanalysis now and can recite them articulately in the midst of our own experience of them. As does this narrator: "I have noticed, if you'll forgive me a digression, that every hurt delivered to a child is returned to the world with interest later on. The fat, the weak, the accidentally bald, the acne-stricken swallow their rage until later, when they are grown up and have power, then they deliver back every humiliation, and they are not careful of their victims" (57).

But what grabbed me, sitting on my verandah on Jessie Avenue reading "Mary Yvette," was not its note of sophistication and self-awareness, impressive and instructive as that is, but something else, something that's missing, if you look for it, in the Sad Phoenician's embroidered litanies. It began to tug at me in the delicate beautiful passage where the father describes going fishing with his young daughter May, when "the mean and brutal lovers had not yet appeared on the horizon," as he says, and they begin to catch "tiny, golden perch" (58). Competing to see who can catch the most, the father prays for his defeat, and "whatever gods there are who look out for fathers and daughters," writes Arnason of this narrator, "answered. She led me home, my tiny victor, consoling me for my loss" (58). A tender moment of practising relinquishing power to the daughter, without possession or abandonment. It is not a moment without its cost: the daughter playfully promises him "another chance" to win, not yet recognizing the irrevocable shift in their relationship, the real inversion of their powers in relation to each other, that their game has begun to enact, and that will continue the rest of their lives. The father recognizes it, however, with a sharp twinge of grief and regret, adding, retrospectively, "though of course there never was. There never is" (58).

The story goes on to spell out the father's sequential rage at the various inadequate suitors who arrive to usurp his position as her first love—though rage is too large a word for it, it is more an eyebrows-raised, hands-in-the-air exasperation. It is anger that points reflexively back to himself: their inadequacies reflect, he is fair-minded enough to recognize, his own inadequacy as a father, both in the general sense of being unable to protect his daughter from life experience—as none of us can our children, or anyone—but also in the specific sense of having himself failed her through acts of parental clumsiness, if nothing else, by "wanting too much" (53). He briefly mentions, then studiously avoids, "a night of rage I'd sooner not remember" (57), but after listing the suitor's failures, arrives in due fairness at his own. Mary Yvette was falsely accused by a police officer of stealing a blouse, and he not only believed the charges without question but added, he confesses to us with engaging candour, "some charges of my own that were equally false, but even meaner" (61). "Nothing since," he concludes sadly, "has undone that breach" (61).

The story ends with Mary Yvette turning away from men altogether and becoming happily involved with a woman, pregnant by an unknown father. Instead of punishing her with absolute abandonment for this eloquent rejection of patriarchy, fatherhood and himself, the narrator reflects, post-confessionally, that he is "almost radiant" with expectation, anticipating in the prospect of a granddaughter "another chance" after all, at "fishing lines and poles, for, yes, love, drawn up like golden perch out of the immaculate water" (61). This ending left me in tears when I first read it, sitting on my verandah on Jessie Avenue, in Winnipeg, and it leaves me in tears now, writing this in Toronto all these years later. Like this father, like most fathers in patriarchally structured families, mine couldn't negotiate the emotional territory of paternal loss, that painful, tender moment of giving away his daughters to the world, without blame and judgment, without inserting his unreasonable desire for paternal immortality into a moment that is not rightfully his, that belongs, in celebration, to her. It's a confusing and deeply hurtful response for a daughter verging on adult independence, as most women could tell you.

Unlike this father, mine didn't have the privilege of self-reflexivity and the luxury of time in which to rewrite this story. He died before our "breach" could be bridged through the mediating relationship of grandchildren, or the mellowing of age and time. (Though, if you'll "forgive me a digression" of my own, I confess that Martha Henry's harried Lear at the Manitoba Theatre

Centre a few years ago jolted me into the recognition that I had crossed the divide of generations and identified with the king's agony now as much as with the daughters—"Hads't daughters, and gav'st them all?"—a reversal I could not in my wildest imaginings have foreseen, encountering that play for the first time as a twenty-year-old daughter in exile from an equally unreasonable father and his territory, nearly three decades ago.)

What Arnason gives us here, looking imaginatively beyond the oedipal bind of the patriarchal family, is a model of paternal love that risks emotional vulnerability, humiliation and tenderness, and which promises freedom from and for "the flawed and flailing father," not by running away from paternal responsibility but by embracing it in its gentlest, most caretaking sense. Along with it comes the poignant acknowledgement of clumsiness and failure, and acceptance of the pain of loss. This is Joyce's moment of epiphany, at the end of the century whose course he so profoundly influenced, completely turned around: instead of falling from the myth of heroes and saints into irony and exile, Arnason's characters skate lightly across the slough of despond and begin to dance there. Arnason does not write in isolation. Hélène Cixous said that the mother story is not a quest but a giveaway ("Castration or Decapitation?" 1981, 53). Told the way Arnason tells it here, the father's story is not oppositional to the mother's, but in creative partnership with it. This is a model that the recent generation of men, brought up with patriarchal expectations but encountering the adventurous revisions of the sixties and the challenges of feminism after that, floundering in triple confusion in their fatherly responsibilities, would do well to study.

Sandra Sabatini has argued that Arnason's stories, "Mary Yvette" and " A Good Baby," along with Leon Rooke's novel, *A Good Baby*, and Thomas King's *Medicine River*, illustrate "a momentous change in the way men write about babies. This is a change not only in the quantity of babies written into the literary text, but more importantly, a change in quality. The babies have more concrete value in these tests; they are uniquely valued, even precious to the male protagonists" (138). The significance of this change cannot be overestimated, writes Sabatini; there are simply "no examples in Canadian prose fiction of such writing before 1980 (140). The emergence of caretaking fathers of infants in our literature signals what philosopher Mary O'Brien might call a "world-historical event," as momentous as the women's movement and directly related to it, in that women began to insist on greater equality both in the workplace and at home. This event also coincides with changes in theories of child development, with psychologists like Daniel Stern insisting on a much more consolidated sense of infant subjectivity than had previously been theorized, arguing for the intentionality and agency of even newborn infants (Stern 18-22). Sabatini worries, however, whether the "new father" stories (my term) valorize paternal relationships with young children at the expense of the mothers, that is, "whether men are appropriating the female caregiving role" by exclud[ing] the mother as a figure of importance" (158). In particular, she points at Arnason's story, "My Baby and Me," where the narrator and his wife fight over parental rights in the manner of many separating young couples in our time; in this case, the story ends with the father running off with the baby and "all the equipment you need to operate a baby," against the mother's wishes (35).

Sabatini points out the ambivalent value of such father stories for women: on the one hand, we have wanted nothing more than for men to become more involved in the tendernesses of early childrearing, in order to share the burden of double careers, and in order to encourage the development of stronger nurturing capabilities in men. On the other hand, our great-grandmothers fought long and hard for our legal "mother right," that is, custodial privilege as primary caretakers in the eyes of the law; it is our twentieth-century legacy. Are we willing to give up this privilege in the name of "equality," as feminists like Ann Ferguson, Dorothy Dinnerstein and Nancy Chodorow have argued we should?[2] Frankly, I don't buy Dinnerstein's and Chodorow's argument that equally shared parenting of young children by both parents is the solution to matrophobia or the denigration of the mother; it doesn't make sense to say let's take away the mother's hard-fought-for right to legal recognition for her maternal reproductive labour and history of equally hard-earned nurturing expertise, and that will make us honour her more. Given our long history in Western culture of "matricide," to use Irigaray's term for the repeated delegitimation, and indeed often literal murder (or neglect to the point of death), of the mother in our social and legal arrangements, we would do well, as Sabatini cautions us, to beware of any male-initiated revisions of parental privilege that don't include overt recognition of the mother's unique agency and expertise—and presence!—in the reproductive process, in both its childbearing and childrearing aspects.[3] A very different strategy of maternal empowerment is offered by theorists like Mary O'Brien,

Luce Irigaray and Paula Gunn Allen (in whose company I count myself), who argue strongly against egalitarian ideals that depend on the neutralization of gender, however problematic our negotiations of sexual difference continue to be: this difference lies after all at the heart of our biological/social/spiritual identity as sexually engendered erotic beings. Instead, we wish to expand the sphere of women's rights and influence to include a greater celebration of maternal agency not only at home but in the public sphere, in philosophy, the sciences and art. Irigaray argues that women should have equal representation in public governing bodies, and is working hard to make this happen in the European Union; we should do the same in North America. Paradoxically, enlarging women's sphere of power and influence in these ways, as Irigaray and O'Brien point out, does not diminish men's access to feminine knowledge and creativity and capacity for nurturing. Rather, it makes it more available as a governing principle in all our cultural arrangements, and as a result has the potential to improve the quality of men's lives immensely.[4]

What about the parental rights of the father? If indeed men discover they not only like looking after young children but occasionally excel at it, and if, as we have challenged them to, they share equal access to the workplace and equal domestic labour at home with us, then do we also need to share equal parental custody rights, and our rich archive of (traditionally closely guarded) childrearing expertise with them? But in a world where men have greater socio-economic power than women, and still receive a lot of social rewards for macho dominator behaviours, would that disadvantage women (and children) all over again, swinging the culture back into granting patriarchal privilege over the custody of children at the expense of the mother and her relational interests and expertise? Arnason's story, Sabatini observes, "does not indicate an equality of relationship between mother and father concerning the care of the baby [much less mother right]. It reads like payback. [The narrator] does not experience pregnancy or childbirth, but his connection to the infant, a connection solicited and sustained by the infant's gaze and engagement behaviours, is vital. But his love for the baby is complicated by his animosity toward Patsy and the power he can exert over her by being a better 'mother' than she is" (161). Will his nurturance of the baby be characterized similarly by the fostering of macho qualities of dominance and power, as per the traditional Western male model, asks Sabatini, rather than skills of cooperation and relationship, as per the female one?

True, I say, Arnason's narrator may be emotionally immature in all these ways. Nevertheless, his neo-parental questions about who gets the baby if the parents split up, and why, and even who the primary caretaker is, in cases where the father is or wishes to be fully involved in parenting, all these are surely critical questions in contemporary discourse on gender "equality," currently being fought out in the divorce courts more precisely than in our fictions, where this story is only now beginning to be written, burnished in the fiery furnaces of our new age. I defend the narrative outcome of the story therefore not on practical or ideological grounds but on emotional ones: here Arnason is probing the tenderest insecurities of the paternal psyche (is not men's exclusion from the heroism and magic of childbearing their greatest envy?) with his characteristic mixture of sensitivity and bravado, and comes through the moment of grief gently laughing. The father's clumsiness as a father to his previous children, by his own numerous admissions, is not entirely mitigated by his deep affection for the new baby. Surely running off with the baby and its "equipment"—despite the narrator's happy gurgle, "[W]e're going for a walk by the river, me and my baby, my baby and me" (35)—cannot be read as an unproblematic happy ending, nor even as realism, but rather as the profoundly revisionary (and bewildering) discovery that yes, indeed, fathers can bond emotionally with infants, and even to some extent take care of them. We can assume extended custody and parental visitation negotiations are about to begin.

Note that Leon Rooke's *A Good Baby*, by comparison, avoids the difficult custody question by having the mother die in good old Victorian fashion, thereby proposing the new fatherhood without disturbing the old patriarchal pattern of maternal absence through death. It is adoptive fatherhood in this case, since the nurturing father figure, Toker, is not the child's biological parent. But how is this different from, say, *Silas Marner*, or the ending of *Dombey and Son*, where the death of the mother (and expulsion of her threatening replacement in the form of the attractive stepmother Edith) enables the distant father to become more sensitive to his children? The narrative outcome in maternal terms is the same. It is the proximity of the father to diapers and baby bottles that is different (and how much of that has to do with the invention of automatic washing machines?). Thomas King's *Medicine River*, on the other hand, avoids the nastiness of the parental custody battle by drawing on the more traditional Native sense of the extended family community, presided over by the grandmothers. Martha Oldcrow, the matriarch in the novel, interviews Will, the adopting "new father," and approves his inclusion in the child's family on the basis of his presence at the baby's birth and his declared love for her, both signifying his commitment to mother as well as baby. He becomes, as Arnold Davidson has commented, "part of Joyce Bluehorn's 'big family,' where 'by Native definitions, a big family is everyone—every cousin's cousin, every brother-in-law's ex-wife's new stepchild. The distinctions don't matter" (195). Extending parental rights and responsibilities in the direction of shared arrangements in a larger community, as King's novel suggests, seems like a good idea. It should be explored much more in contemporary parenting theory and practices than it has been, even if it is not a readily available option for most urban families at present, isolated as they are in fragmented, nuclear family arrangements.

None of these authors agree, nor do I, with sociologist David Popinoe's recent argument that "traditional marital gender roles are necessary if the good of society—and of individuals—is to be advanced" (166). Popinoe bases his conclusions on the higher divorce rate in families where traditional gender roles are reversed or even moderately modified; as well as on the typical gendered behaviour that documents females as more responsive to infants than males. He also argues for the universal normativity of the nuclear family, ignoring the radical changes that have occurred in modern industrialized cultures that created the nuclear family in the first place (relatively recently in the history of humankind, after all), and are now putting such drastic pressures on it by isolating the domestic realm ever further from the centres of contemporary social and cultural life. Here is an interesting illustration of the advantages literary fiction has over sociological studies, which are incapable of documenting utopian or revisionary ideas unless they have already been successfully enacted in significant numbers, and unless their outcome is clear.

An energetic alternative view is offered by visionary science writer Natalie Angier's "call for a revolutionary psychology," in her brilliant bestselling *Woman: An Intimate Geography*:

> Men can love babies madly, and the more they sit and smell
> and clutch their babies against them, the more sensorily
> embellished the love becomes. How often, though, does

the average father sit and rock his baby against his naked breast? Not often enough, and not nearly as often as the average mother does. Mothers tend to monopolize their babies. . . . The nursery is still the mother's domain. There, she is poobah. Yet if we want men to do their share and to shine at it, it's unfair to give them the handicap of our doubt, to practice a reverse form of discrimination: 'we suckle; you suck.' If women expect men to dive into the warm, rich waters of body love and to feel the tug of baby bondage, we must give over the infant again and again. Between feedings, between breasts, play touch football, baby as pigskin—pass it along. (400)

Angier rejects arguments promoted by influential sociobiologists like Stephen Pinker, "that men are inevitably less invested in their children than women are, that because there is always a chance to do better reproductively, to conquer new wombs, their feet are always shod and halfway out the door" (Angier 400). Cleverly turning the Darwinian notion of the survival of the fittest, newly popularized by the trendy proponents of "evolutionary psychology," on its head with an impressive array of biologically convincing counterstatistics, Angier demonstrates that "In this murderously competitive habitat of ours, this teeming global agora, men's reproductive success may well hinge on their capacity to do just the opposite, to pay attention to every offspring, to shower each child with every possible advantage. Men need women and children now, just as women and children are always thought to need their men" (400-401). Arnason's "new father" stories are impressively in the front lines of exploring just such an important shift in masculine thinking.

My other favourite stories of Arnason's add further refinements and details to his transformative revision of the family drama. I don't want to give the impression that all his stories are about families, or that there aren't many other marvellous things to talk about in his work. It's just that his rewriting of the family story is what strikes me with greatest wonder, looking back over his oeuvre here. "Sons and Fathers, Fathers and Sons," another small masterpiece, acknowledges its revisionary intentions right at the start: "there is something about fathers and sons that could do with an explanation a little less mechanical than Freud's" (*The Circus Performers' Bar*, 37). As in

"Mary Yvette," it's quite one thing to be self-conscious and reflective, and another to negotiate the deep waters of inherited relational patterns, in this case the highly competitive nature of fathers and sons, without merely falling into them. "It's a devious business," the narrator comments, spiritedly, "this sending your genes out into the world in a body over which you no longer have control. It calls for extreme measures, and any relationship between a father and a son is organized around extremes. Nothing is unfair" (37).

The story goes on to tell us of an ill-fated moose hunt, filled with misunderstandings and bravado and near disasters and bottles of Scotch—and no moose. This is a finely tuned parody of North American male initiatory and bonding rites, roughing it in the bush, undergoing various endurance tests, finding a sense of brotherhood amid intense jostling for power. But what gives this story its revisionary edge is not its parodic inflation/deflation of a familiar story, entertaining as that is. The botched encounter by citified wannabe hunters with a pretend frontier is after all itself one of Hollywood's favourite themes. Instead, what shines in this story is its surprise narrative twist. For all its self-reflexive framing of the traditional western, Hollywood has done little to challenge the old underlying gender biases, a rejection of domesticity and all that it implies, femininity and emotional vulnerability and the intricacies of family relationships, in favour of wordless rugged masculine strength. Arnason brings home, so to speak, along on the trip. The boys, it turns out here, are not an adolescent peer gang boisterously proclaiming its independence from the family, but an uncomfortable, sweaty, emotionally enmeshed triad of father, son and grandfather. The narrator, caught between the conflicting demands of elder and progeny, twists this way and that, trying to assert his own place of importance in the family story. After the son rescues the grandfather from drowning, they find an emotional connection that excludes the father, who finds himself suddenly odd man out: "They looked at each other like new lovers," the narrator sniffs, "they sidestepped me like you might sidestep an aggressive puppy" (46).

Here is where Freud's (and Darwin's) competitive model gives out. Jealousy, as Shakespeare knew well, cannot be resolved through feats of strength. Love cannot be decreed. If conquered, it disappears. The solution to men's loneliness and deep need for love is not silence and escape into a nostalgic and regressive fantasy of the wild, where hunting replaces negotiation with the other. Rather, as Arnason tells it, what is needed is precisely men's courage to accept their own vulnerability and desires, and to nurture their emotional bonds. The narrator, after small bouts of self-confessed peevishness, clumsiness and petty jealousy, chooses to open his heart to both his father and his son. "I had determined," he declares with typical Arnasonian bluster and optimism, after an afternoon of sulking, "that I would wrest forgiveness from them if I had to wrestle them to the ground to get it." He prepares a meal for them, feeling "brimful of love" (47). When they don't return even after it's dark, he goes out to find them, and miraculously locates them, by sheer effort of will it seems—or perhaps by what biologist Rupert Sheldrake calls "morphic resonance," the magnetic, intuitive connection that people and animals who care about each other carry. Though I prefer Arnason's term for it, reuniting, as he tells us, "in a little dance of joy and love" (47). After dinner they sit around the fire and tell stories, "telling and retelling what had happened, until we had a single version that belonged to us all, carved into the wordless night" (47). This is intersubjective, communal, artistic identity building at its finest. "There was no need to forgive or ask forgiveness," the narrator says. "The story did that for us all" (47). It is storytelling at its most simple and ancient and profound, contrasting dramatically with the ritualistic silences of cowboy and explorer and pioneer.

Love, as Hélène Cixous might say, at the site of death: it is where knowledge of the beloved's mortality seizes us with its terror, and we leap beyond ourselves to know the other (*Three Steps on the Ladder of Writing*, 12-13). Indeed, Arnason acknowledges Cixous as one of his tutors in an epigraph to *The Happiest Man in the World*, quoting her famous mantra from "The Laugh of the Medusa": "All you have to do to see the Medusa is look her in the face: and she isn't deadly. She is beautiful, and she laughs" (n.p.). It's a hell of a challenge to live up to, but Arnason rises to it beautifully. There are few contemporary writers who know how to write about love better than he does. There are few contemporary writers who know how to write about love at all: it seems we have lost the context, and perhaps the will, for it.

So this is one of Arnason's great gifts to us, his capacity for joy with its full range of dark and radiant undertones, his capacity for love. Oh, and there is a moose after all, glimpsed from the car window as they're leaving for home. "After a brief flurry of excitement as we reached for guns," reports the narrator, "we decided that the hunt had been too much of a success to ruin it now by killing a moose" (87). The quest, the hunt, is quietly reabsorbed here back into a story of love, of home. Aeschylus, who wrote eloquently and ambivalently about the destruction of the hearth as power centre all those centuries ago, would be happy to know that the shambles of patriarchy can offer us, all these millennia later, this tentative, delicately constructed return. Does the new masculinity as envisioned by Arnason not bode well also for our now radically endangered natural environment, due to human overkill of other species? If men can figure out how to appreciate each other, especially reproductively, across generations, "Sons and Fathers, Fathers and Sons" suggests, their need to conquer each other, and the rest of the world, including the natural environment, in order to prove themselves worthy of recognition in each other's eyes, may be transformed into more useful survival strategies than the testosterone flexing that has become such a hazard to the whole planet now, in its tragic über-application. (Though I am not one of those writers, and neither, I think, is Arnason, who think hunting is "bad," indeed, hunting can help preserve wildness by sharpening our human attention to the health of animal habitats and populations, and our kinship with them as interdependent species.)

It wouldn't be right to stop this meditation without mentioning the beautifully crafted title story of *The Happiest Man in the World*. Here, Arnason lets us in on the intimate life of the narrator, the same intelligent, urbane, witty, clumsy and occasionally comical character we've seen in the other stories. Much has been made lately of Carol Shields' gift for describing the domestic; it's much less common to notice its presence in men's writing, but here Arnason shows himself an adept. The story begins with Sharon, the narrator's wife, removing an infected sliver from his foot, goes on to describe a dinner party with friends at the lake, and ends with a late night swim and the anticipation of lovemaking. What drives this story, besides the lighthearted wealth of domestic detail—strawberry flans, chicken casseroles wrapped in aluminum foil, babies' colic medicine, dog food, interesting guests and a delicious feast of barbecued lamb—is the good-humoured jostling and arguing between husband and wife throughout, much of it going on inside the narrator husband's head, in reflection and anticipation of previous and impending skirmishes. He mocks their "fifty-fifty" arrangement of domestic responsibility, by describing the spectacle of his wife shovelling her half of the snow on the driveway while he is forced to sit on the front steps watching her, nursing Scotch, enduring the neighbours' scorn. But he doesn't really mean it. He is a dog worrying a bone, with frustration and pleasure. There is no ennui, no sense of impending doom, no feeling of alienation or emptiness or angst. The title sounds inflated, parodic, but is not. Arnason's narrator, like his author, thinks big, talks big and treads ever so lightly. The skirmishes turn out to be minor, erotic squirmish, foreplay. The gender war disarmed, delightfully and ending in love: it doesn't get much happier than that.

Thank you, David Arnason.

The poet and the wild city

A few years ago, Wayne Grady published a marvellous book entitled *Toronto the Wild*. In Grady's portrait of Canada's largest, most cosmopolitan city, the urban does not represent an escape from or conquest over nature and wild animals and plants and trees, but rather a haven for them. In Grady's Toronto, among and between streets and houses, and cars and bridges and high-rises, and the lives of people, thrive raccoons and sparrows and seagulls and pigeons, and bats and coyotes and rats and termites and snakes, and starlings and cockroaches and mosquitoes, and trees and grasses and wildflowers and weeds, and rivers and lakes and beaches and ravines, each with their own independent species organizations, happily co-existing through the seasons on terms that are only partially sanctioned by their human neighbours.

When I set out to write this essay, this was the meaning of "wild" I had in my mind: I was thinking of the way the city appears in my poetry mostly in the form of rivers and parks and trees and grass, and only occasionally as bridges and libraries and highways and airports and sidewalks, and rarely, if ever, as office buildings or high-rises or movie theatres or shopping centres or department stores or bars. I was thinking that in fact I experience the city, in a physical way, much as my beloved dog Maddie did, through our fondly remembered decade together, the way my children did when they were very young, as grey blurs interspersed with living patches of sweet-smelling, endlessly fascinating damp or wet or dry patches of earth, and grass and riverbanks and squirrels and cats and birds and earthworms and acorns and twigs and pebbles and snowflakes and puddles and mud and clouds and rain and sun. How I've spent all these years trying to adapt from my peasant prairie village farm upbringing to the life of the modern Canadian city, and how after all those major lifestyle revisions and years of intense culture shock, and fielding so much criticism from my family and the Mennonite community for abandoning the culture, I haven't really gotten very far away from my sensuous childhood love of prairie silence and four leggeds and green places after all. I wanted to confess that, despite my practised urbanity,

I'm still country in my imagination and my bones, that it takes a lot more than a couple of decades and a handful of books and university degrees to make the transition from a deeply rooted peasant life to modern post-industrial urban culture.

But then I remembered that the word "wild" had a whole other meaning in our traditional Mennonite lexicon, something quite other than Grady's benign covert urban wildlife. Wildness, in the stern eyes of our Mennonite fathers and grandfathers, denoted social disorderliness, lack of control, unsubmissiveness, wilfulness, stubborn resistance to reason, disobedience. Who of us, I thought, at least among those who grew up before television and the end of Mennonite cultural separatism, who does not remember the huge and sometimes desperate efforts our parents and grandparents undertook to wring these seemingly inherent, lurking qualities out of us, by hook or by crook (to use an expression of my mother's), that is, by seduction and teaching and violence? Not for any erratic or unsociable reason but rather to replace them, dutifully and painstakingly, with their desired and respected opposites which, unlike qualities of wildness, apparently had to be instructed and learned, that is to say: orderliness, self-control, submissiveness, yieldingness to the will of the group or its leaders, reasonableness and obedience. Now I don't know how much anyone else thought about this when they were being brought up and instructed in these proper Mennonite social behaviours, but I know I pondered this question a lot: why was it that the behaviours considered essential to the making and sustaining of human community and goodness did not seem to come naturally to the human species, while the behaviours that seemed so undesirable flourished unbidden, like weeds, in us?

But after all the same was true for the cows, and the cats and dogs and pigs and chickens, and the vegetables in our gardens, and the wheat and barley in the fields, all of which exhibited the same inclination toward waywardness: how was it that the good, submissive, reasonable behaviours of all these creatures (for their own good and ours) required so much conscientious labour from humans, and despite all our care they were always on the verge of slipping out of the pasture, tearing down the pig barn, flying the coop, wandering off to join the lives of the wild foxes and gophers in their burrows and lairs; how was it that our neatly laid out pretty fields and gardens were constantly under threat of being overrun by pigweed and wild mustard and milkweed and thistles, and dandelions and potato beetles, and grasshoppers and blackbirds, who apparently, unlike us and our farms, needed no keepers or teachers and knew nothing of straight lines or submissiveness to the human collective good, and yet who seemed to be having a darn good time in their lawlessness?

Indeed, there seemed to be two different and opposite ways of being in the world, one governed by externally imposed rules stemming from our fathers and the Bible and God, the other by unpredictable, uncontrollable energies inherent in every living thing. This dichotomy held right through the great chain of being, from the lowliest creatures to the angels: it wasn't as simple as a dichotomy of nature versus culture, as contemporary theorists have characterized the binary nature of Western thought, nor was it about individuality versus collectivity, or randomness versus order, since wildness could be found as easily in cultural settings as in natural ones, and certain groups of people were considered especially dangerous: pagan drum-beating African tribes, say, and, especially dangerous for us, the shaggy-haired irreverent Beatles who stirred up eroticism and hysteria in crowds of young people and scandalously claimed to rival Jesus Christ in popularity.

Cities were considered havens of wildness in my village, not in Wayne Grady's sense of providing intentional or inadvertent refuge for bits of forest and wild animals and weeds, but in the sense of providing all kinds of avenues of escape from the eyes of the church and our own fathers. Cities challenged, in a direct way, Menno Simons' injunction to avoid daily association with unbelievers, which was after all the cornerstone of the Mennonite practice of cultural separatism. Multiculturalism, plurality, relativism, notions of fragmented identity, transitory communities and relationships, aesthetic superficiality, addiction to novelty, discontinuity, transience, mobility, intense momentary pleasures, and simultaneous gestures of primitivism and futurism—all these buzzwords and values of modernity and postmodernity, amply exemplified in the cultural organization of our Canadian cities, ran directly counter to Mennonite values, as we understood them, of cultural unity, extended families, the primacy of the local community, respect for tradition, orality, sobriety, emotional depth, spirituality, and a deep, long-term relationship to the land.

Of course we knew, everyone knew, there were some practising Mennonites living in cities, including some of our own close relatives, but in the villages, they were understood to be playing with fire, as evidenced in the worldliness of their children growing up surrounded by strangers, often unable to speak Plautdietsch or perform all six verses of twenty German hymns verbatim, on demand, and unclear about the subtle rules of plain style dress or other kinds of proper decorum, such as a demeanour of silence and lowered eyes before elders, and most importantly, virtually no knowledge of the seasons and the land.

Later, around the time of adolescence, the notion of wildness acquired a whole new range of meanings, mysteriously connected to something our parents were suddenly very worried about, a powerful erotic energy rising up in us that threatened to disrupt all that carefully tended obedience and reasonableness in us with new and unexpected force. Suddenly we were in need of taming all over again. Wildness, in this context, was connected with sexuality—yes, particularly in its aspect of fertility, an amazing prospect—but equally worrisome to our parents, with intellectual curiosity and the desire for adventure and travel and independence. How extraordinary and extravagant it was to discover that our awkward gawky trembling selves apparently harboured the potential to publicly shame our families and all-powerful fathers, simply by relaxing a portion of our taught vigilance, by allowing ourselves to get carried away with these new desires growing entirely unbidden and unforeseen (though certainly not unwelcome!) in us.

Much of our desire, my sister's and mine, was connected with our fantasies of escape to the wild city with its worldly enticements, in particular, the seduction of questionable places like libraries, bookstores, movie theatres, and the university, and folk festivals and rock music concerts, and bars with glittering dance floors, and live theatre, all of which were designed precisely so as to distract our attentions away from loyalty to Mennonite tradition. And thus it was that the leap from rural to urban, and traditional to contemporary—confusing and difficult and even dreary as it was in so many practical ways, having to learn how to negotiate cafeterias and bus schedules and apartment leases and job contracts and many other completely foreign inventions and arrangements, with no prior understanding of them, and having to negotiate at the same time strong family opposition to our heedless abandonment of the old village ways—was coloured by a delicious erotic flavour, nicely fanned by the "free love" rhetoric of '60s counterculture, and the complex rhetorics of feminism and multiculturalism and other negotiations of plurality coming after that, similarly inflected by notions of desire.

I'm remembering, as I'm writing this, so many poignant moments in those first confusing years of city life, how when I got married at the age of nineteen my father wanted to give the newlyweds a side of beef as a wedding present, even though we were living in a one-room apartment in the basement of the student residence at the Canadian Mennonite Bible College with a tiny shared freezer at the end of the hall, and professed to be vegetarians. How suddenly people around me were asking seriously whether it was appropriate for married women to work—an astonishing question to me, having grown up surrounded by strong, cheerful, highly skilled and hard-working farm women who managed large flourishing farm households, cooking, baking, laundering, gardening, tending cows and pigs and chickens, canning vegetables, sewing, decorating our houses and organizing social events, while raising numerous children, often singing lustily at the top of their voices. Women, as I knew them, never seemed to stop working, and singing, even on Sundays when our fathers obediently hung up their hats, even while visiting each other, pleasurably fussing over embroidery or knitting or crocheting. How my idea of quiet contemplation in those first years of city life was taking a nice long walk in the small forest behind the college or in Assiniboine Park, after dark, until my friends found me out, furious at my stupid lack of caution in dangerous urban places. Not only were women not supposed to work in cities, it seemed, but they weren't even supposed to walk around. How I practised, consciously and pointedly, shutting down my senses enough to be able to ride city buses and walk along downtown sidewalks without tremendous information overload. How severely city people frowned upon singing or even humming in public places, a deeply ingrained habit inherited from my mother and aunts and grandmothers, that took me years of concentration and tongue biting to undo. How odd it seemed to me, when I first began frequenting restaurants, to have people sitting right next to each other, pretending they weren't there.

How the John T. Robarts Library appeared in my parents' eyes when they came to visit me at the University of Toronto, as rooms full of inexplicably flimsy, poorly built shelves, far below my father's sturdy carpenter's standards. How pitiful and culturally impoverished my MA graduation reception seemed to them, and also to me, where hardly anyone knew anyone else and where neither singing nor beautiful oratory nor an elaborately prepared meal sweetened the hours of routine ceremony. How my mother kept asking me, after my children were born, what are you doing these days, Mrs. Friesen was asking me the other day and I just couldn't remember, and I'd say again, I'm going to school, Mom, I'm studying to earn a Ph.D. in English literature, and I could see her trying to translate this information into something useful and practical and reasonable enough to tell Mrs. Friesen, when it mostly appeared to her, and also sometimes to me, as nothing more than a monumental and tragic forgetting of our carefully guarded family treasury of detailed and powerful peasant skills and ceremonies. How nervous she was, attending my graduation ceremony, hoping no one from the village would see her there and witness this latest embarrassing act of her daughter's. As it turned out, there was someone there who knew her, and she did have to face that no doubt extremely painful moment of simultaneous pride and shame as the mother of a daughter who broke so many of the village rules in pursuit of dubious and incomprehensible achievements with mostly negative currency in the villages.

She didn't have that same confusion about my poetry. Unlike literary criticism, which is after all a kind of priestly, institutionally controlled, textual commentary deemed unnecessary by traditional Mennonites, as it is also to some extent in the contemporary Canadian popular mind, poetry was cherished and revered in our villages, both in its "high" incarnations as recited texts by Goethe or Heinrich Heine or hymn lyrics or the Bible itself, and its "low" versions as the children's recitations performed for Grandma at Christmas, or the freely improvised adaptations of "Parlez-vous" we made up for weddings and birthdays, or the endless ribald ballads our uncles scribbled on the machine shed walls during harness season, trying to parody and outdo each other with naughty rhymes, and checking every few days with great laughter to see the latest addition. (What wouldn't I give for a transcription of one of those summer-long twenty-stanza burlesque poetic compositions now!) Everyone in the villages knew exactly what poetry was, and understood precisely its imaginative power. Unlike, for example, most of my undergraduate students in southern Ontario, where I lived this past decade, the sons and daughters of factory workers for whom poetry was a mysterious foreign language with zero context outside the classroom, needing endless decoding into more rationalist, information-based, functionalist terms (or less easily, seduction into more erotically, mythically inflected vistas). But it didn't mean a young Mennonite village woman with no public credentials should be writing it, and especially she shouldn't be writing it about them, scattering our cultural secrets to strangers, blatantly selling us out to the world.

I never did successfully integrate the reversal of private and public spheres in moving from Mennonite country life, where work is private and family and church are public, to modern city life, where it's the other way around, a failure that has caused much misunderstanding between me and other people in both places over the years. And also much grief, in the sense of deep loss of the gathered community that knows each of its members intimately. Nor have I assimilated successfully the notion that emotional expressiveness is generally considered a bad thing, at least in Anglo-dominated urban circles, and that if you say or write something with feeling, your reasoning is probably suspect or, at the very least, you've been caught out in a humiliating act. A famous contemporary example would be American television anchorman Dan Rather's unintentional small sob during a David Letterman interview shortly after the events of September 11, 2001, in New York, which was portrayed as a serious professional lapse a few weeks later in an interview on *Larry King Live*. I will not apologize, said the recovered Dan Rather, slightly defiantly, what happened happened. I watched this with a pang, remembering how often both men and women in my village would cry in public when they were particularly moved by something, how those instances were honoured as communally shared moments of personal strength and truth telling, and how the separation of feeling from thinking would have been considered a dangerous splitting off in home community, as indeed I still believe it is. Would we be living in a safer world just now if the New Yorkers and Americans generally had allowed themselves to cry and wail and sob together in those first few days instead of biting their lips and imagining revenge?

Nor did I ever get used to the notion, characteristic of contemporary North American urban life, that art and literature are mostly decorative and have little bearing on our actual belief systems or the governance of the nation. It was hard, very hard—I am not exaggerating when I say it nearly killed me—to field so much deep criticism from my family and the larger Mennonite community for daring to break many of our cultural taboos in writing *questions i asked my mother*, and the books that followed, but I remember also how many of my artist friends at the time said, we envy you this audience who thinks what you write about matters that much.

It is impossible to think about the differences between rural Mennonite and contemporary Canadian urban cultures in these ways without reflecting on our different cultural genealogies. Many of my friends who grew up in Anglo urban households with puritan histories and resonances assume, because we Mennonites had strict rules of behaviour that included plain style dress and demeanour, and restrictions on education and use of electronic media, that we were puritan, that is to say, sexually and emotionally repressed, more at home in our heads than our feelings or bodies, and taught, like they were, to be obsessed with cleanliness and look down on dirt, that we shared their Enlightenment-derived Victorian-style ideas about the superiority of theory over practice, individuality over community, the abstract over the physical, logical proof over intuition and belief, earnestness over laughter, and the urban and urbane over the rural and simple. They also assume we share their notions of gender, that women are the weaker, more vulnerable sex, that we aren't made for hard or dirty work but for beauty and entertainment, that women are less intelligent than men, that men mustn't allow themselves tender feelings because they may be called upon to make war to defend the weak women, that men are the main keepers of public space and cultural life, that complexity is better than simplicity, that social change is necessarily a good thing and superior to preserving the old ways, that ordinary people have no right or means to challenge government decisions or the cultural implications of intellectual expertise, and so on.

But none of this is true. Surely the reason for our cultural separatism and numerous migrations and endurance of so much political persecution over centuries was to protect and preserve our deep connection to the land and the veneration of our traditional cultural ways, which included the following: an irreverent comic distrust of cultural hierarchies and so-called authority and expertise, whether bureaucratic, technological or intellectual; pacifism and the willingness to practise civil disobedience or migration to avoid military conflict; delight in physicality, sexuality, practicality and dirt; emotional and artistic expressiveness in music and poetic language; and a deep belief in the spiritual economy of "love," understood erotically and familially, and as a practice of toleration and loyalty to the village community. For everyone who missed out on the Mennonite celebration of dirt, let me describe some of my favourite remembered moments of it for you: how our mother would send us out on summer days after a rain shower to leap around in the puddles on the yard—Quick! she'd say, before they're gone! How our father's side of the bedroom would sprout little dirt hills from his trousers and shoes during harvest season, to everyone's great amusement. How coming into the house after an afternoon's hard play covered from top to toe in mud would be greeted by our mothers with approval and pleasure. How tenderly our fathers caressed the black earth in their fields around newly sprouted grain. (It was Australian writer Sylvie Shaw who made me realize how beautiful and valuable this celebration of dirt was, after hearing her paper, "Reclaiming the Eco-Erotic," at a conference in Scotland a few years ago, in which she complained about the degradation of dirt and therefore loss of eroticism and earthiness in industrialized countries.)

Our resistance to textualization and industrialization therefore happened not because we were intellectually backward, as the contemporary world has depicted us, but rather because we valued our oral peasant culture enough to want to preserve it, originally in resistance to the violent multinational globalizing tactics of the seventeenth and eighteenth centuries, not wanting to be shepherded into factories and crowded city ghettoes or culturally alienated suburbs as the peasants of England and Scotland were forced to do at that time. We have practised our traditionalism ever since, migrating from one country to another in search of political/cultural freedom, in resistance to whatever sources threatened it, including the pressures of citizenship in the modern national state, and the cultural investments of text and electronic media.

I began to understand something of the materialist aspect of our Mennonite origins and practice of separatism, when I read Carolyn Merchant's environmentalist history of Western agriculture and the rise of modern science in *The Death of Nature*, particularly her description of the communitarian movements of Europe during the Reformation, among which she includes the Anabaptists, our forebears. These movements, she argues, which are often described in religious, millenarian terms, were in fact peasant-led resistance movements to corporate takeovers by expansionist landlords during the early modern period, when mechanization of labour was revolutionizing European agriculture, and the Catholic church was suppressing pagan cultural practices all over Europe through the Spanish-driven Inquisition. The communitarian movements of northern Europe, writes Merchant, were much better organized to resist takeovers than were their less fortunate neighbours on the British Isles, who suffered eviction in large numbers during the enclosures of the commons. These resistance movements subscribed to an "organic" view of society, organized on democratic, egalitarian, communally interdependent principles, "modeled on nature's prime examples of communal colonies—bees and ants" (71).

I didn't learn about this materialist history in the villages of my childhood, where our separatism was theorized and enforced, quite sternly, in aesthetic, "feminine" terms—involving food and dress and language and demeanour—while farming itself, during the postwar years of the 1950s and '60s while I was growing up, was cheerfully and unquestioningly assimilating to Canadian mainstream agricultural practice through intense and rapid mechanization and chemicalization and corporatization. If our fathers had any ambivalence about this commercial selling out of our materialist separatism, or about the violent, multinational and even military resonances of these practices that so dramatically contradicted our pacifist and separatist beliefs in other areas of our lives, we never heard about it. And yet, there was a fierce ongoing attunement, throughout this period of accelerated modernization of farming methods in the villages, to the rhythms of the seasons and the weather, a profound appreciation of how deeply our lives as humans were intertwined with and dependent on nature, understood by us not in the English Romantic sense of a picturesque landscape to be gazed at with sublime appreciation, but rather in a quasi-pagan way as a fierce, fertile, living, wilful, dare I say, female and maternal presence to be fought with and feared and loved and revered, and hungrily, pleasurably suckled by.

I realize I am offering a slightly different genealogy of our Mennonite cultural affiliations than the one typically written about by Mennonite historians. James Urry, for example, has influentially claimed that the Russländer Mennonites had become enthusiastic industrialists by the end of the nineteenth century in Russia, and that their settlements in Canada in the 1920s were located strategically close to cities, with an eye to not only direct commercial links but also the urbanization and education of their children (123-54). The version I'm giving you here is perhaps more typical of the Chortitza group, which emigrated to Canada from Ukraine in the 1870s, that was less interested in urbanization or industrialization, and has continued, stubbornly, to practise a version of separatism despite the pressures of television and market globalization. But I would argue, as the sometimes loyal daughter of stubborn peasants whose roots in the land were deep, deep, transplanted as they were from the Flemish flatlands, our primal landscape, to the Russian steppes, to the Canadian prairies (similar enough bio-regions to make the transplants hugely successful), and whose oral memories were long, long, reaching back to the Burning Times and the exhortations of Menno Simons (whom we could quote nearly verbatim even though we didn't know he'd written books, only that he'd been a visionary and leader), that the peasant version is, culturally speaking, the predominant one, at least in the following ways: it is closer to the original vision of the Mennonite movement, at least the Menno Simons version of it; it is psychically accurate, if only in a guilty or nostalgic sense, even for those Mennonites who did flirt with urbanization and industrialization over the past two centuries; it provided the agricultural backbone in our difficult migrations from one underdeveloped landscape to another over four centuries of repeated pioneering; and most importantly, it has been the source of most of the influential Mennonite literary writing in Canada during the past two decades.

Here I am faced with a confusing question: if the genealogy I have traced here is an accurate one, then for my WASP and northern European friends it is we Mennonites whose values are "wild," unruly, anarchistic and socially dangerous to their status quo. We remember that fact with vividness, do we not, how we were persecuted in large numbers in northern Europe in the sixteenth and seventeenth centuries, tortured and burned at the stake, and drowned in rivers, and hounded out of our mother countries for precisely these reasons. So then I ask myself, did we, do we really hate and fear wildness, we Mennonites, haven't we in fact loved it, haven't we located ourselves geographically on the edge of it, the edge of the wild prairie, the Ukrainian steppes, the Chaco, the Mexican desert, whenever we found ourselves moving due to changed political circumstances? Isn't that where we have been most comfortable, balancing on the precarious edge between so-called "civilization" and "wildness"? Haven't we, socially speaking, been more comfortable locating ourselves next to Turkish and Aboriginal and Métis communities with their oral, tribal, hunting-gathering sensibilities than within modern post-industrial hierarchical bureaucracies?

Isn't this, I ask myself, what I'm most nostalgic about when I think of my Mennonite heritage, from the staid, organized factory culture of southern Ontario, where my students and their families rarely dream of challenging the practices of large-scale manufacturing or corporate multinationalism or the war in Afghanistan; in the eastern side of our continent where it is said that 90 per cent of the women don't know what sexual orgasm is; where strong feelings and physicality and emotional expressiveness and spontaneous laughter and dirt are frowned upon as inappropriate and possibly obscene, while the extensive degradation of air and water through heavy industry is regarded, institutionally at least, as reasonable and respectable? Isn't this what I am most grateful for to my ancestors, to have grown up in a culture that claimed for itself the right to hold onto its economic and cultural self-determination despite overwhelming pressures to give them up? Then why at the same time were we so nervous about other kinds of wildness, nervous enough to allow ourselves extensive violence in the attempted eradication of it in our children and animals and fields and gardens? Nervous enough to drive our artists and visionaries from our communities, even shunning them from family gatherings and personal relationships with family members—as has been done to me for over a decade now?

What is wildness, exactly? Obviously it is not just disorder or chaos or negativity or evil, since when we look it in the eye, we see that one community's wildness is the other's social organization, and one person's or species' wildness is another's carefully preserved and necessary life spirit. Wildness seems to be profoundly about otherness: a radical irreducible difference at the heart of all living beings and organisms and communities. But, as those of us who were brought up wrestling with wildness know deeply, it is more radically dynamic than that: an energetic fiery free-spiritedness that also connects these differences in unexpected, erotic and magical ways, and that resides at the very heart of life on this planet. Aboriginal people call this energy variously the trickster, Raven, the shapeshifter, Changing Woman, and so on, and honour these beings and this energy in and among us with fear and reverence and laughter, as god (Allen 1986, Hyde 1998). Mayan trained shaman Martín Prechtel calls this wild spirit "the indigenous soul," and exhorts us all to cultivate it as a way of reversing the ravages of overindustrialization in the contemporary arena (2001, 109-25).

Western culture, by contrast, has been obsessed with domesticating and/ or eradicating wildness in people, plants, animals and ecosystems, while at the same time desiring and needing its power. There have been many theories to justify the human-centred project of planetary domestication through the centuries, including, recently, the Gaian theory of earth management made popular by James E. Lovelock and his followers, who call themselves environmentalists. But as critic John Livingston observes, the Gaian theorists still hold to the belief that "only through human agency does planet Earth become whole and complete, self-aware in the human image" (211, n.8). Livingston proposes, as an alternative to "the destiny of earth as a human monoculture," the cultivation of respect for the inherent wildness of all living beings, which he describes eloquently as follows: "Wildness is not acquired through covenant or dispensation. Wildness is, and has been, from the beginning. It is not merely an evolved phenomenon; it is a quality of being, and a precondition of having become. As such, it is beyond the reach of rationality; it is previous, and transcendent. It has no missing parts, either through mutation or amputation. It requires no prosthetic devices, no fixing, no reordering, no moral overlays. Wildness requires no organizational intervention, even of the purest and highest democratic sort. Wildness is whole. It is the antithesis of the domesticated human state, uncontaminated by power, claims to power, or the need for power." (172)

What if we spent our imaginative energies celebrating and honouring wildness, and locating ourselves within it, as Métis poet Gregory Scofield does in his poem, "Oskan-Acimowina (Bone Stories)":

Before I was flesh and bone,
I was magpie
in her blood, singing
in her belly

all winter.

Before
I had bone songs, stories
of weeds and stones
there was a great sky
shimmering with stars.

(114)

It was freedom, akin to wildness understood in this way, that I came to the city in search of, when I abandoned—or perhaps I should say fled—the peasant Mennonite village culture of my heritage at age seventeen, bereft, heartbroken, terrified, but also hugely optimistic and ready for adventure. I can say that I found it in Winnipeg, this city that I love, with its beautiful parks and forests and rivers, haven to wild deer and beavers and rabbits and squirrels and numerous kinds of birds and fish and other creatures, its tree-lined streets, its rich cultural life, its urban offer of anonymity and experimentation and encounters with diversity, its fierce struggle to exist and flourish against numerous environmental and economic obstacles. I also found here that other necessary ingredient to the artist's life, a strongly supportive artistic community, interested in every kind of creative expression, with generous mentors and peers—Les Brandt, Patrick Friesen, Robert Kroetsch, Carol Shields, Sandra Birdsell, Smaro Kamboureli, Armin Wiebe, Pamela Banting, Kristjana Gunnars, Jan Horner, Marie Annharte Baker, Aganetha Dyck, Diana Thorneycroft, Miriam Toews and many others—most of whom were negotiating interesting cultural leaps of their own, and who taught me, among other things, that discontinuities and contradictions in my cultural identity were occasions of celebration as well as lament, and who shared with me the joy and terror of learning to dance with the words, and make them shake.

Some urban theorists are now arguing that the city is obsolete, having been replaced by homogeneous conglomerates of highways and suburban hamlets, that "place" in this sense has been replaced by "space" (cf. MacLean, Landry and Ward, "Introduction," 1-23). While this is true of much of central and eastern North America, including southern Ontario, it is decidedly not true of the prairies, where cities have distinct circumferences, and possess strongly identifiable characters in the manner of the great cities established in previous eras: Paris, London, Barcelona, New York. One of the reasons our prairie cities have retained their distinctive characters is surely because of the distance between them, but another, ironically, is because they were left out of the great economic boom of eastern Canada and the US during the past few decades. This fact has created economic hardship for many citizens and forced some people, including me, to leave, but it also means that the population size has been relatively stable, housing prices have remained low, and pollution and industry have been kept at a much more manageable level than in the east. In Windsor, Ontario, for example, where I lived from the mid '90s until recently, you can get a chemical burn from putting your hands into the silt of the Detroit River (reported on the front page of *The Windsor Star*, September 8, 2001). Still, it is nice to see cicadas, butterflies and fireflies still flourishing in eastern Canada and the United States, when we've sprayed most of them to death on the prairies.

Winnipeg has been able to hold onto its established character as, among other things, a cultural gateway, a meeting place, the Forks, elegantly poised on the axis between eastern and western North America with their different geographical and cultural orientations, and also vitally located on the dynamic, creative and tragic edge between prairie First Nations and settler cultures, at the place where we must negotiate together our separate and shared destinies. Perhaps it is this unique mix of cultural and geographical factors that has nurtured Winnipeg's strong creative character and turned it into a solidly established artists' mecca, with more music, drama, film, literary festivals, bookstores and theatres per capita than any other city I know of. When I think of "city," therefore, it is Winnipeg, the city I have lived in the longest and love the most—proud, stubborn, elegant, shabby, gracious, desperate, playful, violent, flourishing, hot, cold, easy, struggling— that I think of. I feel lucky to have had my artistic apprenticeship and to have been able to raise my children in Winnipeg, surrounded by the great singing prairie. Though it was once a place of great spatial and cultural confusion for me, as a newly arrived village peasant girl from Reinland, Manitoba, and though I will spend the rest of my life mourning the loss of my beloved mother culture, mother tongue, mother lands, this city became home for me, and I consider it so still.

Berlin notes

Berlin came into me like a mist, a garden, a knife, a flame. It was early April, the trees were newly green, the wind cold, tasting of winter. I went to Berlin because of Jenny Erpenbeck. Because the women she invented, A and B, skewer each other scene after scene with cruel word games, extreme cruelty disguised as love. Nothing gets fixed up in her play, *Katzen haben sieben Leben*. (Cats have seven lives. English cats get nine chances: why is that?) There is no mitigation, resolution. There is expectation, betrayal, rapid escalation of threats, sudden violence. Silence. There is no pretense of innocence. Neither is there apology, penance, renewal. A and B are generic, fastened neither to place nor calendar, only to each other, their own shadows, themselves. They are us.

I wanted to go to the city that made this play possible: that let a woman brush up so close to the murderous impulse that gets paraded as love, sometimes, between people, that let her touch it, flirt with it, play, like a cat with its stunned bird, without self-destructing. The grace of it. Not in the script, but in the watching of it. See, it's speakable, it happened to them, too. Funny, even. Entertaining, witty. Or, no, they don't survive it, the characters kill each other, *kalt tot*, over and over, but the play goes on. Their violence exceeds them, outlives them, but by that very fact is redeemed, in our witnessing of it, the playwright's stylish retrieval of it from denial, the underworld, oblivion. Not distracted, clogged up, by technology, drugs, petroleum, glamour, the endless frightening parade of things, products, as we mostly are, hard to escape it now, in our lives and fictions, in North America.

Is this a safe time to go, my Toronto friends asked. After all there is a war on. Berlin? And there's SARS. It was the spring of 2003. Berlin is safer, now, I heard this thought resonating somewhere deep in my bones, safer than Toronto or Detroit. It is we in North America who have become dangerous to the rest of the world, and to ourselves, though we insist loudly and repeatedly on pronouncing our innocence. Innocence is the eighth deadly sin, Margaret Laurence said.

I stepped off the plane, no forms to fill out, no questions to answer, no border hysteria, paranoia, formalities. Collect your suitcases from the moving ramp and walk out. Is this Germany? Is this Berlin? Famed city of walls, guns, borders, surveillance, xenophobia? *Achtung! Jawohl!* Kneejerk impulses bred into the world by countless Hollywood portraits of robotic army commanders, *das angeführte Volk*. All those forms and questions in Toronto. The helpless gesture of surveillance against SARS. Who were you in contact with last week? Which doorknobs did you touch? When did you sneeze? All those bizarre subjectless defence alerts across the American border now, yellow, orange, red, stepped up surveillance, tapped telephone lines, opened mail, guilt about the war in Iraq and Afghanistan and godknowswhere next, disguised as huge, nameless, faceless fear.

When did I fall in love, was it that first week, in the blur of finding out where everything was, getting used to the euro, the map, the S-Bahn, the building sites on every corner, colourful new buildings going up everywhere among the still visible ruins of that other terrible war half a century ago, the lovely thick Berliner accent spoken everywhere around me, having to retreat to bed in my little apartment sometimes in the middle of the day to recover from the sensual information overload? Was it the second week, the third? Realizing suddenly, with a start, I'm living on an island! Right in the middle of the placid Spree River, a famous island, in the heart of Alt Berlin, surrounded by what's left of the great old museums and statues and gardens of Museeninsel, in the historic Nikolaiviertel, the very Mitte of the Mitte. For some reason it made me think of Anaïs Nin, in her houseboat on the Seine, rocking in a new age from her little haven. I've always wanted to live on an island.

And then Berlin broke into blossom, huge scented flowers and shrubs on every street, the great parks with multicoloured greens, mauve lilacs, bright pink chestnut blossoms, purple and pink and white hibiscus, rose tinted apple and dark red plum, the mysterious pervasive scent of linden blossoms, nearly invisible under their broad leaves, and then the roses, not the hothouse cultivated thick petalled roses of North America but thin delicate ones, bright red, yellow, white, on every large and small city square, surrounding the arabesque fountains, weeds growing between the patterned cobblestones, the granite slabs of sidewalk, no pesticides in the famous *Champagner Luft* of Berlin, the champagne air. A third of the famous city is forests and parks. There are occasionally ornate Chinese gates and Prussian stone lions and bridges inscribed with bronze medallions, the winged Victory column, military symbol turned angel for the celluloid generation, techno muse for the colourful children of the Love Parade, a few imitation French gardens, so much simpler, more casual than Versailles, cotton shirts and sensible shoes instead of corsets and pointy toes and high heels. But most of the parkland is tangled, overgrown, a beautiful northern wildness right there in the midst of streets and churches and buses and riverboats and trains and embassies and office buildings. You can touch the grass here! exclaimed my daughter Lisa, visiting for the weekend from Paris. Not just touch it, I said, look, the signs say *Liegewiese* and *Lustgarten*, meadows to lie in, these are, officially, pleasure gardens.

It was the *Gurkensalat*, made with cream, thinly sliced cucumbers, served in little glass bowls in a supermarket restaurant. It was the rich sugared purple *Pflaumenkuchen*, served heated up on a little plate with a paper lace doily in the Alexanderplatz Tourist Information coffee shop. It was the *Kaffee mit Sahne*, served in countless street cafes, at little tables with coloured straw chairs, in the middle of the afternoon, on a decorated cup and saucer. Ceremonies of innocence, as Yeats called them, lamenting their erosion, still beautifully intact here on this northern edge of modernity. It was the polite earnest manner of the waiters and post office clerks and people on the street. Earthy, hearty, passionate, neat, orderly. Traditionalist, stylish, modern. (How can they be both?) It was the Berliner dialect, with its Huguenot inflections and traces of *Plautdietsch*, my lost mother tongue, *Jo, nay, daut ish ja nit*.

It was the theatre, with its full-bodied emotional expressiveness. *Schrei Theater*, Sara called it, disparagingly, citing the press, but to me it was robust. Ah! What a relief to be surrounded by expressionists, bodies at home in their skin, big bellies, lungs. All that nakedness in the public baths, young, old, everyone walking around proudly, frankly looking at each other, assessing, interested, casual, relaxed. The theatre of Brecht and Weill and zany Max Frisch. The poetics of *die Brücke*, with its war-time paintings in deep bright colours. Red grass. Yellow sky. Purple trees. Blue houses. The startling fiercely surreal paintings of postwar East Berlin at the National Museum, filled with screams and howls and streaks of terror, dramatically unlike the cliché stylized Communist propoganda paintings we've been shown in the West.

Lorca's achingly beautiful medieval Spanish tragedy, *Bluthochzeit, Bodas de Sangre, Blood Wedding*, in the newly renovated chandeliered red-carpeted Deutsches Theater in passionate surrealist German tones, hotblooded flamenco transformed into haunting postmodern lyric movements. The glitter spangled love oil dribbled over the suffering dancers, their thrilling desire. Near the end of the first act, the bride disappears with her ex-lover, who has appeared uninvited at the wedding party. The evocative scene I will never forget, the doomed lovers in their long night of ecstasy, he twirls her around on a high rope swing, his blood reaches after her, the shining folds of her silk dress, his outstretched hands, her head bent back, long blonde hair falling to the ground, her arched throat. Wanting love so badly they are willing to risk their lives for it. Would I have done the same, I asked myself, to escape burial in a stultifying marriage? Yes, I thought, yes.

Why is it that we can't imagine passionate love in our stories, even now, even after centuries of romance narratives, and romantic marriage conventions, so many variations of erotic art, without it ending in death? Perhaps it is, as Jeanette Winterson says, simply a biological imperative: the difference between those organisms that reproduce by multiplication, like bacteria, versus those who reproduce through copulation, and therefore die (2004). Perhaps it is, as Hélène Cixous said, that only dogs among this planet's species have evolved enough to know what love is, unconditionally, and because it hurts us to see it, to be the undeserving recipients of it, we beat them, we crucify those among us who aspire to reach that same depth of affiliation, loyalty, ecstasy (Cixous, 1998, 257-9). The word made flesh: we still cannot bear it. The audience weeps through the intermission in the courtyard, into our *Rotwein* in the candlelit cobblestone courtyard, watching the fire eater performing his death defying tricks, his threadbare life lived so close to the ground, *Maurice von Parice*. We weep over the doomed lovers, knowing what will come next, the outraged relatives dressed in black, *schwarze Geier*, the vultures moving in.

Later, Michael, sweet *Heilpraktiker* of Dortmund, in gentle farming country, close, very close to my ancestral lands, at the Dutch border, we might have been cousins, whose hands I love, whose touch I live for on my broken spirit/bones in this long, centuries long, healing, Tuesday afternoons at two o'clock, Michael says this word *Geier*, as in *O, O, der Pleitegeier kommt*, when I tell him my health insurance has run out and I won't be able to afford more chiropractic/acupuncture/homeopathic treatments. The German eagle stamped on the repossessed furniture of the poor, he smiles, *die Pleite*. You will have to hold out a hat on the street.

I had never once, in the year before I left Canada, thought of my Berlin travel adventure as a homecoming. I came after all for the exotic experience of otherness, to immerse myself in a famous city's rich cultural scene, to feed my restless hungry muse, whose fierce dictations lost me my strict traditionalist German-speaking Mennonite family, my village homeland, my mother tongue, in a series of shunnings and economic dislocations that terrified me, then broke my heart. I came to escape for awhile the dreadful pollution, both spiritual and cultural, of the clogged industrialized urban Ontario landscape where I was living, at the border to Detroit, on the NAFTA Superhighway. *NAFTA, we worship you.* Trucks and trucks and cars and cars and border guards and border guards. Thick grey air. The house across the street from my apartment swathed in a haze. Particulate matter, settling into every living cell, burrowing for cancer.

Berlin rose up from the earth around me, from the cadences of the language, the dark hauntings spiralling out from back alleys, courtyards, street corners, the gold cobblestones naming where Jewish family lives and homes were lost during the war, the spooky remnants of the wall, flaunted by West Berlin, winced at in the *Ost*. Daniel Libeskind's lead-coloured broken Star of David museum, sharp gashes of light through windowless walls of cement, jewel of remembrance, grieving, sprawled at the heart of the city. The pain of that dark memory in every stone and tree. The gravity of people who have lived through catastrophe, or inherited its imprint, even the teenagers, children. Very little of the infamous neo-Nazi movement so popular in the North American media. Small handfuls of punks with dogs and spiked collars and chains drink beer on the park benches at Alexanderplatz, bothering no one except perhaps their own women: the girl I saw at the Friedrichstrasse subway station on a dog leash, a joke, but still. The kid on the S-Bahn with his ghetto blaster at full volume, all the old people scurrying to another car. His light blue eyes looked at Lisa and me, his belligerence gradually turned to curiosity and even affection, when he saw we weren't afraid, only bemused. *Kann ich das haben?* he asked me, pointing to the anti-Bush pin on my sweater. *Nein*, I said, *Ich will es behalten.* I want to keep it myself. On May Day each year, hoodlums dig up cobblestones in Kreuzberg to throw at the cops, overturn cars, set them on fire, a predictable yearly ritual. If this is anarchy it is well orchestrated and contained. In Poland, not far away geographically, but in another paradigm altogether, young people kiss under flowering trees and on rooftops on this day, variations on ancient spring rituals, goddess worship. (Are revolutions really commemorations of spring that have forgotten their origin?)

The beautiful wounded heart of a great nation recovering from a half century of internal division, and the terrible tragedy of the war before that, the "wall of shame" separating cousins and lovers, guarded by rifle-toting nineteen-year-old boys in uniforms, at the other end of the spectrum of public boy behaviour. Wall of protection, to the Ossies, of a high minded anti-Faschistik, anti-Kapitalistik vision: a communist utopia despite the various failures in its enactment. The bewildering rearrangements after it came down, another heap of rubble to sweep up. Trying, as few modern peoples are willing to do, to face up to that dark heritage, not only as victim but also as perpetrator, the bank robber left holding the gold. Eloquent memorials on every major city site. This happened to us, this is what we did.

You mean, you are going to find out how to write about your own cruel side, my other daughter Ali said in Toronto, with the perceptiveness of children who carry the secrets of their mother's belly around with them as memory of their first surround. This is what happened to me and this is what I did. *Ich bin ein Berliner.* Or maybe she means it communally, the collective heritage of our Mennonite people's long history of persecution and, yes, cruelty. Martyrs turned perpetrators, the heritage turned inward. (And outward: we may have disagreed with North American expansionism, but we still occupy land that belonged to indigenous peoples not long ago. Can history ever be fixed up or atoned for or undone? We haven't even begun to memorialize the cultural cost of occupying Turtle Island, let alone negotiate amends.)

Jenny could write a play about women fighting each other, scratching each other's eyes out, hanging themselves in front of each other with rope, because of the trees, the great whispering oaks, the sweet smelling lindens, the gorgeous blossomed *Kastanienbäume*. The rich comfort of the wild grown roses along the banks of the Spree, on Iburger Ufer, splashes of crimson among tangles of green. Because of the robust theatre, the great sense of the *Bühne* of the German people. The stage is dead, Leonard Cohen said. There is no more poetry after Auschwitz. But it's not true, not here, not in Berlin. The stage lives, as nothing else, here. The sacred sense of public space, eloquent utterance, performance art. (How could it not? The whole world watches Berlin.) From the snappy high art of the Berliner Ensemble and Maxim Gorki Theater to the low art of the Ku'Damm. Half naked dancers, pretty boys, flaunting their gayness, dressed in sunflowers. Circus trapeze. The heritage of a city exempt from the rest of the country's conscription laws, haven of dropouts, peaceniks, new-agers. (The women weaving in and out, between.) And a long tradition of serious play, before that. This was after all the City of Sin, the city of gays and lesbians in the '20s, the city of jazz, of interracial nightclub decadence and experimentation, a particular object of Hitler's puritanical Aryan wrath. Ironic that America prefers to remember Hitler instead of the artists, or perhaps, sadly, not so ironic in this age of George Bush, the American Reich. Barbara wasn't interested in the Love Parade, too techno, too popular culture, not political enough, she said. Ah, but what about its pacifist anarchist erotic Black Detroit homosexual connections, all that colour dancing under the golden wings of the Victory Column? It's why I came.

Surprise! They still have professional elocutionists reciting classic German poetry in Berlin theatres! *Ich weiss nicht, was soll es bedeuten*, the audience gasping or prompting or chuckling as appropriate. *Und in seinen Armen das Kind war tot*, everyone knowing all the lines, including me. The *unheimlich* thrill of Goethe's *Der Erlkönig*, which we memorized in grade five German class in Manitoba without pedagogical commentary. Why didn't the father see him in the forest following his horse? Why did the Erlkönig demand the life of the child in his arms, against the father's warm safe embrace? The collective pleasure of anticipating that well known dreadful ending. When did we stop reciting poetry in North America? So many things have disappeared. I remember reciting "The Assyrian came down like the wolf on the fold" (from Lord Byron's poem, "The Destruction of Sennacherib") at a festival competition in grade nine, their shining antique gold armour alarmingly out of place in the plain style Winkler Collegiate auditorium. That would have been in the mid '60s, in Manitoba, the same festival where Loreena McKennitt honed her tremulous Celtic lilt, surrounded by Mennonite farm childen playing Bach and Mendelssohn, some brilliantly, going on to become world renowned professional musicians. All that is gone. *Wir haben so viel verloren*, one of Jenny Erpenbeck's Ossie characters from another story says. We have lost so much. *Ja, wir auch.*

The first thing that was rebuilt amidst the great heaps of rubble that was Berlin after the war was the theatre. *Poesie*. Then the trams, then everything else. Oh, but that's a myth, said a tall blond German economist with the *Financial Times* I spoke with at a politically charged poetry reading by Slovenian poet Boris Novak, at the well appointed Literaturhaus on Fasanenstrasse. The first thing must have been the sewers and waterpipes. But theatre is catharsis and water for the spirit. How otherwise get enough strength to rebuild a city, a nation, a country, after so much tragedy, friends killing friends in the Lustgarten in front of the Dom, Nazis and *Antifaschisten* violently deploying the rub of East against West? How else gather together long lines of women painstakingly removing the rubble of a shattered city in tin pails? A half century of work, the Americans and Brits gleefully predicted, having shot out their new war toys pornographically on the staggering nation, faltering by then under the inflated weight of their own misguided dictator. Some people fear the Germans for their dominator aspirations, but it's not the Deutsche who have ruled the world for the most part, their modern attempts at takeovers botched beyond thinkability. Berliner women in handsewn '50s cotton dresses and braided hair, singing folksongs, *Das Wandern ist des Müllers Lust*, cleaning up those high heaps of rubble, their hundreds of thousands of dead, to the surprise of the watching world, in a mere handful of years.

The great Berliner Stadtschloss would have still been here then, across the tree-lined Unter den Linden, though bombed into ruins, where the big cement parking lot is now. Next to the abandoned Palast der Republik, dilapidated remnant of the DDR days, with its rust-coloured mirror glass facade, still beautiful at sunset despite plywood in many of the windows, weeds growing all around, waiting for renovation or destruction, overlooking the formidable bronze figures of the eerie Marx Engels Forum across the Spree River, uncomfortable Communist art from a bygone era, now turned museum, a popular tourist photo site. My communist mother always rushes over there to get her photo taken when she comes to visit me in Berlin, says Algerian-born Hocine. Along with a million other tourists from around the world.

It wasn't a local family quarrel, was it, though we like to think of it that way in North America. Scared hungry Berliners got caught between ideologies, relatives got turned tragically against each other, along that ragged seam of earthly bipolar differences, the planetary right brain/left brain split. The gypsies and Jews and gays were caught in between: modernist experimentalism, aesthetic decadence, philosophy and jazz, bred through the lineage of black American ex-slaves in the smoky bars of New York, all became suspect. Frightening to think of how easily a beleagured people can turn inhumane, falling back on that old European script, the witch hunt, the faggot, the Anabaptist, the Jew hunt, re-enactments of the Inquisition.

I couldn't get a clear sense of geographical direction in Berlin. I understood where Ost and West were, had been, but I couldn't understand how the Atlantic could be in the west. I repeated it to myself at night: the Atlantic Ocean is west of Berlin, Paris is over there. Museeninsel, I realized, is not a real island, flanked on one side by a canal. Oh, but a really old canal, Jenny said, old enough to count as a river: it's a real island now, see how many old bridges there are across to it. And showed me the real live bears in the little bear pit on Fischerinsel at the east end of the island: the old mascot of Berlin. Bears are no longer paraded in the streets in chains as they once were, having been replaced for the most part now by little plush teddy bear toys, greatly diminishing their totemic effect. But here they still are, real living bears, keepers of the wild heart of the city, disguised princes and lovers from the old stories, with their hearts of gold. And around the corner from my Ossi apartment (reputedly a *Gasthaus* of the Stasi during the Communist years), a sweet old redstone sculpture features a mother bear sitting on her haunches calmly, sensuously, her little bears tumbling around her in playful rivalry and embrace.

How strange to feel such great ancestral connection to this land. How strange to feel so protective of it with my visitors from North America, wanting to hug it close, safe from outsiders' comments (even from other Germans,' Mark of Hannover's comment on the train to Paris: Oh, in Berlin everything is an argument). How unsurprising to hear Americans here repeating all the old Hollywood clichés about *die Deutschew*, easy target of satire after decades of *Hogan's Heroes* and Schwarzenegger, from a country now embroiled in its own dictatorial scandals, its muzzled news media.

Henri Chopin, the father of sound poetry and guest star of the Poesiefestival, is now a bright-eyed, spry eighty-three-year-old man in a wheelchair, who drinks wine, smokes Gauloises, and offers kisses to women fans like me. After the war, he says, in which I was interned in a series of POW camps, some of them in this country, often narrowly escaping with my life when hundreds of

Fig. 4 "Di with the bears of Alt Berlin." Photo: Eunice Scarfe, 2003.

thousands of my comrades were blown to bits, I lost my faith in philosophy. I believed only in the body, and rhythm and sound: the body as a sound machine. I come back here now, he says, and see that the German people are the only people among rich nations to have the capacity and will to ask why it happened, to think about the past in a profoundly revisionary way. I thank you, he says (a bit disingenuously), if you hadn't put me in prison here, I would never have discovered sound poetry. And: You are the nation that will show the rest of the world what remorse is, what mourning is, how to revisit the past, memorialize it, undo the effects of it, insofar as it is possible. Someone asks, does he think his vision of a global sound poetry revolution has been fulfilled? He looks straight at us with those lively blue eyes. I have lived my life with integrity, he says energetically. I have never compromised my beliefs, or my vision. (It is how I am trying to live, too.)

How strange to think of my Dutch German Mennonite heritage filtered through the lens of this grand landscape, this complicated past. The great statue of the warlike Friedrich the Great on his mighty horse and Friedrich Wilhelm III in effeminate artsy poses on Under den Linden avenue was built around the time my people had to leave yet another poverty-stricken landscape, cultivated from bare steppes into rugged farmland by their strong hands, to begin all over again on the Canadian prairies. One exile after another. Northern Germany, Prussia (Poland), Ukraine. How did they manage to preserve so many northern German customs so perfectly? The *Pflaumenkuchen* recipes, the *Gurkensalat*, the ancient inflections of *Plautdietsch*, our mother tongue. I am overwhelmed by the thought of my ancestors' stubborn faithfulness, their anarchistic traditionalism, that crazy beautiful heritage, still flourishing in the old ways in the Canadian prairie, surrounded by First Nations history, the resonance of drumbeats on buffalo hide, the modern world of machinery and chemicals gradually moving in. The Germans have worked harder at understanding their occupations and genocides than we have.

I scour the public library in Rotterdam, where I have come to visit my friend Arnold Schalks and attend the Rotterdam Poetry Festival, for histories of my people: crazy Anabaptists, sensuous naked libertines sprawled in communal orgies according to one engraving, crazy Münsterites, Waco-type fanatics, eager to blow up the world in apocalyptic fanaticism, in another. Witches, burned in the town squares. If the Mennonites weren't so *Plaut* minded, one writer offers, they'd fly off into never-never land with their utopian ideas. As it is, they're too prosaic and sensible to get completely carried away. (If they hadn't been tortured, burned, drowned, hounded out of their homes, I think.) Holland has long been known for its broadmindedness and tolerance of difference, the editor of a collection of essays on religious pluralism in the Netherlands offers, as it still is, allowing public marijuana use and state sanctioned prostitution. (I think of Arnold's apartment in the Kunst en Complex co-op on the Keileweg, in the heart of the Tipple district: the girls next door, sitting up all night on the sidewalk, arms around each other, trying to get through a bad drug trip, boys of every colour loitering on the street in front of the pink neon lit brothel, making deals. It was quite the bike ride for me, returning from the Rotterdam poetry festival to his apartment late at night.) Could we have come back, then, those raggedy traumatized few who lost their relatives at the stakes, after the furor of the Burning Times died down, we with our fierce peasant tribal-minded anti-nationalism? We could have come to Berlin, I think, with the Huguenots, instead of trekking to the open fields of Poland, the desolate steppes of Ukraine. You could have saved yourself centuries of wandering, Paul says, chuckling, instead of just arriving here now: Would it have been any easier? Would we have ended up *im Osten oder Westen*? But much as we talked about homeland and honouring the ancestors, preserving our custom and language and love of the land, the Mennonites of my upbringing weren't interested in going back. It never even came up as an idea. Our whole outlook was frontier-oriented, at the same time fiercely traditionalist and cheerfully pioneering. *Heimat*, home, was an idea, the nostalgic motif of an old song, tinged with the memory of flames.

I apologize on behalf of the Dutch people, writer, publisher and political activist Maria Jacobs said to me over breakfast in her apartment on Bleeker Street in Toronto, when I told her about the trouble in my family, my shunning, the traumatic history of domestic violence, for having caused so much suffering among your people, by taking your lands. It was over then, I saw, breaking the soft-boiled eggs in their delicate shells, spreading strawberry jam on the perfectly warmed French bread, the whole heritage of suffering, the need to re-enact it upon each other. That was Maria's gift to me, to my people. We don't have to stay in that story forever. We could go back home if we wanted to, to the land where our deep ancestral roots are. (But could we? Would we end up like the Israelis, fighting to the death for our return home?) We could invent other stories.

Katzen haben sieben Leben had played for three years at the Deutsches Theater, a media hit, by the time I arrived in Berlin. The company had not followed the script carefully, as we did, workshopping my English translation of it with a handful of talented Drama students and director Lionel Walsh at the University of Windsor the previous winter. They had moved the order of scenes around. They cut and sliced and pasted, they took extravagant liberties in their interpretation. When the manager grills the shop girl, her employee, about her career aspirations and commitment to the job, which requires nothing more or less than a Pozzo/Lucky slavish mindlessness, she adds: Imagine, we didn't have any stores. With those five words the whole history and location of Berlin comes flooding into the play, the overwhelming changes of the *Wendezeit*. How ironic, from a Western point of view, to know that communism was better for tradition and social ceremony than capitalism, at least here in Berlin. The "free" West, free to seek out new communities to exploit. The "closed" East. Closed to commercial ventures that would bulldoze social conventions into the ground, ever in search of the new, the bigger, the better, the improved.

What should we say about Canadian poet activist Dorothy Livesay's naive socialist optimism in her '30s poetry in light of the failure of communism? Barbara Godard and I discussed this statement of Pamela McCallum's (in an unpublished essay) in my Berlin apartment, over tea. Socialism isn't dead, I keep protesting to my Canadian visitors. Live here among the Ossies for awhile: you will see, the dream hasn't died. There are demonstrations along the street every month. Cells, study groups, political rallies: the vision of communalism will never die. (It is my heritage too.) Globalization in the capitalist mode may be an unstoppable force around the world at the moment, but look at the opposition. The world's poor, the disgruntled, the visionaries, are reorganizing quietly (on occasion noisily), with some bewilderment, but lots of high passion. Just because socialism didn't win, didn't survive its own excesses, doesn't mean it wasn't a worthy aspiration. There is a change coming, a cataclysmic change, in the way the world is organized: one can feel the energy of it bubbling up, tangibly, from below the ground, here, among the open spaces created by the fallen Wall, the vanished Iron Curtain.

Instead of angels flying across a desert in the poetic interludes between scenes, as Jenny's script dictates, we see a plastic doll on a cable, moving clumsily, battery-operated, from right to left above the stage. The intertwined spirit voices of A and B, reconnoitering somewhere above earth between incarnations, merged in an electronically altered midget's voice. Parodic, technologically profane, shades of Weimar and Weill. They are dressed in black velvet evening dresses and white silk gloves throughout, even while vacuuming, even in the dying grandmother scene. Instead of lying in bed, emaciated, too weak to hold the pistol she begs her granddaughter to shoot her with, as the script suggests, she stands at the back of the stage, golden-haired, sexy, pistols in both hands like a Western fashion model turned gangster. The granddaughter, played by the much older-looking other woman, takes a pistol from her gently, and puts it into the grandmother's mouth. Violence as an ultimate act of love. The script turning in on itself, spinning, quantumly, into another register.

Somewhere in the middle of a scene, someone sings, *Sah ein Knab' ein Röslein stehn, Röslein auf der Heide,* and I snap back into my childhood, three years old, sitting on my affectionate grandma's lap. We never got sung to like that, Eunice said, my Norwegian Midwest American ancestors gave up all the old folksongs for Luther, the Bible, good works, and hymns. A rose on the wild meadow sticks her thorn sternly into the destructive little boy's finger. (Why do little boys throw sticks at swans in the park? Scattering them, eliciting disapproval, instead of enticing them to come closer, to tame them, as girls and old women do.) Rilke claimed he died of a rose thorn. It was how he discovered his fatal blood illness, fatally caressing his beloved blooms. *Rose, oh reiner Widerspruch, Lust,/Niemandes Schlaf zu sein unter soviel/Lidern:* the enigmatic epitaph he wrote for himself, roses still blooming on his grave on the high rock overlooking the exquisite vine-covered slopes of Raron, at the foot of the Swiss Alps. It sounds like "songs" but he meant lids, as in the eyelids of sleep, comments Ragni, who reads us "Der Panther" under the tree next to it on our poets' pilgrimage up the mountain, that weary coiled up vision of a wild being caught behind prison bars. (The caged bears of Berlin.) I reply with the opening of the First Elegy, and its terrible angels.

"Rose, oh pure contradiction, joy/of being No-one's sleep under so many/lids." Stephen Mitchell's eloquent translation hopscotches us backwards, over Gertrude Stein's modernist irony, to the unmediated agony of Romantic bliss. "O Rose, thou art sick," Blake mourned in that other landscape, in the environmental catastrophe Rilke, too, saw as coming, though he held out even more stoically against it: the worm of industrialism having infected eros, beauty, forever among the Satanic mills of England, the laughing peasants now unsmiling, clock-punching, urban waged labourers. The rose is still the old woman here, in the underdeveloped northern lands next to the Ostsee, Mother Hulda, who makes snow fall when she shakes her feather pillows in her little hovel in the hills, the voice of plenitude, weather, the earth, speaking her robust truth, stern warning against wannabe soldiers and entrepreneurs. If you hurt me, I will hurt you.

They haven't thrown away the old here. They have woven it in with the new. Jazz is flourishing, the burned books are being reprinted, the synagogue has been rebuilt, looking eerily like the mosque on the Jerusalem Temple Mount (how we resemble our enemies), Jews are holding Yiddish cabarets again in the Hackischer Hof where the *Blindenwerkstatt* was, hundreds of Jews hidden from the Nazis in a brush factory, a workplace for the "blind." (Who lives in their dispossessed houses now?) A rainbow-coloured sign on Unter den Linden protests daily the war in Iraq. Every week I negotiate several more trips into the underworld of my endless back injury and the unthinkable family hurt that fed it, with Michael, sweet *Heilpraktiker*, some days, and in Suzanne's golden masseuse hands, other days, overlooked by her granite Egyptian cat, just down the street from the Ägyptisches Museum. There the original cat sits, beside the bust of the unbelievably beautiful queen Nefertiti (whom the Egyptians, understandably, want back). I try to imagine how I can understand Margareta, the character I am trying to write (in a libretto I'm working on), analog of my wounded, wounding mother, dark alter-ego of Goethe's golden-haired muse, and other face of Celan's ashen haired Sulamith, swirling smokily in her grave of air. I listen, through the open window, to amateur guitar lessons of the old people who live in a seniors' complex next to Suzanne's office, across from Iburger Ufer. The canal banks are a paradise of riotous blossoms in the spring. Suzanne's face shines with love. The old songs are badly harmonized, and strangely beautiful: *I love to go a-wandering, along the mountain track, and as I go I love to sing, my knapsack on my back, falari, falara, falari, falarahahahahaha, falari. . . .*

Je jelieda, je vechieda:
Canadian Mennonite (Alter)Identifications

Je jelieda, je vechieda is a popular saying among Plautdietsch-speaking Canadian Mennonites, a traditionalist, separatist religious sect and farming community of northern European peasant origin, living mainly on the Canadian prairies, but with communities also in Ontario and British Columbia. It means, roughly, "the more educated you are, the more corrupt," though it is funnier and more provocative, with its comic, cocky little rhyme, than my translation suggests. Its purpose is not to cultivate stupidity or anti-intellectualism, though it is sometimes understood that way, both inside the community and outside it, and sometimes, alas, practised that way. Its more serious purpose, as I understand it, is to cut through the perceived false posturings of people who have allowed themselves to be split off from their earthy physical/emotional lives through institutionalized "higher" education. This aim is both aesthetic and political: to undercut the pomposity and authority of hierarchical bureaucratic systems and people who represent them, holding themselves "above" other people in some way, in favour of a radically communalist, embodied sensibility, lived flat, *plaut*, close to the ground.

There are many other such sayings among the village Mennonites, such as the joke that the letters of the Ph.D. degree stand for "piled higher and deeper," a metaphor that is all the more pungent and resonant if you've spent time on a traditional Mennonite farm, noisily surrounded by the lively, smelly warmth of kept animals, and sweet hay stacks and alfalfa fields beyond, brushed by hot dry wind, under a wide blue steppe-like prairie sky. This typical Mennonite peasant joke is intended, I suppose, to reflect on the contrasting modes of labour involved in farming and white collar professions, both of which involve shovelling around large piles of "stuff," but with very different affects, the one wet and dirty and fertile, the other chemically bleached, clean and dry. Following the industrial model, we call the hoped for results of such activity "productivity" rather than "fertility," and we think of the never ending increase of stacks of bound paper, following the logic of the Enlightenment, collections of ideas, rather than slowly moldering gatherings of pressed wood. Is the metaphor of productivity inherently more exploitive and colonialist, more falsely idealistic in aspiration, than the sexual, reproductive, literalist agrarian, hunting-gathering one? Certainly it is less erotic and less earthy, less honouring of its resources, in both their aspects of plenitude and environmental limitations.

Now You Care is the title of my most recent poetry collection, and is a phrase lifted from "Dog Days in Maribor," a sequence of "anti-ghazals" (a term I borrowed from Phyllis Webb, who invented it to give herself permission to play around with the ancient venerable Persian and Urdu ghazal form in her poetry). "Now that it's much much too late, /now you care" (38) is an expression of the pollution panic running through this book, inspired most directly by the hyper-industrialized landscape of the Great Lakes region of North America, in particular, Windsor-Detroit, where I lived for nearly a decade, fearing daily for my health as I breathed in, along with everyone else, the thick toxic fumes of factory smoke and agricultural chemicals that have made this region infamous for decades. The phrase was also inspired, more obliquely, by recent travels to such countries as Slovenia and Poland, and the opportunity to witness the long arm of American-driven multinational globalization tactics, which we experience in such a dramatic way daily, close up, on the biggest border of the NAFTA Superhighway, also abroad, especially along the shifting outer edges of the European Union. The worry in this book is that we're not doing enough to stop the "mad drive toward death" inherent in the push toward ever greater, faster technologization and violent colonization of what few independent local cultures and economies still exist on this planet, that even though we are concerned about the future now, we don't seem to know how to turn this dynamic around.

But in the back of my mind, I always hear these words in the voice of my mother, who said them in response to my lament to her a few years ago, Isn't it sad that we lost our ancestral mother tongue, Plautdietsch, in this generation? Through all these centuries of migration from one country to another we were able to preserve it, perfectly. And now, our children don't speak it anymore. All of a sudden, just like that, it's gone. Her unsaid response, which I read in her eyes, and expressive body language, was perhaps the more striking: We told you and told you, what do you think all those admonishments were for, when you were young and itching to get away from the village, from our people, from us? All this time you've been going around talking and writing about us as if we were stupid and backward. Don't you know what it was we were trying to protect and defend?

So, now that it's much much too late, now that I really have made an irrevocable break with my Mennonite heritage and deep-rooted renegade prairie upbringing, and defected shamelessly, though not without grief, to the papered and electronically wired hierarchically organized academy, now that I have lived in the midst of the air-choking "satanic mills" of southern Ontario, and escaped periodically from there via the noisy, petroleum-fuelled airways into the world at large, now that our Plautdietsche ways of living low to the ground with fierce communal independence are lost, at least to my family, I am trying to understand what that stern, proud, humble, retrograde, free-spirited heritage and the irreverent comically and bawdily inflected mother tongue that expressed it were really about.

Let me go back to the beginning and propose, impertinently, that it was not the beginning, in the way that perhaps we are not now at the end, of the legacy of that stubborn cultural heritage, nor in another register, of our hope for the world's future. These two things are directly related in my mind in a way they perhaps are not in everyone's, where the identity of my people and the shattered, scattered hybridity that marked my coming out of it got somehow entwined with my sense of foreboding about our endangered landscapes (connected as they are, in oblique but literal ways, to the shattering, scattering of similarly earthy local communities on the other side of the world in the present). Perhaps my personal sense of shattered scatteredness, passing liminally over the threshold of this particular communal identity, had to do with re-encountering, on my way out, the violent founding moment that marked our way in. This historic era was passed on in our collective memory in stories of the clever but tragic figures who, alone and in groups, tried to evade the judgment of the sixteenth century Spanish Catholic Inquisitors and local state officials, as members of the grassroots Anabaptist religious political movement that was wildly popular throughout Europe. Many of these heroes ended up as martyrs, drowned in rivers or burned at the stake in hundreds of town squares across the continent. I am trying, in this account, to stay close to the embodied, living, oral version of this heritage as we experienced it in the villages, in dialogue with the textually documented, historically recalled version of the *jelieda* and *vechieda*, written by scholars with or without Mennonite affiliation.[1] This feels like a risky venture, risky in its evocation of contradictory epistemologies in an academic context which is clearly committed to the latter, risky also to me personally in stretching my ability to straddle opposing knowledge paradigms simultaneously.

The founding events of Mennonite culture were told and retold to us as children. They were also memorialized in the one book that nearly every Mennonite peasant village household owned, no matter what the literacy level of its occupants, second only to the Bible, though I don't recall anyone ever actually consulting it except to look at the pictures. This was T.J. van Braght's monumental catalogue of Anabaptist martyr stories, *The Martyrs Mirror*, which came complete with graphic illustrations and inspiring death scene testimonials by the condemned. It was first published in Dutch in Holland in 1660, and republished in German in Pennsylvania 1748–49, and in English in 1837.[2] The Anabaptist movement was strongest in Switzerland, northern Germany and Holland, but its influence extended as far as England in the north and Austria in the south. These events, to put them in the larger historical context, happened during the time remembered variously now as the birth of modernity and the Enlightenment; the invention of the printing press and proliferation of international text culture; the beginning of European expansion into the Americas and Africa and the enslavement and genocide of their indigenous peoples; the flowering of the sugar trade, the machine and modern capitalism; the Renaissance of classical ideals of art and beauty; and the Burning Times, with its violent disruption of traditional practices of midwifery, bio-energetic healing and communal farming, and attendant loss of property rights and other privileges for women dating back to medieval times.

Much of the separatist energy of the Mennonites in North America has been connected, right into the present time, with its traumatic origins as a refugee people fleeing their ancestral peasant homelands during that watershed moment of the birth of modernity and its attendant enslavements. What was it they wanted to preserve so badly that they were willing to leave their beloved homelands, that meant the world to them, and risk their lives defending through centuries of extremely difficult pioneering labour in inhospitable landscapes, moving from one to another, enduring all kinds of privation and public shaming? In the story we told ourselves in church on

Sunday mornings, we did it in the name of Christianity, of God, following the leadership of our founding father, Menno Simons. Simons, a defecting Catholic priest, organized a diverse collection of northern European Anabaptist refugees into a coherent separatist religious community, as part of what came to be known as the "Radical Reformation," conceived in the same moment as Luther's Protestantism, but very quickly and dramatically divorced from it. Thereafter, we became an itinerant people, settling temporarily and uneasily in remote lands that would allow us religious freedom in exchange for agricultural development, something we were good at, being resourceful, hardworking and committed to plain style living, first in Poland, then Prussia, later in Russian and Ukraine, and still later, the Canadian prairies. But who were these originary Anabaptists? Scholars disagree on their identity and profile, and Mennonite oral histories have largely sanitized their profile and marginalized their radical edges, their reputation for Luddite protests, staged revolutions, apocalyptic visions and, according to some, polygamous orgies, in order to valorize a more sober profile of humble serious hardworking folk: really, we don't scare anyone, we keep to ourselves, please, don't think about hounding us out of our homes again or burning us at stakes, leave us alone. All the same, we bow to no one, except God. If you force us to work in your factories or fight in your armies, we will pick up our things and move somewhere else to start over again.

If you ask Mennonite historians or theologians about the pre-history to our traumatic founding moment as a people, their typical response is to skip over the patristic and pre-Christian medieval centuries with their extensive famines and plagues and peasant wars, right back to the anointed Pentecostal Apostles in the newly formed Christian church in Jerusalem. They will likely quote its expansionist, forward-looking vision, "Go ye into all the world and preach the gospel . . ." This didn't make sense to me as a kid, and doesn't make sense to me now. There was just far too much emphasis among us on land ties and kinship loyalty, understood more or less tribally, that is to say, locally, even matrilocally, with ancestral resonances and emphasis on preserving the ways of the past in resolutely separatist ways. There was also far too much antipathy pointed at us as a religious and ethnic group from both Catholic and Protestant churches, both during the early modern period and later, to explain it entirely in terms of doctrinal differences.

Our ancestral ways included various folk customs to celebrate and sustain the intergenerationally woman-centered extended family, village committees to look after the sick and the poor, and gender-equitable inheritance, land acquisition and farming practices. We specifically did not believe in huge idealistic ahistorical leaps from one landscape and cultural history to another. Neither did we believe in expansionist enterprise. We carried our traditionalist northern European cultural identifications, inflected with local flavours from the Prussian/Polish and Russian/Ukrainian cultures, with pride. We did not see ourselves as related, ideologically or culturally, to other Christian groups, whom we considered, for the most part, too institutionally rigid and hierarchical for our taste. We kept to ourselves. We prided ourselves on our separatism from the modern world. We called ourselves *die Stillen im Lande*, the Quiet in the Land, in the face we presented to the rest of the world. But at home, we spoke our several languages with ease, adept at code switching at a moment's notice, as indeed most minority peoples are.

And while we distrusted fancy architecture and bureaucratic hierarchies, whether secular or church related, while we distrusted the modern distinction between sacred and secular, public and private or personal (distinctions I have trouble understanding or maintaining even now, in this radically other cultural landscape), we also insisted on traditionalist ceremonies that fostered intergenerational respect and ecstatic communal celebration, centred on frequent extended family gatherings. These gatherings were presided over by the grandmothers and prominently featured communal singing, which we were extremely good at, in perfect four-part harmonies, and performances by even the youngest children, reciting poetry "for Oma" and the gathered clan. There was also the central ritual of baptism, which for us was not a sacrament performed at birth but an initiation in late youth into adulthood and full participation in village life. The *Älteste*, elders who sat on committees to oversee the proper care of widows and orphans and economic assistance for young people interested in farming, were locally elected, as were the church ministers. There was no central office of any kind. Elections are generally held by ballot now, but during the time of my childhood they were still often cast by lot, with the expectation that God, who was very closely aligned with Fate, would direct the proper choosing of the new leaders. Often, a person chosen by lot would receive a dream during the previous week, forewarning him of his imminent calling, and instructing him in the proper enactment of it. There was perhaps a contradiction in our theology around the notion of sacrament. While we famously (and infamously) rejected the notion of "transubstantiation" in the serving of the host, insisting *This is my body and my blood* should be understood metaphorically rather than literally, we believed in many other magical processes: accidents were "acts of God," "divining" could be done by rod or other intuitive processes such as opening the Bible to a random passage to find out the answer to a burning question. I have always understood the resistance to "transubstantiation" to be a political rather than aesthetic one: we weren't rejecting the magic of the mass so much as its institutionalization by a priesthood.

There was altogether a huge discrepancy between our founding stories, told in the language of evangelical Christianity in increasingly pseudo-rationalist terms, and our fiercely defended, ritually understood old village customs, connected to the rhythms of the seasons, superstitiously so. The farmers in my village were enthusiastically married to their field work, and strongly tempted to harvest on Sundays during the far too short August harvest season. But they all knew of farmers who had dared to disobey the gods of weather and fertility, and their crops had failed the next season, or their barns had been struck by lightning, or their children became sick a year later. One of my vivid childhood memories is of my father chafing in his Sunday shirt, uneasily participating in family summer games like baseball and lawn croquet in Oma's generously shaded yard, when he wanted desperately to be on his combine in the sun-blasted yellow prairie wheat fields, sweating, gathering in brimming truckfuls of ripe grain as fast as possible before the first September frost. The men's presence in the domestic sphere all these long Sunday afternoons was considered crucial, however, lending an air of authority to the gatherings of women and children with their celebrations of song and food and play, and ensuring the ongoing pleasure of playful interactions between the generations and genders.

In my family, I was the first person to refuse the daily acts of translation required to negotiate the cross-cultural tensions of the culture successfully. I just decided one day, at age twelve or so, that I didn't want to exist in three languages, that it was "stupid" to hop back and forth between Plautdietsch at home, Hochdeutsch in German school and church and English in school. English was not considered an innocent language; it belonged to *de Englische*, and was therefore tainted in our eyes by its military investments in modern nationhood, only provisionally friendly to our pacifist tribal political identifications, but it was nevertheless the necessary language of commerce outside the community, though I rarely encountered representatives of it during my childhood, so sheltered were we. I decided I wanted to exist in one language only, and it would be English. No doubt I was already planning my getaway. My family strongly disapproved of my breaking of the strict rules we had about which language could be spoken where, but I stubbornly persisted. My conversations with my parents, brother, sisters, grandparents, aunts, uncles and cousins were pointedly bilingual after that, they speaking Plautdietsch and I replying in English. Immediately, I began to see how inherently contradictory our cultural identifications were: how each of the three languages carried a different personality and represented a different cultural paradigm. In Plautdietsch, we were funny, irreverent, bawdy; it was an elemental dialect, filled with humorous trickster-like reversals and jokes. It was impossible to say anything abstract or even earnest in Plautdietsch, an intimate familiar language with nuanced relational terms and modes of address.[3] People were never addressed by their proper names in Plautdietsch, only by nicknames. Spouses would refer to each other, whether they were present or not, as *sei* or *hei*. Children were required to address their elders in the polite form, *Yee*, rather than the direct form, *dü*. Should our mother address her own mother, Oma, as *Yee* or *dü*? She politely offered *Yee*, and Oma impatiently waved her off, insisting on *dü*. It was a game they both seemed to enjoy. (It seemed appropriate, then, that elders should be addressed in the plural. Later, in my *vechieda* rationalist phase, I thought it strange. Now that I'm approaching elderhood myself, it seems appropriate again: sweet that some languages have retained that sense of address of elders as representative of the community, not only themselves.) The aspirations of imagism, as practised by William Carlos Williams and Ezra Pound in another culture, in another place, the paring down to essential elemental things, "no ideas but in things," so as to mobilize the energetic aura of the physical world into poetic consciousness, were active in our language—though we were much more expressionist, even baroque, in our emotional utterances than the American or English modernists allowed. (I claim H.D. as ancestral and spiritual kin in this context: she is imagist and extravagant, visionary and was the daughter of Moravians, cousins to the Mennonites, historically speaking.)

High German, our second language, was elevated, Biblical, literary, reserved for church and the memorization of hymn lyrics and German folksongs and poetry. It was impossible not to be earnest or proper or sad in this language. Our grandfather, Peter S. Zacharias, one of the co-founders of the Rudnerweider Gemeinde, was a stern preacher on Sunday mornings. We children were often chided after the service for wriggling and giggling too much during his sermons. Our grandmother, too, was a famous giggler, and would sometimes giggle and laugh outright for minutes on end, until there were tears streaming down her face, though this usually happened at home in the company of her daughters as opposed to church, where it would have been unseemly. Surely we were laughing in Plautdietsch! English, on the other hand, was functional, rationalist, unadorned, carrying far less subtlety in terms of familial relations or modes of address than either Plautdietsch or German, but endlessly useful and temptingly modern. It was also the language of Chaucer and Shakespeare, with their gorgeous early modern rhythms and nearly Biblical status in our minds. It was Shakespeare, more than any other writer, whose works sustained me in my cross-cultural cross-temporal investigations across the years. All those kings and kings' daughters poised on the cusp of the new age, tragically invested in a dying paradigm of royalty and ceremony, unwilling to give up their dreams of a visionary existence, yet unable to bring it forward into the new rationalist age.

The identity of the Mennonite people who eventually came to western Canada in several group migrations, in the 1870s, and 1920s, and thereafter in much smaller groups, as displaced peoples of the great wars, was a complex, hybrid one, which preserved its inner contradictions through a strictly enforced multilingual cultural practice. Though I was annoyed as a young adolescent by the intricacies and perceived strictures of this practice, I see it retrospectively, and admittedly from an insulated distance, as a clever, if frustratingly pastiched, strategy of cultural survival that enabled the Mennonites to practise stubbornly traditionalist, locally defined, peasant ways while appearing to conform to the universalist Christian rhetoric of the Bible, and successfully participating in the surrounding market economy to the extent that was necessary. I remember a game I made up in grade three, to entertain my school friends at recess, where we tried to find cross-linguistic homonyms in English and Plautdietsch, for example, "come" and *Com* ("bowl"). The (Mennonite) teacher caught us in this clever bpNicholesque word game and threatened to spank us for subverting the "no Plautdietsch at school rule" so deviously. It was long before the age of "multiculturalism" in Canada. We knew how to hang onto our kerchiefs!

The Bible was regarded among the orally minded Mennonites, even in my lifetime, not so much as a literary text to be read in scholarly fashion among other texts, but as a sacred object, a talisman. Its sudden appearance among illiterate peasant peoples of northern Europe at the time of the development of the printing press would have offered them a badly needed rhetoric to use against the big colonizing churches, even if they had not had much access to these stories previously, and their subscription to them was therefore defensive and—I am speaking heresy now—to a large extent superficial. This view is corroborated by a small, but growing, number of historians of the period interested in reading the religious movement of Anabaptism in social-materialist terms. James Stayer, for example, has argued, in direct contradiction to established views on the period by such historians as Claus-Peter Clasen and his classic text, *Anabaptism: A Social History*, that the Anabaptist "community of goods," a village-based communitarianism, as it was practised in Switzerland, Austria and Moravia, and is still quietly practised in North America among Hutterites and Amish, cousins of the Mennonites, was crucially influenced by the German Peasants' War, particularly in its aspect of anti-clericism (3, 35).[4]

The more flamboyant communalist experiment of Münster, in northern Germany, which included polygamy to encourage the rapid proliferation of offspring to people the self-styled apocalyptic walled city of God, suggests Stayer, was further removed from the Peasants' War. For that reason, it was far less sustainable, socially and politically, lasting only a year in its militant phase, from 1534 to 1535, following a decade of more peaceful organizing, before it was violently suppressed, most of its members of both genders and all ages slaughtered by soldiers and police. But here, too, the Anabaptist Münsterites were initially supported by local authorities in order to preserve the endangered religious and political freedoms of their town against domination by an externally appointed overlord (123–138).

Carolyn Merchant, however, argues that the northern European peasants were more independent and egalitarian minded than those in the south, or in England, and for this reason were not drawn into the extensive violence of the Peasants' War. "Here, where the nobility was weak," she writes, "the peasantry was individualistic and autonomous, owning and leasing land, lending money to other peasants, and engaging in urban market trade. Some villages maintained a homogeneous, egalitarian character" (52). Interestingly, Merchant links Anabaptism with a wide range of other "utopian millenarian" movements across Europe, ranging from the medieval crusades of the poor to the religious sects of the English Civil War. "Millenarianism," she suggests, "represented a pre-industrial form of social revolution. It differed from the movements of the industrial revolution by preparing people, through revelation, to accept revolutionary change, as opposed to politicizing the working class" (79). These groups "shared a belief in the emergence of a new age of liberty and love in which God would appear from within and there would be equal sharing of food, clothing, and property among all people" (79).

Benjamin Kaplan points out that the Dutch revolt against Spain was understood at the time to be specifically rooted in ancient local "privileges" or "liberties" among the Dutch peasantry. These laws or customs came to be variously interpreted during the Reformation and Spanish occupation, but included the frequently invoked *jus de non evocando*, which guaranteed that "a burgher accused of a crime would not be tried by a court outside his province," invoking a more ancient time when cities and provinces had enjoyed judicial autonomy (10). Another was the beautifully titled Joyous Entry of Brabant, a medieval oath taken by the Duke of Brabant in 1356, and each successive duke after him, promising to "do no violence or abuse to any person in any manner." The oath was interpreted in an anonymous pamphlet published in 1579 to mean "[no] violence or abuse, be it to property, body, or soul, so that the king is bound by virtue of the Joyous Entry to leave every person in possession of their freedom, not only of property or body but also of soul, that is, of conscience" (11). Kaplan considers the religious interpretation, that is, the right to worship according to conscience, "far-fetched" given that "the variety of beliefs spawned by the Reformation was scarcely older than the placards outlawing them" (10). Nevertheless, his point corroborates my hypothesis that the stubborn fight for communal independence that was so deeply part of Anabaptism had pre-Christian antecedents and was rooted in ancient peasant loyalties to traditionalist local land and community practices.

Figures like Balthazar Hübmaier and Thomas Müntzer, then, who have been marginalized in our popular Mennonite histories, along with the infamous Münsterites, because of their involvements with militarism, strongly disapproved of by the predominantly pacifist contemporary Mennonite community, perhaps were not aberrant but rather central to the concerns of the Anabaptists, namely, to secure political independence for their people against outside rule. Stayer goes so far as to suggest that pacifism was not a central tenet of Anabaptism, in the way that the community of goods and separatism from the outside world were (123). If that is so, then there has been a sea change in thinking over several centuries of migration from one hosting country to another. In the Mennonite community of my childhood, community of goods fell far behind these other two ideals, though it is still practised among Swiss-based Hutterites and the American Amish, both groups also pacifist. Hübmaier is depicted in *The Martyrs Mirror* as a religious leader who "through the enlightenment of the Holy Spirit" rejected the "abomination of popery" and "self-invented infant baptism" and "taught with all his might the baptism of believers, as commanded by Christ" (465). Stayer describes him as a community leader who encouraged his fellow countrymen to oppose enclosure of the commons and unfair taxation, and, indeed, take up arms against local authorities. He was the reputed anonymous author of the Twelve Articles which fuelled the Peasants' Revolt in the Black Forest region. He was burned at the stake in Vienna in 1528; his wife was thrown into the Danube a few days later with a stone around her neck (Weaver 66). Thomas Müntzer is not listed in the *Mirror*, but is nevertheless frequently named in Mennonite rosters of Anabaptist origins, for example, in Mennonite historian Denny Weaver's popular history, *Becoming Anabaptist: The Origin and Significance of Sixteenth-Century Anabaptism*. Müntzer was even more directly involved in the Peasants' War, joining the Battle of Frankenhausen of 1525, where 6000 peasants were slaughtered by a small group of well armed princes. Müntzer escaped the battle, but was discovered in hiding a few days later, and was tortured and executed (55–56).

For Merchant, the real question of the meaning of the utopian millenarian movements of the late medieval and early modern period is not whether they were driven by religious or economic concerns (as it is for Stayer and to some extent for me), since obviously they included elements of both. The driving question of her pioneering study of European environmental history, *The Death of Nature*, is the relationship between traditionalist farming practices and holistic views of nature, prevalent, as she claims, all over Europe and indeed, the world, from ancient to medieval times, and the disruption of both through industrialism and the rise of modern science. "The image of the earth as a living organism and nurturing mother had served as a cultural constraint restricting the actions of human beings," she observes. "As long as the earth was considered to be alive and sensitive, it could be considered a breach of human ethical behaviour to carry out destructive acts against it" (3). Merchant critiques Francis Bacon's elucidation of the principles of the new "scientific method," in a justly famous chapter, as courtroom derived, with strong inquisitorial flavours, urging its practitioners to bind nature into service, to torture her to reveal her innermost secrets, to dissect her in order to yield up her powers to the human mind (ch. 7, "Dominion over Nature," 164–190). Traditionalist constraints against the misuse of nature, observes Merchant, have now been overturned as "sanctions in language that legitimate the exploitation and 'rape' of nature for human good" (171).

Merchant links the violent suppression of Anabaptists and other utopian millenarians with the witch burnings that swept through Europe in the same era. While they were reported differently in the court records, it is clear that the women tortured and burned as witches belonged to the same class of insubordinates who understood nature and God as living entities and themselves as able to have ecstatic relationships with them, in direct worship, unmediated by church hierarchies. The subordination and exploitation of First Nations peoples in North America and Africa, which followed closely upon the introduction of industrialism and the new mechanistic view of nature, belong to this same historical moment. The principles of dissection, torture and despiriting of nature for human use are still the guiding principles of science today, Merchant observes, and are perhaps the greatest obstacle to responsible ecological thinking and action in our environmentally threatened age. The subordination of women and people of colour, not incidentally, also continues, so that "If nature and women, [and indigenous peoples around the world] are to be liberated from the strictures of this ideology a radical critique of the very categories *nature* and *culture*, as organizing concepts in all disciplines, must be undertaken" (144).

Mennonite historians have been reluctant to examine Anabaptist martyrdom in relation to the witch burnings. I asked Arnold Snyder, an historian of the period and one of the editors of *Profiles of Anabaptist Women*, a collective scholarly project, whether he had ever thought to do so. "Never," he replied. I asked another prominent historian of Mennonite history the same question and he exclaimed, "Too bad the history departments let fiction writers into their ranks, the witch burnings are a complete fabrication." I didn't ask him whether the Mennonite martyr stories were also a fabrication, but I doubt very much that he would want to contradict our official history in that way. Marie Conn, in her study of religious women martyrs in Western Christianity from the thirteenth to the eighteenth centuries, *Noble Daughters*, has a chapter on "Anabaptist Women Martyrs" and a different chapter on "Victims of the Witch Craze." Conn studied theology at the University of Notre Dame in South Bend, Indiana, which is closely associated with Associated Mennonite Biblical Seminaries in nearby Elkhart, a fact she points out in her prologue, poetically describing the drive from noisy, urban South Bend to the idyllic rural Mennonite Indiana countryside as a metaphorical journey into a less complicated way of life. In orthodox Mennonite fashion, she identifies the "cause" of Anabaptist persecution to be "an earnest and uncompromising endeavor to live a life of true discipleship of Christ," and the cause of the witch burnings to be "paganism" and "folk culture," which were gradually transformed, under the pressure of "200 years of terror," into images of devil workshop and heresy (49, 70).

This is the sort of separation of Anabaptist and Mennonite faith principles from folk customs and farming practices I wish, remembering their deep connection in the village culture of my Mennonite childhood, to oppose. Conn speculates in her epilogue that "It would be instructive to map out the houses of the beguines [members of a medieval Catholic women's movement that came under heavy criticism because of the freedom it offered women from men, church and state], the sites of the Anabaptist martyrdoms, and the squares where the so-called witches were burned, to see if there is a high degree of correlation" (104). Her hunch, "I suspect there is," is marred, in my view, by her surprising attack a moment later on the victims of violent political suppression and the—surely innocent—landscapes they lived in as the originators of the violence that was inflicted upon them: "Was it the harsher climate of the north that led to harsher judgments? Do rougher terrains breed rougher minds that see no other way to deal with perceived opposition than to stamp it out?" (104).[5]

I tried to find other examples, besides Conn's brief comment, of historical analyses that examine the witch burnings and Anabaptism in the same frame. I am astonished that the two literatures, given their high coincidence of

Fig. 5 Jan van Kuykens, "Twelve Christians Burned at the Stake," 1660, from
Thielemann J. van Braght, The Martyrs Mirror, *1964. 886.*
Reprinted in Marie-Sylvie Dupont-Bouchat, Heksen in de Zuidelijke Nederlanden
(16de-17de eeuw). *1000 Brussel: Algemeen Rijksarchief, 1989. 16.*

commonalities, exist as separately as they do, and are typically housed, in both North America and Europe, in separate sections in the library. I found one instance of their conflation in the Rotterdam Public Library. Marie-Sylvie Dupont-Bouchat identifies the public execution of twelve peasants at Deventer in 1571 as a witch burning site (16), and illustrates it with Jan van Luykens' engraving of the event as printed in *The Martyrs Mirror* (886), [fig. 5].

In van Braght's telling, the martyrs were hunted out of their houses by "the Spaniards" with "swords, halberds, guns, and many other implements" because they were "sheep of Christ" (885). Interestingly, however, the accusation levelled at the victims by the "Spaniards," as told by van Braght, is "O you heretical dogs, because you deny the Roman Catholic faith you will have to die," an accusation which identifies the victims by what they are not rather than by what they are, suggesting that the targets of their wrath could have been various, and leaving the door open to interpretations like Dupont-Bouchat's and Merchant's. Solis and Aldegraver's satiric 1536 engraving of the Anabaptists of northern Europe, *De Anabaptistengemeente*, as a gathering of naked women, children and men in the throes of group ecstasy offers another intriguing example (115), [fig. 6].

The engraving is meant to comment negatively on Anabaptist communitarianism, and is no doubt a reference to the polygamous experiment of the Münsterites. The image also suggests their exultation in physicality and religious ecstasy, in a way that is reminiscent of the critiques of witches as sexually profligate and aligned with the wild forces of nature, forces that rationalist science has been intent on controlling and subduing right into the present (see Merchant 127–148). Indeed, historian Lyndal Roper recalls that Anabaptists were commonly dubbed the "flesh-loving sect," and cites their widespread experimental sexual practices and communal living arrangements as a major reason for the Calvinist backlash against them (81). Donna Read's 1990 film documentary of the witchburning sites of Europe, *The Burning Times*, closely follows Conn's description of the period, yet many of the instruments of torture displayed in the film are notoriously known in connection with Mennonite martyrdom.[6]

As I remember it, "paganism," vaguely understood as a pre-Christian celebration of intuition, bodily pleasure and reverence for the natural world, itself inhabited by magical entities and spirits, was both greatly feared in the Mennonite community of my childhood and at the same time extensively,

*Fig. 6 Solis and Aldegraver, "De Anabaptistengemeente," 1536.
Bibliothèque Nationale, Paris. Reprinted in Pierre Chaunu,* De Reformatie: De 16de-eeuwse Revolutie in de Kerk, *transl. into Dutch by S. Groenveld and S.B.J. Zilverberg.
Netherlands: Uitgeverij Uniepers, 1986. 115.*

albeit covertly, practised: in the form of herbal and bio-energetic folk healing and midwifery customs; in superstitious rituals of planting and harvesting on auspicious days coinciding with the rhythms of the moon; in communal rituals emphasizing the gathering of the clan; in singing and folk dancing circles; in prophecy through dreams and divining rituals; in magical interpretations of natural and spiritual phenomena; and in relaxed attitudes toward the body and sexual pleasure. Roper's description of medieval European cultures as much less anxious about bodily functions and emotional expression than contemporary attitudes, supports my hunch that at the heart of Mennonite culture lies a much older world view than the early modern (23). Albrecht Dürer's well known engraving "Peasants Dancing," aptly describes the exuberance of the medieval northern European peasantry [fig. 7]. And it is interesting, too, that the people the Mennonites have found themselves closest to, and felt the most affinity with, are the indigenous and tribal peoples of those lands, with similar attachments to land, communalism and ancestors, superstitious beliefs in the paranormal, and carnivalesque celebration of the body. This has certainly been true in the Americas (and was true of Mennonite-Turkish relations in Russia/Ukraine in the eighteenth and nineteenth centuries, according to our passed down stories), even though in other ways the agricultural investments of the Mennonites locate us squarely on the modern side of the great industrialist divide.[7]

And what are we to make of the fact that so many of our Mennonite surnames are also recognizably Jewish names? Almost half of the names listed in the catalogue of Holocaust victims in the Jewish Museum in Berlin, as Paul and Hildi Tiessen pointed out to me when we visited it together, are also Mennonite names. R. Po-Chia Hsia in his Introduction to the essay collection, *Calvinism and Religious Toleration in the Dutch Golden Age*, documents the extensive presence of Jews, both Sephardim and Ashkenazi, in Holland during the time of the Reformation, living in close proximity with Mennonites. The Sephardim arrived there as merchants in flight from the Jewish Expulsion Edict of 1492 in Spain and a similar edict in Portugal in 1497 (1). There was already an established Ashkenazi community in Holland, having migrated from Germany, and later from Poland, escaping violent persecution there (Schoenberg, www.us-israel.org, 2004). Many of the Sephardic Jews were Conversos, nominally Christian but privately still practising Jewish customs, having been forced to do so by Spanish law during the century before expulsion. It is hard to say exactly how many of the Ashkenazi passed as New Christians

Fig. 7 Albrecht Dürer, "Peasants Dancing," 1514.

in Holland, though Hsia makes the point that by the mid-1600s, the so-called Golden Age of the Netherlands, there was a flourishing "religious pluralism" in the country, in which "individuals found porous boundaries" (2).

Again, I find it surprising that studies of Jews, Anabaptists, and "witches," given the commonalities of their persecutions and close-knit community arrangements and proximity of migration patterns, have not occurred in greater dialogue with each other. In the case of Jews and Mennonites, these commonalities also include shared landscapes over several centuries of forced migration, from Prussia/Poland to Russia/Ukraine to Canada, and marked similarities between Yiddish and Plautdietsch. No doubt this lapse in attention is due to the heritage of trauma and ongoing survival issues suffered by the survivors of these similarly persecuted groups, who were its first historians, only recently in command of the resources that would allow a more scholarly and secular discussion of their interconnections. There are some exceptions. The website *Sephardic Genealogy*, maintained by Jeff Malka, casually conflates early modern witch burning with Jewish martyrdom, suggesting that, perhaps in the popular mind, these histories are more consonant than most scholars have allowed. The Spanish Inquisition, writes Malka, "lasted for 350 years. Its last victim was a woman burnt at the stake in 1821 for allegedly having sex with the devil and producing eggs that prophecised [sic] the future" (2006).

A famous related argument is made by Arthur Koestler in his controversial history of medieval Europe, *The Thirteenth Tribe*, which offers the radical thesis that the large Ashkenazi population of Poland in the early modern period derived mostly from descendants of the Khazars. The medieval Khazar Empire was powerfully located on the eastern confines of Europe between the Caucasus and the Volga at the time Charlemagne was crowned Emperor of the West, in 800 CE. These were people of Turkic, i.e., nomadic Caucasian, stock, according to Koestler, who converted to Judaism en masse in 740 CE. During the Crusades they came under heavy persecution and, in the late 1300s, emigrated in large numbers to Poland under the patronage of Casimir the Great. This history leads Koestler to the startling and controversial claim that "the bulk of modern Jewry is not of Palestinian, but of Caucasian origin" (180), and that the Nazi preoccupation with ethnic cleansing was therefore tragically, and foolishly, "based on a misapprehension [of ethnic differences] shared by both the killers and their victims" (17).

Could it be that our mysterious Anabaptist origins are somehow connected with underground early modern European Judaism, and with perhaps Khazarian roots, which included elements of "witchcraft," that is to say, remnants of ancient woman-centred shamanic healing practices?[8] That would make us a profoundly hybrid people, as I think we are, despite our insistence on communal identity and historical continuity and blood kinship, and would explain some of our internal cultural contradictions between our ironic insistence on embodied experience rather than book learning, on the one hand, and our reverence for textual knowledge and aesthetic performance, on the other, between our peasant loyalties and sense of origin, and our alternative image of ourselves as an urban intellectual movement that was driven out of doors, outside the early modern city walls, on the other, contradictions Rudy Wiebe explores at some length in his recent novel, *Sweeter Than All The World*.[9]

One of the striking aspects of Mennonite identity in North America is our almost complete lack of interest in going back to the ancestral lands that are still so much part of our cultural imagination, despite or perhaps because of our deep sense of exile from them. We have not felt the need to return there in order to preserve our language or customs or sense of ourselves as a people. And indeed, until my defecting generation, which was unable to circumvent the impact of the media, radio and television, and the enticements of mainstream North American '60s and '70s mass culture, we practised our Plautdietsch and our traditionalist northern German cuisine with confidence and aplomb. I was impressed, when I visited Berlin, to see how accurately we had preserved our mother tongue, Plautdietsch, precisely as it appears, for example, in Clemens Brentano and Achim von Arnim's nineteenth century scholarly gathering of old folk songs, *Des Knaben Wunderhorn*. I was lucky to see these performed at the Berliner Ensemble by Günter Grass, together with his daughter Hélène. They interspersed their performance with citations from the Brentano/von Arnim correspondence, including a well-known argument about which dialect was superior when it came to *echt* originary lyrical material, von Arnim insisting on Plautdietsch, Brentano countering with the observation that those same Plautdietsche lyrics that so excited von Arnim had been sung by his own grandmother in High German during his childhood (and could have been translated into the older language just as easily as the other way around).

A related argument about authenticity and superiority of Plautdiestche dialects is still carried on, mostly with good-natured humour but sometimes with furious standoffs, in Canadian Mennonite communities. In rural Manitoba, where I grew up, there were two Plautdietsch-speaking communities, divided by the Red River that runs from North Dakota north across the Canadian-American border up to Winnipeg and into Lake Winnipeg. There was a third, more urban-minded, group living in Winnipeg, which practised High German as the language of every day, to the strong criticism of the Plautdietsch speakers from both sides of the river, who considered this a kind of defection and putting on of airs, not unrelated to the mistrust of higher education I described earlier (and no doubt dating back to the German/Prussian occupation of local communities in northern Europe in the eighteenth century, German representing the language of occupation). Here is the Plautdietsche version of "You say tomato, I say tomahto," a fondly remembered saying from my childhood: *Maeken, kaecken, Schinken, Knaecken, daut sent goude Spraeken. Moawken, koawken, Schinken, Knoawken, daut sent schleichte Sproawken*. If you lived on Yantzeed, the other side of the river, you would say it the other way around: *Moawken, koawken, Schinken, Knoawken, daut sent goude Sproawken. Maeken, kaeken, Schinken, Knaeken, daut sent schleichte Spraeken*. Making, cooking, bones, ham, are good turns of speech. Making, cooking, bones, ham (in the other pronunciation), are bad turns of speech.

While, on the one hand, we Mennonites practised a kind of "indigenosity," a sense of ethnicity that puts high stakes on embodied physicality, ancestral loyalty, wild-minded communal interdependence, separatism from the rest of the world, and an intimate relationship to land, we adhered rigorously, on the other hand, to a post-exilic narrative identity that insists we can put it all in a suitcase, or a Red River cart at least, and take it with us, to any other similar landscape, that "homeland" in this sense is a transplantable metaphor rather than a literal place. This contradiction can be explained in part by our pacifism, which supersedes our sense of land attachment, but within the culture our migratory history is understood in poetic and mythical terms, as a re-enactment of the Hebrews' forty years of wandering in the desert, followed later by centuries of wandering all over the earth.

In his book, *The Spell of The Sensuous*, American Jewish philosopher-magician David Abram proposes that what has got us into the present environmentalist mess is our Western tendency to divorce story from place, in a way that pre-alphabetic cultures did not and do not. In oral communities, says Abram, memory is understood to be literally embodied in place. For example, if you want to remember something that happened you go to the place where it did happen and it will come to you, it will be given to you by the rock or tree that has kept that memory for you. Bruce Chatwin's *Song Lines* made the ancient Australian Aboriginal version of this concept well known to the modern world.

In shamanic cultures, Abram claims, this capacity to hear the memories held by the tree or rock is much more extensive than in ours, where we have invested so much of our imaginative energies in transliterating thoughts and experiences into alphabetic signs written down on pieces of paper and bound together into books, and now, increasingly, recorded as electronic markings on computer chips. Our capacity to read little black marks on pieces of paper or flickering electronic screens, thereby recreating thoughts and experiences that originated in the physical world, is no less magical than the capacity to read trees and rocks, suggests Abram. Both require a kind of Gestalt approach to entering a strange code outside our immediate sensibility. The problem with text memory is that it allows us to forget that these thoughts and experiences did indeed originate in the natural world, the living earth, and that they belong to it. And so we tell our stories and live our lives increasingly divorced from embodied physicality and erotic spiritual connection to the earth.

Abram suggests that in order to recover our sense of place as living environment we need to practise language in erotically, emotionally, physically charged ways so that we can learn to "re-inhabit" the earth as reciprocal beings in delicately balanced and complex ecosystems, instead of living several inches or feet or miles above it, as we do both conceptually and literally in the modern world. This sounds like poetry to me—and also like Plautdietsch, and Cree, and Ojibwa, and Gaelic, and any other language that has retained its humorously embodied oral qualities. Abram doesn't spell out the kinds of communal arrangements that might sustain such a practice of "re-inhabitation"—and has been rightly criticized for this omission by First Nations philosophers Lorraine F. Brundige and J. Douglas Rabb, who charge him with "pan-primitivism" for focusing too exclusively on linguistic practices and not enough on socio/geopolitics (79–88). However, it is easy to think of numerous fictional depictions in contemporary Canadian literature that still remember old versions of living communally, and close to the earth, which barely survived their forced entries into industrialized modernity, and are now, like the Mennonite community I have been describing here, tragically on the verge of extinction—and therefore, perhaps, at last publicly speakable. Maybe, their authors speculate, with hard imaginative work and trickster logic and some luck, they are even translateable into contemporary terms. Thomas King's wild-minded Blackfoot in Alberta, for example, who practise extended family arrangements, and rituals of gift-giving, sacrifice, and homecoming (as well as judicious political standoffs with the Canadian government about the misuse of First Nations lands), as part of their effort to regain indigenous cultural strength and spiritual vision; Alistair MacLeod's unrepentant Scots in Cape Breton, who retain many of their visionary Gaelic beliefs and relational environmental practices while at the same time participating uneasily in exploitative contemporary economic life; Hiromi Goto's renegade Japanese Canadians in Alberta, who despite concerted efforts by the Canadian government to break their communal solidarity by incarcerating and then scattering them across the country in the '40s, joyously practise traditionalist Japanese cuisine in their enforced assimilations, exhibiting traces of ancient Shinto nature worship, and exuberantly retelling and revising old Japanese folk tales and classic literary texts to suit their present hybrid purposes; and even Mordecai Richler's thoroughly contemporary cosmopolitan Montreal Jews, who misremember the indigenous meaning of land ownership as an exploitative commercial venture, but nevertheless struggle heroically to inhabit the New World in emotionally and earth-connected, embodied, ways.

Interestingly, Martin Heidegger, one of the European intellectuals Abram admires for his investigations into poetic dwelling on the earth in a non-exploitive way, looked to early Anabaptism, as I am doing here, for inspiration in reconceptualizing our human place on earth in the throes of violent modernity. George Steiner, in the Introduction to his study of Martin Heidegger, locates Heidegger in the company of a group of giant thinkers who sought to address the German "crisis of spirit" after the First World War, including Karl Barth, Ernst Bloch, Oswald Spengler, Franz Rosenzweig—and in another tenor, Adolf Hitler—by returning to the roots of modernity. Their monumental works on the meaning of history, Steiner points out, are, like the vision of the Anabaptists who occupied such a dramatic place in the negotiation of early European modernity, both ecstatic and apocalyptic: "They address themselves to 'the last things.'" In Rosenzweig's writing, the "light of God's immediacy breaks almost unbearably upon human consciousness." Bloch's *Spirit of Utopia* leads directly to his "fiery celebration of Thomas Müntzer and the sixteenth-century insurrections of peasant-saints and millenarians" (ix). For Heidegger, the call for a revolution in thinking and cultural practice leads to that other stream of Anabaptist thinking and practice, a celebration of orality and rhapsodic poetry. His readings of Sophocles, Hölderlin and Trakl, writes Steiner, are "attempts to reclaim for language of ontological presentness, of *Gegenwart*, the high ground illictly (according to Heidegger) occupied by the onto-theology and metaphysics which perpetuate our 'forgetting of Being.' They are, to use a celebrated Heidegger-trope, the labors of a woodcutter, seeking to hack out a path to the 'clearing,' to the luminous 'thereness of what is'" (xix).[10] As Anne Carson puts it in her long poem, "Canicula di Anna," in a witty parody of a contemporary European philosophers' conference, "'A sort of phenomenological pastoral . . .' / 'Heidegger, *ja*, liked farmers very much'" (61). He would have liked us, I think, practising our version of immediacy and immanence on the Canadian prairies stubbornly, wild-mindedly, far from our ancestral lands in Europe.[11]

I have been trying to highlight the joyfully indigenous-minded aspect of the Mennonites and other analogous cultural communities in Canada and elsewhere, in part, to quarrel with the stream of thinking amongst contemporary theorists of ethnicity and postcolonialism that valorizes hybridity as the solution to tribal and ethnic misunderstanding and hostilities. Such arguments are often made without paying enough attention to the far-reaching violence that goes into the forcible creation of hybridities in the first place, nor, perhaps, to their resulting vulnerability to further capitalist and multinationalist exploitation. European cultural theorist Rosi Braidotti, for example, argues idealistically that "linguistic promiscuity" in the form of polyglotism might prevent the kind of ethnic quarrels over motherlands and mother tongues that continue to bedevil Europe's outer edges, and to some extent inner borders as well. She also counsels a nomadic—that is, enthusiastically hybrid and easily transportable—sensibility as more effective for displaced peoples than exilic or migrant attachments to lost homelands and cultural practices: as though grief and rage over such steep losses were easily expendable; as though the political implications of historical violations of homeland security were easily forgivable! American critic Werner Sollors argues that notions of ethnic authenticity, however traditionalist in definition, are nevertheless modernist in character, since it is only in the modern context of proximity of cultures, and therefore resulting hybridities, that the question of ethnic identity even arises (*Beyond Ethnicity*, 241–58). Sollors' argument, while hugely insightful in locating the discourse of ethnicity within discussions of modernity, discounts the strong role that trade and cultural exchange played in traditional economies, and thus bizarrely risks crediting the destroyers of traditional cultural identifications with their belated defence.

Canadian critic Winfried Siemerling, citing Sollors, argues that any notions of authenticity or segregationalist belonging to a group on the basis of blood kinship or other homogeneous definitions run the risk of racism, and posits proximity of cultures, intersections and hybridity as guarantors against it (*Writing Ethnicity*, 16–17). Siemerling does not explain why cross-cultural or hybrid situations should be less conducive to anxieties of identity and belonging or to fantasies of domination than homogeneous or blood-related ones. Indeed, it would be easy to argue the opposite, would it not, that it is precisely anxious border situations that flare up quickly into group hostilities, and that violent domination fantasies are nurtured by insecure identities, not secure ones. Nancy Chodorow makes this point in a recent essay on masculinity and violence: "When social wholes fracture, and identity, via conscious and unconscious concepts of peoplehood, nation, or ethnos, is threatened, for men, especially, [the threat to selfhood leads to] reactive, hate-filled violence" (256). Or, as American sociologist Georgi M. Derluguian dramatically puts it in the title of the Introduction to his recent analysis of the rise and collapse of Soviet socialism, "Does Globalization Breed Ethnic Violence?" (*Bourdieu's Secret Admirer in the Caucasus: A World-System Biography*, 1). Nor does Siemerling question the implicit identification of blood kinship with homogeneity, when here, too, we could argue the opposite: that extended families represent the proliferation, literally, of difference in both genetic and social terms, and it is universalizing rhetorics and associations centred on ideas, rather than local flesh and blood realities, that nurture uniformity and erasure of difference. Neither does Siemerling consider the pertinent fact that many cross-cultural intersections are the direct result of racist acts of domination and displacement, and that cultural hybridities in this sense are often necessary responses to uncomfortable situations, that were violently imposed rather than chosen. Hybridity in this sense is often a painful cultural experience until it has been absorbed into a kind of unity of understanding, which often takes several generations to accomplish, and then only through the intensive mediation of the creative arts.

In his quirky comparative study of social patterns, *Children of the Earth*, Marc Shell argues that it is universalizing rhetorics like Christianity, with its high flying notion of the brotherhood of all mankind—and its contemporary version, multinational economic globalization—that are most vulnerable to slipping into racialist violence, rather than particularist ideologies that openly acknowledge that not everyone belongs to their fraternity, that know from the beginning that there are "others" in the playing field outside their family circle. This is so, offers Shell, because the universalist ideal is simply too difficult to attain, that we are, like all species on this planet, created to desire and cultivate local affiliations and kinship networks, however fictional and unprovable they might be in biological terms, and to "admit in good faith as ours the particularist likes and dislikes that constitute political and sexual being" (304). (What was wrong with the Nazi vision, in Shell's terms, then, was not the desire for more embodied ways of living on the earth, as their slogan *Blut und Boden* signified, but rather, their attempt to impose a locally informed vision violently and absolutely on the rest of the world.) Fred Wah echoes Shell's particularist ethics in *Faking It: Poetics & Hybridity*, when he suggests that "To write (or live) ethnically is also to write (or live) ethically, in pursuit of right value, right place, right home, right otherness" (58). Indigenous peoples in North America take the notion of local community a radical step further to include other species of their bio-region, regarding nearby "four legged, winged and standing people" as their kin (Paula Gunn Allen 1986, 7), in contrast to the postindustrial model of identification based on structural similarities alone. Local and bioregional identifications obviously carry a much greater sense of interspecies respect and need for human constraint in the use of natural resources than the universalist model.

Hybridity, it would seem, is a natural state of affairs among humans, in that kinship structures are always being modified by exogamous liaisons for reproductive and commercial purposes, and in that our natural curiosity, adaptability and interdependence with other living beings predispose us to travel and interact with others unlike us. Perhaps it is a natural state of affairs among all living beings on this planet. It is also a central characteristic of postmodernity which has witnessed extensive displacements of local peoples around the globe. However, to posit unmediated hybridity as a political solution to the problem of ethnic differences sounds too much like the assimilationist rhetoric that created so many of the violent disruptions of traditionalist identities around the world in the first place. It also runs the risk of throwing away the rich archive of particularist traditionalist knowledge that made it possible for our ancestors to live in specific landscapes in stable, environmentally committed and ecologically sustainable ways, which are being rapidly lost in the technologized urban nomadic present. To what extent is linguistic and cultural diversity related to species and bioregional biodiversity? Perhaps we need to relearn the practice of honouring local loyalties and their specific ancestries more fiercely, and more dialogically, one alongside the other, rather than climbing unquestioningly onto the universalizing globalization wagon, that is ravaging the earth now.

Nü waut sai Yee, Mame, waut saigst dü dann?

Souwestoegg on Winnipuzz:
James Reaney's Winnipeg

The first professionally produced Canadian play I ever saw was *The Sun and the Moon* by James Reaney, at the Manitoba Theatre Centre in Winnipeg in 1973. The MTC archives record it as having taken place in February 1972 (Laurie Lam, email to Di Brandt, August 30, 2004), but I remember discussing it afterward in several English Honours classes at the University of Manitoba. I didn't enroll there until the fall of 1972, so it must have been the following winter. This was when CanLit was just coming into being in our universities and still considered a Mickey Mouse option. All of us keeners in Honours English at Manitoba hugged away from it, and stuck to British and American, though even American was considered brash and loudmouthed and not really couth.[1] Seeing a Canadian play on stage in the early '70s gave us all queasy shivers of familiarity and what I would call now a kind of shame, that feeling of being somehow found out, exposed, caught in the act, of existing in the public literary discourse that had until then excluded us. That felt safer. We understood we were readers of literature, critics in training, not its subject, and never its authors. New Criticism, with its emphasis on the text, sans socio-biographical context, was then at its height. Northrop Frye ruled the halls of the University of Manitoba through his numerous acolytes as he did the University of Toronto. Literature, in our apprentice-critical eyes, could be divided into neat conceptual periods—Renaissance, Neo-Classical, Romantic, Victorian, Modern. Texts could be read according to orderly, pre-defined interpretive levels—literal, metaphoric, symbolic, anagogic. Through the veins of English literature flowed the ancient blood of the Romans and Hebrews and Greeks. There was rare mention of our various ethnic and First Nations ancestries. We were not players on the stage of world history. We were its endline observers in a faraway country. We liked it that way.

Those of us with writerly dreams and murkily intuited creative manuscripts in the making bit our tongues, and hid them in mental caves and study drawers. Where did we get such self-important ideas? There were no

writer residencies, no visiting writers on our campuses—though I recall well
the deep impression made by a youngish chain-smoking Mordecai Richler,
and a brilliantly nervous, articulate young R.D. Laing, at the University of
Manitoba's experimental Festival of Life and Learning. The city was then
beginning to pulse with the kinds of theatre and street and film festivals it
has since become famous for. Creative writing classes were just beginning
to be taught in Canadian universities. At Manitoba they were relegated to a
minor category, over with CanLit. There were several published writers in our
department, notably George Amabile and Ed Kleiman and Mike Turner, and
even a composer, Chester Duncan. Mike Turner ran his own literary press,
Four Humours. Turner and Amabile also published a semi-annual literary
journal, *The Far Point*, which featured work by new Canadian writers as well
as established ones like Livesay and Ralph Gustafson; very few of its writers
were local, very few of their works were set on the prairies.

These professors taught British and American literature as well, and the
gulf between their creative and critical work, and so between our own student
efforts in these different directions, seemed unbridgeable and immense. Twice
Governor General's Award winning poet and playwright James Reaney had
taught creative writing at Manitoba from 1949 to 1960, and his play, *Names
and Nicknames*, had been performed at the Manitoba Theatre Centre in
1963. Frye himself was promoting new Canadian writing in his reviews,
collected in *The Bush Garden*. We were all reading Richler and Atwood and
listening to Leonard Cohen in our dorm rooms. But mostly, we scribbled
away in secret, hugging our sheaves of literary fragments surreptitiously
under our jackets.[2]

Reaney's play embarrassed us with its familiarity, its small-town
religiosity, and its symbolism, recognizably Frygian but applied so startlingly
to a quintessentially Canadian setting. We discussed it in our Shakespeare
and Victorian Lit classes, shivering over its invasion of our safe critical spaces
with local contemporaneity. Reaney's Mill Bank and United Church were
set in anglo-southwestern Ontario, far from our own much more sparsely
settled but far more multicultural Manitoba prairie. His colourful Mrs.
Shade and fair-minded Kingbird were allegorical figures in a metaphysical
redemption story, a contest between good and evil, that evoked Blake and
James Frazer's mythologies, rooted in other places and times. They were
also, hilariously, uncomfortably, the kind of church-going Bible-quoting

people we might expect to meet on our Winnipeg and small town streets.

Did we notice then, as we can't help noticing now, the problematic genderedness of Reaney's implied metaphysical realms in *The Sun and the Moon*, the enlightened calm male sunny daytime realm chaotically impinged upon and enlivened by but ultimately prevailing against the energetic demonic female night realm? I took a course in "Literary Symbolism" with Frye at the University of Toronto in the mid '70s. Frye persistently refused to address the potentially misogynist and anti-ecological bias in his great symbolic code, his equation of "male" with divinity and heroism and cultural enlightenment, and "female" with nature, nightmare, chaos and darkness. When challenged on this point, as he sometimes was, then, though not as often as he would be now, he insisted on a metaphorical understanding of gender, culture and nature: we are all females in relation to God, he would say, and all males in relation to the earth. An interesting answer, making cross-dressers and transsexuals of us all, when we are not in fact repeating old habits of dominance and submission so widely sustained historically by this old binary equation. Reaney put Frye's archetypal paradigm to the test, in many ways, by applying it to the telling of stories; his gender politics, like Frye's, remains questionable.

In 1960 Reaney moved to London, Ontario, to take up a teaching post at the University of Western Ontario, where he continued to produce prolifically and win more awards. That same year he wrote the poetic sequence, *A Message to Winnipeg*, which was later collected in *Selected Longer Poems* edited by Germaine Warkentin (30-38). A section of Part VI, "Winnipeg as a Chess Game" reappeared as a chant in his surreal play, *Colours in the Dark*, produced in Stratford in 1967. *A Message to Winnipeg* is the kind of "longer poem" (as he called it) you'd want to write when leaving a city, not when trying to live in it, with its alarming apocalyptic vision of the city's imminent doom: "Destruction cometh—a sucking cloud,/Your towers will tumble down//Child's Restaurant will be consumed/Eaton's and Hudson's Bay/Grass will grow on your neon signs/And the rivers dry away," accompanied by loud warnings, "Leave the burning city/Leave this burning town" (37)! There is no reason given for the poem's dire prediction, except Winnipeg's similarity to every other city: "the same as the London of the/Empire that spawned you, the Athens and Rome/that still/transmit some of their patterns to you sitting in the /swamp/at the forks of the river You are like Babylon and like/Nineveh You are any city" (37). Reaney gives this fiery doomsday message right after a marvellously conceived, humorous, site specific line like "Winnipeg is a loutish giant sucking a sugar beet beside/the two winding rivers" (36).

The juxtaposition encapsulates precisely the best and worst of Reaney as he sounds to us now, several decades removed from the archetypalizing influence of Frye, forced to listen as we are to predictions and ecological warnings of doom on a weekly basis, and hungry as ever for stories and images that reflect our own time and place with clarity and affection, but also a sense of hope. Puckish humour, brash pronouncements, affectionate local colour, and heavy-handed structural manipulation of plot in the name of a shadowy metaphysics that borrows heavily from fundamentalist Christianity while at the same time disavowing its influence, all these signature effects running through Reaney's oeuvre are present in this dramatic little sequence that nevertheless still delights with its provocative voice and vivid sense of detail: "ice glitter[ing] on the gargoyles and statues/High up on the 1913 boom business buildings" (33).

It is hard to believe now that it was his interest in regionalism Reaney was most criticized for in his early career, as can be seen from his own passionate defense of the same in a 1971 essay in *Maclean's*: "If, however, you go in for too much taking the Big Picture you miss something very valuable in the smaller picture" (18). Terry Griggs, writing in 1983, repeats the anti-regionalist bias he was replying to in the *Maclean's* essay. Griggs defends Reaney against the charge of localism by championing his archetypalism: "Reaney mines atoms— small towns, children, the bare stage—to get at the giants lying foetal within" (28), evoking the very kind of universalizing we have come to distrust now in the age of cultural and economic globalization, which claims to act in the interests of all yet so blatantly works for the few. We long now, even in our psychological and ontological paradigms, for "thick" overviews rather than reductively "thin" ones, not because we're not interested in the big picture, or indeed inner giants, but because we don't, now, believe we can access them through confident universalist assertions—except tragically annihilating ones. We recognize that we must locate our theories in specificities of time and place and their randomly collected intertexts, including meticulously open-minded proprioception, the "movement of life into language" (to use Robin Blaser's phrase), and then work like hell at trying to understand how our theories might interface with others that began elsewhere (cited in Dragland 220). Or to quote cultural theorist Eve Sedgwick, there may be "benefit in exploring the extremely varied, dynamic, and historically contingent ways that strong theoretical constructs interact with weak ones in the ecology of knowing—an exploration that obviously can't proceed without a respectful interest in weak as well as strong theoretical acts" (23).

Margaret Atwood, who was interested in both Frygian archetypalism and Canadian regionalism but knew how to juggle them in a more cosmopolitan, sophisticated fashion than Reaney did, wrote wittily and witheringly of Reaney's *Poems* in 1973: "I have long entertained a private vision of Frye reading through Reaney while muttering 'What have I wrought?' or 'This is not what I meant, at all,' and this collection confirms it" (114). Her criticism seems more directed at his clumsiness in melding the two, though, than at his interest in them as such: "If you can see a world in a grain of sand, well, good; but you shouldn't stick one on just because you think it ought to be there" (117). What she praises, on the other hand, is his "uniqueness, power, peculiarity and, sometimes, unprecedented weirdness." (I second the weirdness! You have no idea what is coming next in most of his poems and plays, and drawings, foro that matter. There is nothing else like it.)

Reaney's sense of apocalypse in *A Message to Winnipeg* borrows heavily from Eliotic motifs of modernity as wasteland to describe the logical outcome of and just punishment for the sins of industrial overdevelopment of the recently wild prairie landscape.[3] It echoes further, alarmingly, what theologian Catherine Keller calls the "apocalypse habit" of Western culture, rooted in its "master script," the Book of Revelation, a habit Eliot's modernist vision was not immune to. "I have wondered," writes Keller, "whether Revelation voices a darkly lucid and quite valid intuition into [what Richard Horsely has called the Western] 'spiral of violence' or whether Western civilization has been acting out a self-fulfilling prophecy" (12). The apocalypse habit is pervasive in the positivist sciences as much as the nihilist humanities, writes Keller; it exhibits a tendency to respond to situations of dire need, such as the current eco-crisis, with unrealistic hopes of instantaneous large scale transformation, which flip inevitably, disappointed, into despair. "We wish for messianic solutions and end up doing nothing. If we can't save the world, then to hell with it" (14). Against such absolutist either/or thinking, Keller proposes the practice of "finitude" rather than final solutions, the celebration and nurturance of "trickster logic," the spirit of mimicry and metamorphosis, of laughter and survival (306). And where this logic comes too late, the practice of grief, which can bring with it "productive rage and even a primal laughter" (310).[4]

Fig. 8 James Reaney, "When the clouds cross the sky . . . ," 1976.
From Selected Longer Poems, *ed. Germaine Warkentin.*
Erin, ON: Press Porcepic, 1976. 94.

On the other hand, some version of apocalyptic thinking seems pervasive in cultures around the globe, figuring most prominently in periods of profound cultural shift, when it does feel as if the world itself is coming to an end. Frank Kermode has suggested that apocalyptic thinking, "the sense of an ending," is really a projection of our own sense of mortality onto the rest of the universe (93-124). Carolyn Merchant connects it with fear of pervasive cultural and environmental disaster, but also, on the other side, the hope for revolutionary change through divine intervention or radical transformation from within (79-83). The "fire and brimstone" version seems particularly punitive, and is popular in North America through the wide influence of the Christian Right. But there are numerous other versions. Hindu cosmology proposes vast cycles of time, or *yugas*, which mark the beginning and middle and end of entire universes (we are currently in the middle of the Kali Yuga); Hopis believe in the repeated creation and destruction and recreation of the world (we are now living in the fifth creation); the Mayan calendar of cosmic and world events famously ends on December 21, 2012. Climate change and the rising sea as the polar icecaps melt is the widely accepted catastrophic narrative of our time. Some version of apocalypse is perhaps necessary and useful for us to understand the cycles of birth and death and possibly rebirth that mark our lives and histories, and to mobilize us into action of one kind and another in times of crisis. It is the fundamentalist overtones of the apocalypse Reaney imagines for Winnipeg, which call forth fear and judgment rather than agency and understanding, that I object to.

Remarkably, though, Reaney also captures, alongside and in counterpoint to Christian motifs, the flavour of the Métis rebellion against eastern Canadian nationalist interests that have so coloured our cultural identifications in the West in his poem. Reaney's Winnipeg is haunted by the ghosts of the defeated Bois-Brûles; it is bogged down by the proliferation of factories and "Glittering/ Hard merciless cars. Glittering hard merciless/Cars. Extremely useful, extremely depressing," where there were once "ravens in flocks," and indigenous peoples, "Who did what the stars did and the sun" (31). The apocalyptic ending of the poem, nevertheless, in the bombastic voice of the unnamed "Messenger," disturbingly resembles the very excesses he decries in the figure of "old Canon Bastion" who rides on the streetcar and "never understands but has a voice/Fit for anything in the King James Version" (35-38).

Perhaps there is an element of revenge in *A Message to Winnipeg* for "the city," as Reaney complains in the preface, "where noone [sic] listened to the poet made up of one thousand rice paper Bible pages" (30). Such lack of audience response, looking back, is not after all surprising in a city that didn't know itself yet, the way it does now, as a rich cultural site that sustains a large lively writing community, internationally renowned literary presses, journals and festivals, and Pulitzer-, Governor General's Award- and Giller Prize-winning literary careers of the stature of Carol Shields, Robert Kroetsch, Miriam Toews and David Bergen. For Reaney, coming from Toronto with its much larger and more established cultural playing field, Winnipeg in the '50s may have felt unbearably parochial.

Nevertheless, Winnipeg deserves credit for shaping Reaney's oeuvre during his early academic and writerly years. Toronto may have instilled in him universalist archetypal ideas, and may have published his Governor General's Award-winning mythopoetic poetry collections, *The Red Heart* and *A Suit of Nettles*, but it was in Winnipeg that he developed his own regionally flavoured symbolism. It was in conversation with colleagues and students at the University of Manitoba during the '50s that he developed his signature sense of regionalism as "an area of subtle zoning [of the] *here and now*," as he put it in the editorial of the inaugural issue of *Alphabet*, the influential literary journal he began editing there shortly before his move to London.

Among Reaney's students at Manitoba were Ed Kleiman, Jack Parr and Victor Cowie, themselves to become premier players in the Winnipeg academic and literary scene, as well as Dick Harrison, whose pioneering doctoral dissertation was published as *Unnamed Country: The Struggle for a Canadian Prairie Fiction*. Harrison's study highlighted the multicultural character of western Canadian settlement, and referred, if too obliquely, to the presence of Métis and First Nations peoples in its cultural development. Later Reaney taught Cree playwright and novelist Tomson Highway at the University of Western Ontario. Highway acknowledges Reaney as one of the people who gave him "support, inspiration, faith, and love" during the writing of his novel, *Kiss of the Fur Queen*, in which Winnipeg reveals a hellish face in its treatment of indigenous citizens, worthy of Reaney's direst prophecies.

Reaney's influence on the development of regionally based site-specific writing in Canada and on prairie writing generally thus deserves broad recognition. But so does the prairie's compelling influence on Reaney: the specificity of the local, and the profound influence of particular landscape and region on cultural expression, are pretty hard to avoid in western Canada, though we have also worked hard at cosmopolitanism and transnationalism in our ways. A debate like Griggs', on whether regionalism matters as much as universalism, is simply unthinkable on the prairies where cities are separated from one another by hundreds of miles, and where the landscape and harsh climate exert a strong unavoidable presence, indelibly marked by indigenous cultural mediations. The fact that it took an easterner to bring a growing sense of First Nations indigenosity and immigrant multiculturalism into our academic and public literary discourses says more about the fledgling nature of our cultural institutions in the '50s and '60s than about our local consciousness as such.

Alphabet No. 1 was published in September 1960 with a London address, but the editorial is signed "Winnipeg, July 1960" (Birk Sproxton tells me Walter Swayze remembers Reaney editing copy for it on the bus to the University of Manitoba campus). The inaugural issue included an evocative short story, "Crystal Pillow," by Ed Kleiman, set in the fictional town White Horn, Manitoba, in bush country not far from Winnipeg. The town boasts a small crystalline salt-bed in a circle of trees, mysterious reminder of a vanished geological age, and site of visionary glimpses of bygone times, such as an "Indian brave" leaping on a "fiery pony" (63). The story concludes with a comical-satirical portrait of Winnipeg as "a sinking marshland filled with [dinosaurs]," which turn out to be high rise buildings whose weight cannot be sustained by the swampy ground and are doomed, in the narrator Billy's eyes, to sink "below the silencing muddy surface" (68).

In his editorial, Reaney claimed Kleiman's story as the inspirational text that motivated him to found *Alphabet*: "It was Kleiman's story I first felt I must see published; it was so imaginative and no one was doing a thing about it" (4). The obvious symbolic and regional intertextuality between this story and Reaney's own *A Message to Winnipeg* bespeak a rich cultural dialogue in the halls of the University of Manitoba's English department during the Reaney years. But notice the differences between Kleiman's vision of Winnipeg doom and Reaney's apocalypse: Kleiman's is psychologized by being rooted in a suicidal boy's vision, and his ending for the city does not seem to be fuelled by punitive, angry gods, as does Reaney's, but rather, by its own unsustainability in having been built on muddy ground. It's true: Winnipeg is built on a swamp; most house owners know what that means in terms shifting foundations and basement flooding.

Kleiman comments on the source of the story as follows: "Of course I'd read *Message to Winnipeg*, but am not aware of my story being influenced by his work. It was a period when many of us were taking teaching jobs in rural Manitoba, and I'd heard a story of a pupil taking his life. The story was haunting, and I began to wonder what could have been passing through that student's mind at that time and how he viewed his surroundings. All that concern gave way to a fictional communication with someone I'd never met and never would." He adds, "That ability to submerge one's self totally in one's material—and not let one's own personality get in the way—was a skill that Jamie's class helped us develop. Since then we've kept in touch and are always reading and commenting to one another about each other's work." (Kleiman, email to Di Brandt, December 12, 2004).

George Bowering has reflected wittily on the difference between Reaney's later "souwesto"-inflected regionalist aesthetics and the kind of local writing the TISH poets, under the influence of Olson's Black Mountain poetics, were developing on the west coast in the '60s and '70s. The TISH poets, Bowering writes, were interested in exploring place in the sense of locus, milieu, geographic site, while the "regionalists of London" led by Reaney, as he encountered them in the mid '60s, seemed more interested in region as territory, as property, identifiable address. While the BC poets committed themselves to the notion of "surface" in writing, Reaney and his gang were "intent upon exploring deep, well under the surface of the place where [they lived]" (3).

They did so, observes Bowering, not in order to lift themselves out of place or nature, but indeed to establish themselves more firmly in it, in the interest of "identification . . . and domestication. A sense of being capably at home, and glad of it." Souwesto regionalism thus becomes, in Bowering's definition, the "performance of a social consciousness" (3). It was Reaney, of course, who popularized the term Souwesto, for the particular mannered culture of the densely settled countryside southwest of Toronto, that produced Stephen Leacock and Alice Munro and Christopher Dewdney and Nino Ricci and Don McKay, and only much later non-European writers like André

Alexis and Christopher Curtis, though Reaney claims it was Greg Curnoe who coined the term (1971, 18).

We Winnipeggers took longer to come to our literary sense of the local and regional, beyond the pioneering efforts of Reaney and Kleiman, and writers like John Marlyn and Livesay and Laurence and Wiseman, who had after all gone elsewhere to write about our landscape and us. The Manitoba Writers' Guild was founded in 1981 by a small group of writers centered around the recently organized Turnstone Press and *Prairie Fire* magazine, then *Writers' News Manitoba*. There was similar organizational activity happening in Alberta and Saskatchewan in these years, with the establishment of presses like NeWest, Longspoon, Coteau, Thistledown and Red Deer, and literary magazines like *Dandelion*, *Grain* and *The Dinosaur Review*. Situated at the crossroads between east and west, densely settled Ontario and sparsely settled BC, we Winnipeggers looked in both directions for our bearings. Because we developed our sense of place during the '70s and '80s, under the additional galvanizing influence of feminism and multiculturalism, we did not share Bowering's West Coast sense of a lone (white, male) horse rider surveying an ineffable "phenomenal frontier" (Bowering 4-6) even though we, like the BC writers, remembered the settler experience, and shared their sense of western alienation from the centres of power in the east.

For us on the western prairies, cultural activity did not happen, as we saw it, in an empty landscape waiting to be discovered and explored by solitary wanderers, but rather in domestically inhabited, indigenous-minded and multiculturally inflected territories and communities, Cree, Ojibway, Dakota, Métis, Jewish, Ukrainian, French, Mennonite. Kroetsch's *Stone Hammer*, found on his father's farm, carries as much indigenous hunter/gatherer as settler/agricultural meaning, and his *Seed Catalogue* is maternally inflected. Patrick Friesen's and Kristjana Gunnars' and Eli Mandel's settler communities bear strong nomadic cultural markings that evoke traditional European landscapes, more akin to local indigenous communities than to anglo-derived, Ontario-driven Canadian nationalism. Jan Horner's women are firmly embedded in family and neighbourhood. Anne Szumigalski's world is simultaneously domestic and wild-minded, surreal. Louise Halfe's *Blue Marrow* boldly portrays Native women engaged in daring cultural reclamation acts, asserting their ancient Aboriginal and matriarchal clan rights in and against the invading settler culture.

Like Reaney's regionalists, we were determinedly "we" rather than "I," to use Bowering's terms. Our domesticity, however, was, is, wild-minded, Métis flavoured, independentiste, socialist, shtetl, forever rebellious à la Riel and the General Strike, mistrustful of Ontario capitalist interests. Nevertheless we Winnipeggers tended to see ourselves as more poststructuralist than phenomenologist, more performance poets in the Torontonian tradition than projectivists in the Olsonian, even though in many ways we shared the proprioceptive aims of open field poetics. No doubt this had a lot to do with the affiliations of our leading regional mentors. bpNichol had grown up in Winnipeg, so was legitimately one of ours. Kroetsch had spent years in New York State, reading Heidegger and J. Hillis Miller and Derrida, before returning to the prairies to theorize his interests in local stories vis-à-vis the postmodern. Like them, Laurence and Wiseman had migrated east rather than west, while maintaining geographical loyalties in their writing. Livesay of course had lived a widely cosmopolitan life, in Montreal, Winnipeg, New Jersey, London and Paris, before settling in Vancouver, and spanned a wide geographic and cultural intertext in her long and diverse career, which was reflected in the eclectic editorial policy of *Contemporary Verse 2*, which she founded in Winnipeg in 1979 during a stint as writer-in-residence at the University of Manitoba.

Reaney's acerbic *Message to Winnipeg*, relayed over his shoulder in a huff, so to speak, as he exited the prairies to take up adult abode in his childhood Souwesto in 1960, unnervingly anticipates many of our later Manitoba literary trends. His collage portrait of the city is impressively diverse in its attentions, from factory to river, to indigenous history, to pioneer settlement, to French and Métis presence, to modern traffic, to city politics. His amusing catalogue of citizens on the busy sidewalks of Portage Avenue between Eaton's and the Bay includes a dramatic range of character types which looks forward to both '80s-style identity politics and turn of the millennium ecopoetics, marked by profession, psychology, ethnicity, family configuration, age, gender, even, remarkably, association with animals: "Doctor Horror, Assistant Professor Sulky, and Mother /Neurosis/Some Hutterites with geese under their arms, Father/Monster,/And the Sliver girls: Little Sliver, Just as little Sliver,/Sliver,/ Old Spit, Young Kleenex and twenty-five Albanians" (34).

Should we read Reaney's apocalyptic conclusion as a doomsday vision of the sort environmental activists are now predicting for us in the coming decades, if we continue in our escalating demands on the earth's resources?

Part II, "Winnipeg Seen as a Body of Time & Space," suggests so: "Then on top of you fell/A boneyard wrecked auto gent, his hair/Made of rusted car door handles, his fingernails/Of red Snowflake Pastry signs, his belly/Of buildings downtown; his arms of sewers,/His nerves electric wires, his mouth a telephone,/His backbone—a cracked cement street. His heart/An orange pendulum bus crawling with the human fleas/Of a so-so civilization—half gadget, half flesh" (31). The poem offers no alternative directions, however, admitting helplessly or even flippantly, "I don't know what I would have instead" (31). The Messenger's exhortation to "leave the burning city" in Part VI (38), similarly, offers no solution, since presumably the citizens who left would have to congregate elsewhere and find or create similarly doomed conditions in another city.

As a displaced, homesick Winnipegger living in Souwesto most of the last decade, I can't help noticing how much more industrialized, how much more polluted, how much more car-invested, how much more environmentally burdened the Souwesto landscape is than Winnipeg's, even though the latter is, to be sure, a bigger, busier city than London or Sarnia, or Windsor, or Waterloo. Perhaps it was the proximity of the open prairie, and the recentness of agricultural settlement, that tuned Reaney's environmental consciousness up to a higher frequency than seems to be the case in some of his earlier pre-Winnipeg writings, though the Great Lakes regions come under environmental scrutiny, also, in his earlier 1948 *Great Lakes Suite*: "Lake Erie is weary/Of washing the dreary/Crowds of the cities/That line her shores" (collected in the same volume, *Selected Longer Poems*, 16).

Perhaps surprisingly, Reaney proposed regionalism as a solution to the problems of Souwesto über-industrialization:

> At the present moment hopelessly uncontrolled and undersigned megalopolises are on the march. Politicians cheerfully prophesy that the Detroit complex will one day melt into the Toronto system at London, Ontario! Well, wonderful. And what kind of human rat will scuttle around in this huge maze of freeways and parking lots? Zombies don't know where they are; comforted by such phrases as 'global village' and 'you can't stop progress,' they cheerfully face the prospect of a world where all places are the same

shopping plaza and all the shoppers are interchangeable units. For some reason or other I can't cheerfully face this prospect. One way to fight it is to 'know' where you are, and this means, among other things, your street, your apartment block, your window box, the faces of friends around you. (1971, 18)

This is the opposite solution to Bowering's, for whom cultivating cosmopolitan nomadism in sparsely settled areas offers a better guarantee against over-industrialization than home-making. Temperamentally, I am with him: like Bowering, I find Souwesto domesticity stultifying in its tameness, its large investment in factory life, its calm acceptance of shocking levels of air and water pollution. The easy sceptic's reply to Reaney's proposal of regionalism as a solution to the conundrum of the megalopolis and overcrowding is that knowing where you are, where your street and neighbourhood are, doesn't stop the relentless march of "progress," doesn't stop the fields from being paved over, doesn't stop the excesses of petroleum culture from destroying what little natural beauty and untampered-with ecosystemic vitality are left. Arguably it even enables further overdevelopment, by providing the cultural locale that makes its horrors endurable.

The sceptic's reply to Bowering's alternative is that it applies only to the few, not the many, in its assumption of easily accessible, sparsely settled land; that cosmopolitanism depends on large city environments whose investment in environmental degradation is surely even bigger, or indeed directly related to, small town factory culture, if more buffered by niceties; and that urban nomadism encourages a good time for its privileged practitioners who can leave environmental troubles behind for the locally embedded to deal with. Bowering's vision of BC as sparsely populated and underdeveloped is, further, outmoded now in light of Vancouver's current population overrun and rural BC's overlogging.

What is striking, in light of the current eco-crisis, is Reaney's prescient rage about its coming horrors well before the topic became generally fashionable in North American lit circles, as it is beginning to be now. The "Lake St. Clair" section of the *Great Lakes Suite* declares humorously but emphatically:

I once knew a bear
Who swam in Lake St. Clair

And after the experience
Said, 'Hoity Toit
I don't like the way Detroit
Pollutes the air there.'
Then after a while
He added with a smile,
'And I don't like the way Windsor
Does, either.' (1976, 16).

In "Yonge Street: A Denunciation of Toronto," Scene 15 of *Colours in the Dark*, the character Pa curses "this street where it's increasingly difficult to find a green leaf" (1969, 80). Over and over, Reaney offers the Blakean adage of "Art as mentor of spiritual depths and heights, of rebirth, of combating the boredom of our capitalist, phoney paradise" (1990, 72), in ways that powerfully recapture the spirit of Romantic environmentalism, as recently explicated by Jonathan Bate (1991, 2000), but very pointedly set in the Canadian modern context.

What of Reaney's fanatical attachment to Frye's vertical levels of literary expression and interpretation and existential reality, in our own time which is so much more horizontally inclined, so much more trusting of contiguity than symbolism and metaphor, so much more materialist in its interests, than archetypal and surrealist? A dedicated postmodernist like Stan Dragland has argued that while Reaney appears to adhere to premeditated and imposed formal structures rather than open-ended verse, he nevertheless is "formally eclectic and protean" and "restless" in meaning (220). bpNichol, less reserved in his praise, highlights Reaney's alphabetic self-reflexivity, his concern "with language with the materials of language[. He] comes close to writing writing[. His texts] exist as real objects in the real world" (5).

To these postmodern defences of Reaney's admittedly old-fashioned sounding poetics—because of his penchant for rhyme and predictable rhythms as well as repetitive structural patterns, I suggest—we can add his interest in the generation of experimental literary texts and performance pieces through arbitrary juxtapositions of myth with documentary detail, in ways that anticipate postmodern poetics in technique, if not in effect. Reaney's failure to wed archetypes to realism convincingly is precisely what interests us now. His bipolar landscapes with their frightening figures of bears and interrogators and danses macabre, wedded to familiar realist details, create a nightmarish and suggestive landscape that has impressive historical and psychological scope, unpredictable and often startling effects, and prophetic vocality, of a sort that is often sadly missing in more fashionably circumscribed contemporary work.

I forgive Reaney his imminent Winnipeg apocalypse on these grounds. Anyway, there is the possibility of reading the ending of *Message to Winnipeg* as ironic, a hallucination, a nightmare in the Messenger's head. After all, his vision of the burning city is interrupted by a "wise old idiot," a local guy, who reasonably protests, "But this city is not burning . . . And there's no war we've heard of." At this point, the Messenger "beats his brow," only to get dramatically swallowed up by the "stupid pavement," until "the Babylon becomes him" and the city "disappears" (38). Notably, he does not disappear with it: on he gallops wildly, "Over the plain and under the sky," still shouting his unheeded message of "truthful fear" (38). If Reaney meant to convey a general sense of anxiety and foreboding about the future, in a way that is becoming pervasive in North America and around the world now, using Winnipeg as reflective locus rather than specific source or target for this anxiety, then indeed we can embrace his portrait wholeheartedly, as does the refrain of the poem's communal speaking voice, responding to the Messenger's unconfirmed warnings: "It's the sound of our hearts, say we" (38).

After all, only Guy Maddin and Marcel Dzama have come anywhere close to the kind of inventive zaniness that characterizes Reaney's best work, that allows him to insert, in the middle of the dizzyingly unpredictable *Colours in the Dark*—set in Souwestoland but at any moment zipping out to other parts of the country or dramatically other psychic realms—the following marvellously nutty "Fantasia on the Street Names of Winnipeg." Reaney's brilliant riff on our civic geography encouraged me to practise further nominal conjugations on our fair city's name in my title. I can't resist citing here in full, in the name of (anti-apocalyptic) inter-regionalist cosmopolitan good fun:

> I met a nun coming up Osborne Street
> You met an Osborne coming up Fort Street
> He met a Portage Fort coming down Main
> She carried a Kennedy filled with Dagmar
> It, Broadway, balanced its rows of elms

We are nothing but Pembina all that Wellington Crescent
You Assiniboine far too much about Gertie
They Corydoned their gay Oxfords and Ashes
Beg you Osborne. Portage your Main this conjugation.
To be a city system, Winnipegging the whole thing?
That's exactly what I Main Street South.
For Example:

I Winnipeg	We Winnipegged
You Winnip	You Winnipdown
He Winni	
She Winnipeggied	They Winnipugged
It Winned	

The Past Tense of To Winnipeg?
I'm not quite sure but I think that it would be—

I Winnipuzzed? (70-71)

"Twins are not the same baby twice": Twin intimacies and clone fantasies

David Teplica's photograph, *Ovum (1998)*, shows adult identical twins entwined in a circular embrace, making them look like one being with two heads and four feet. In fact they are women, but you can't tell that from the photograph, the faceless circular being appears androgynous, and perhaps something other than human. Pierre Baldi chose this photograph for the cover of his book, *The Shattered Self*, iconic of what he sees as the crowning achievement of the contemporary technological revolution, the control of human reproduction through cloning and the manipulation of embryonic stem cells.

Baldi celebrates the existential implications of contemporary genomics that many of us fear: the blurring of the distinction between self and other, and human and machine, and the de-eroticization and dehumanization of human reproduction through in vitro processes. Many contemporary artists and cultural theorists are equally enamoured of the increasing mechanization of human and genetic processes. Belgian artist Wim Delvoye garnered international headlines for wittily replicating the process of human digestion in a mechanical installation, *Cloaca* (2000). American feminist science theorist Donna Haraway received much attention for her celebration of the cyborg, and the arrival of the transgenically altered Harvard "oncomouse," and other instances of biotechnological interventions with radical social implications (1989, 1991, 1997). On the other side of the debate, there is increasing opposition to genetic manipulation of living organisms among a vocal group of intellectuals, including Canadian writers Margaret Atwood and Erin Mouré. Atwood's dystopic novel, *Oryx and Crake*, envisions a devastated, nightmarish world where genetic engineering has gone wrong in the hands of a power-hungry scientist, in which humans have morphed into robotic machine-like beings, and animals have turned crafty and human-like. Erin Mouré similarly questions the ethics of contemporary genomics in her tour de force long poem, *Furious*, on the grounds of our biological and

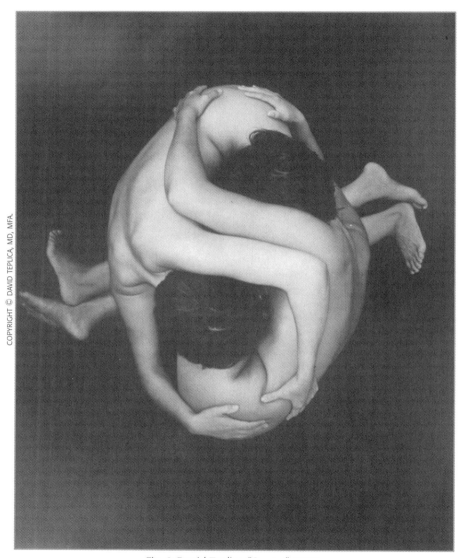

COPYRIGHT © DAVID TEPLICA, MD, MFA.

Fig. 9 David Teplica "Ovum," 1998.

spiritual kinship to animals. Her dramatic image of laboratory animals in "Pure Reason: Science,"

> The day the animals came on the radio, fed-up, the electrodes
>   in their hands
> Beaming, small tubes leading into their brains
>   where chemicals enter,
> . . . showing off into the microphone the cut scars
> of our diet fantasy
> inside which their babies are waiting with our defects
> to be born
>
> (21),

is echoed a few pages later, in "Pure Reason: Femininity," by its human analog:

> The day the women came on the radio, fed-up, electrodes in
>   their purses,
> the bubbling light from that, neuronic balance, the de/
>   pression
> of their inner houses
>
> (24).

In Mouré's vision, the humanist dream of complete dominion over the non-human world is shown to be not only dangerous and wrong-headed on the grounds of hubris, but unethical and wrong-hearted in its disregard of the spiritual and biological integrity and interconnectedness of living beings. It is strange, after all, that according to contemporary medical iconography, our cells and genomic identities are similar enough to those of rats and pigs and other animals to make analogous research possible for medical conditions, and yet, at the same time, our psychic and spiritual identities are regarded as dissimilar enough to warrant human domination of other species. The attitudes we foster toward animals, Mouré suggests, is intimately connected to the attitudes we foster toward humans, particularly women, who are often, illogically, regarded as closer to "nature" than men, at least "white" men. Humans are poetic beings, posits Mouré, we think and act by analogy. It isn't possible for us to step outside or above our own ecological interdependencies as though we came from another planet. Nor is it possible to isolate human respect for one species or one gender or one race only; the categories are interconnected in our minds and actions, as they are also in practice in the intricately reciprocal realm of physical being.

The argument over ethics in genetic engineering is typically constructed in North American public discourse as an argument between progressive, enlightened thinking and retrograde conservatism; scientists are depicted as neutral investigators with open minds, and critics as erroneously self-interested subjects whose childish attachments to traditional processes and relations hamper "evolutionary" change. Haraway, following this trend, provocatively suggests that those who oppose the blurring of organic and machinic processes and categories are akin to racial purists who resist multiculturalism and cross-racial hybridization (1997, 62). In the rhetorical confusion that characterizes contemporary bio-ethical debate, it is refreshing to discover a science writer like Baldi, willing to unequivocally expose the political agenda of innovative biogenetic trends. In Baldi's view, the major cultural aim of the contemporary biotechnological revolution is to relocate the primary locus of reproduction from women's wombs to the petri dishes of scientists, so as to leave behind the "awkward and cumbersome, almost bizarre business" of sex and facilitate "unprecedented degrees of speed, precision, and efficiency" in the reproductive process (43). Why we would wish to introduce more "speed" and "efficiency" in the birth process in our already overpopulated planet, and indeed, why we would want to give up erotic pleasure, reproductive or otherwise, are questions Baldi does not discuss. Nor does he address the issues of power and gender in the construction of the science labs—which belong, after all, mostly to white males—other than to offer the specious observation that taking the provenance of reproduction away from women will achieve "a completely level and equal field between the sexes at the purely reproductive level" (43). Baldi does acknowledge that people might be reluctant to give up the pleasures of intercourse, but, he suggests, there could be "new drugs or new means of electrical or other stimulation" to replace the consolations of sexual excitement and orgasm (46).

Far from dancing adventurously along the highwire of joyful, erotically inflected, open-minded evolutionary change, hard science here acknowledges its aims to be reductionist and counter-evolutionary, married to hard-jawed pre-existent—and puritan—purposes that will be coldly imposed by a few privileged men upon the rest of the species and the planet. Baldi's subtitle, *The End of Natural Evolution*, openly admits to this charge. Sociologist and science critic Barbara Rothman observes that the Human Genome Project does not seem to have progressed beyond the precepts of ancient Greek culture, famously depicted in Aeschylus' *Oresteia*, wherein the paternal "seed," in Apollo's words, is constructed as the sole parent of the child, and the mother downgraded from erstwhile goddess to mindless "vessel." In contemporary genetic theory, writes Rothman, the environment, including the rest of the cell outside the DNA-laden nucleus, and all the rest of the rich contextual factors that sustain the life process and bring it into being, is constructed as possible interference with the expression of the genotype rather than as its evolutionary fulfillment, including the mother who carries the embryo, the community that shelters and nurtures the mother, the society that contains the community, and the Earth itself, which feeds and holds and sustains the entire life process (15).

What does all this have to do with identical twins? For Baldi, twins represent the natural prototype for human cloning, which he considers both inevitable and imminent in contemporary scientific practice. Cloning could increase the appearance of "identical" human beings from the natural incidence of 1 in a 1000 to a commonplace occurrence. What would be the advantages of having many identical cloned siblings (or should they be called sons and daughters) walking around? Twins are "one of the major tools for psychological studies attempting to tease out the roles of nature and nurture in humans," observes Baldi. Cloning could "enable analysis of these difficult questions on an unprecedented scale, [and increase] the chances of producing extremely gifted organisms" (58). Cloning could also increase, in Baldi's view, the chances of achieving the high level of understanding and cooperation often observed in twins, which he attributes to their lack of individuality, "as if they had almost the same self and the distance between their brains were very small" (60). Most grandiosely, cloning offers a form of "genetic immortality" and thus challenges not only our conventional notions of the self and individuality, but our very concepts of life and death. "In time," offers Baldi, "we could imagine a gigantic cloning 'machine' that continuously outputs in parallel new, young clones of all possible genomes. [Thus] any living individual would be assured of having contemporary clones of himself of exactly the same age, and in fact of all possible ages" (66).

What is wrong with this picture? "Twins are not the same baby twice," exclaims Barbara Rothman. "At birth they do not weigh the same; their rates of growth can be dramatically different. Placed here or there, in the same womb in the same woman in the same environment, they're not having the same experience. *Here* isn't *there*, and nothing is ever the same" (26-27). Twin studies in the nature-nurture debates, it appears, often assume a simplistic and absolute divide between "nature" and "nurture" that is not borne out by experience. The emotional closeness of twins is only partially accounted for by their genetic similarity; non-identical twins also share an uncanny level of connection, presumably because of their experiential closeness in the womb, the birth process, and if they're lucky enough to remain together, life thereafter.

The clear distinction between identical and non-identical twins assumed by most of us, in fact, does not hold up under analytical scrutiny. The two-egg origin of non-identical twins has been questioned by researchers who are debating the process and function of twinning in the womb. Identical twins have been found to have discrepancies in their DNA coding, and a full third of all parents of fraternal twins, according to one estimate, may be treating them as if they were identicals.[1] What about the well-known and extensively documented phenomenon of strikingly similar lifestyle choices and illnesses between twins who have been separated for long periods of time, sometimes since birth? Many American biologists are proposing genetic coding as the exclusive explanation for this phenomenon. There is no question that contemporary biogenetic research has offered a needed corrective to earlier modernist theories of human behaviour which were exclusively environmentally and experientially based, by demonstrating a direct link between genetic inheritance and personalities and behaviour. But this is, after all, not a new idea. In the traditionalist Mennonite village culture I grew up in, where families were large and easily observable over long periods of time, everyone played the game of identifying who takes after whom, who inherited whose nose, who inherited whose laugh, or nimble fingers or visionary prose. The idea that our individual lives and identities and destinies are clearly embedded in both our genetic and social inheritance,

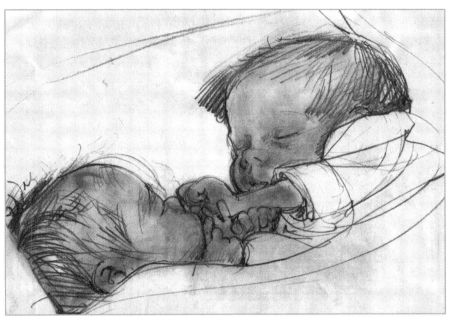

Fig. 10 Heather Spears, "Newborn twins," 1986.

and that these are deeply intertwined, is after all as old as ideas of karma, and fate, and destiny, prevalent in all pre-modernist cultures around the world. In this sense, geneticists' much touted ability to predict people's futures, at least in terms of abilities and strengths, amounts to nothing more than an expensive, mechanicially produced tea leaf reading, with a perhaps similar rate of accuracy, given the exigencies and unpredictabilities of experience and human will (Rothman 27-29). The contemporary biogenetic explanation for heritable traits goes overboard, however, in positing that all human behaviour might be biologically determined, including, as has been famously asserted by researchers at the University of Minnesota's Center for Twin and Adoption Research and their colleagues, not only the same number of crow's feet at the corners of twins' eyes, but also such lifestyle choices as make and colour of cars, cigarette brands and fashion designs. How could genetic coding determine such minute behaviours and choices, and more alarmingly, what happens to free will in such an extensively deterministic paradigm? "Nobody has the vaguest idea how that happens," admits Thomas Bouchard, founder of the Center, whose studies tracked the habits of identical twins separated during early childhood with these astonishing results. "There is tons of stuff to work on here, it's all open territory" (cited in Neimark 43).

British biologist Rupert Sheldrake offers a completely different hypothesis, which he terms "morphic resonance," to explain deep, instantaneous, and nonlocal communication between organisms, commonly observable in such instances as the high level of cooperation among bees in a hive, instantaneous communication between birds in a flock which makes complex cooperative flight patterns possible, animals who know when their human companions are coming home without any physical clues, mothers who know when their children are safe or in danger however near or far away they are from them, and animals who know when earthquakes are coming before any physical indications are present, not even seismic tremors (*Dogs That Know when their Owners are Coming Home and Other Unexplained Powers of Animals*, 1999). Morphic resonance, posits Sheldrake, occurs between organisms sharing deep bonding of some sort, such as species identity or emotional attachment. Sheldrake's hypothesis explains the mechanism that enables disparate but interdependent organisms and ecosystems to communicate with one another, and that allows evolution to occur, by rapidly proliferating individual mutations or leaps in consciousness across an entire species, bioregion, or ecosystem. Sheldrake's theory is consonant with the principles of quantum mechanics, which has demonstrated nonlocal communication between particles on the subatomic level (see Pratt 69-78, 1997). It is a much more believable explanation of coincidences in precise lifestyle choices among twins than absolute biological determinism, which is impossible (and dangerous!) to believe on the level of ordinary experience, where we daily encounter the effects of free will, environmental influence, and chance. Morphic resonance is able to address communication on all levels of existence, from the subatomic and cellular to the highest forms of human consciousness. Twins who have shared the primal experiences of conception, gestation and birth in a single womb, and who share genetic identity as well, would necessarily share a high level of morphic resonance and therefore be able to communicate nonlocally with ease, whether conscious of it or not.

In fact it is frightening to imagine a world in which genetic identicalness is seen, à la Baldi, as the recipe for social cooperation, while traditional forms of intimacy, including sex and the tender gestation of the human fetus inside the mother's womb, are eliminated. Pregnancy is an erotic, psychologically and spiritually profound experience for women, their male partners, and also the developing child. Raising children from infancy through adolescence to adulthood is a long, challenging task; it is where the ethical, emotional, psychic life of the species is nurtured through repeated social interactions and negotiations, and pregnancy is one of the primary loci of emotional preparation for this daunting work. Baldi appears to be oblivious to the realities of raising young, growing children, and the cauldron of emotional and ethical decision-making and steep learning—and also delight, playfulness and joy!—that the parental project is. If it is connectedness he covets, here is the most intense, extended, common, beautiful instance of it available to our species. Anthropologist Evelyn Reed has argued that it is precisely the long dependency of human children, compared to the short infancy of the offspring of other species, that makes us human, in that it enables us to replace instinctual coding with extensive experiential learning (47).

If Reed is right, then Baldi's project of speeding up the reproductive process from gestation onwards bodes very badly for us, amounting to a kind of anti-evolutionary behaviourist regression to more instinctual modes of being. The denial of human mortality in the fantasy of the infinitely clonable self is also alarming: if we lose our psychic, spiritual and biological integrity as a species, do we also lose our capacity to understand, promote and protect life in its individualist and holistic aspects, as part of a vast interconnected cosmic process that is surely much bigger than we can grasp or understand? If we lose our ability to die, are we also, perhaps, already, losing our ability to live?

Jean Baudrillard calls the fantasy of cloning not only a regression of complex beings to the destiny of protozoa, but a reduction of individuality and selfhood and the profound erotics of sexual reproduction with its incorporation of alterity, to a kind of cancerous metastasis, that is, a single base formula proliferating indefinitely without taking into account the Other (100). Rothman, in a related vein, detects the spectre of racism and fascism, reminiscent of Nazi eugenics experiments, rearing its ugly double head in the contemporary biogenetic fantasy of identicalness, and goal of breeding a group of superior people. Hitler was interested in macroeugenics, writes Rothman, "keeping the [gene] pools separate, free of contamination by other, less valued pools" (112); contemporary American medicine is invested in microeugenics, separating "good" from "bad" genes in the reproductive process. The ethical questions raised by the Human Genome Project are huge, and not being widely enough addressed, Rothman feels, outside the medical community that is creating them. Genetically transmitted diseases can now be identified with particular lines of descent in families and racially identifiable groups. Tay-Sachs, for example, has been identified as an "inborn error of metabolism" (114) that runs typically in Jewish families of Ashkenazi descent. Sickle-cell anemia, caused by "point mutation," tends to be thought of as a "black or African disease" (116-19). Should genetically "defective" fetuses be aborted? Should racial groups who show tendencies toward certain genetically transmitted diseases be prevented from reproducing them? Is it good for people to be able to predict illnesses without knowing how to cure or prevent them? Is it accurate or right to predict illnesses in people based on genetic tendencies rather than experience?

There are other problematic instances of biomedical planning that smack of macroeugenics. David Lykken, former Head of the Twin Registry at the University of Minnesota's Center for Twin and Adoption Research, argues that criminality runs in families, specifically single mother families, and is therefore "caused" by fatherless childrearing (197-212). Instead of advocating better financial and social support for mothers and their children,

Lykken advocates the licensing of parents, which would be restricted to heterosexual couples, and has been consulted by federal officials on this idea. As he openly admits, most African American families would not qualify for parenting licenses in his scheme (cited in Wright 59). Sandra Scarr and Richard Weinberg's investigations of twinship in minority racial populations purport to show that African American children from impoverished backgrounds can improve their IQ levels by being adopted into wealthier white families—but only up to a point (726-39). As with Lykken, Scarr and Weinberg's work overlooks the contextual factors involved in parenting, and the many cross-cultural factors involved in the construction of IQ as a measurement of intelligence among minority populations. This branch of genetic research seems to lack an adequate working concept of the intimate, detailed and reciprocal connection between genetics and environment, and between them and the free will of the creative, imaginative human spirit, whose desires and admiration insert randomness into the historical process, and shape it along potentially visionary lines.

What is the profile of superior intelligence we should try to emulate? Baldi suggests not the persona of a saint, or contemplative, or artist, or grandmother, or healer, to be imitated through courage and hard work, as traditional sages have done, but rather the figure of Einstein, mathematician and physicist, to be copied through cloning his genes, as if Einstein's hard work and life experiences had no influence or impact on his intellectual achievements. What happens to less intellectually endowed and disabled children in this paradigm? Rothman reminds us that children under the age of three with Down syndrome were the first population group to be gassed by the Nazis (59). The killing of Jews and other perceived undesirables in Nazi Germany happened, as she observes, "in a context of killing to heal, a biomedical program." The language of the camps was consistently a medical language, based on a social theory of collective decay and biological purification. "There was a logical progression, if the word 'logic' has any meaning here at all: from coercive sterilization, to the killing of 'impaired' children, the killing of 'impaired' adults, the selection and killing of 'impaired' inmates of concentration camps, and finally the mass killing of Jews" (61). Consider what it means to posit mathematical intelligence as the most valuable human trait, divorced from empathy, wisdom, love and social responsibility. Is it relevant to note that Einstein's experiments in relativity contributed directly to the invention of the deadliest weapon on the planet, whose deployment requires wisdom much more crucially than intelligence? Is it pertinent to remember that Plato valorized mathematics as the highest truth in *The Republic*, at the outset of Western culture's long project of progressive domination of the planet, specifically for its ability to reduce experience to analytical concepts, outside the cycle of birth and regeneration, and ordinary mortality? It was precisely this emphasis in Platonic thought, observes Grace Jantzen in her classical study, *Foundations of Violence*, that informed the ancient Greeks' valorization of soldiery, death-dealing and otherworldly "truth," at the tragic expense of eros and beauty (186). It is an orientation that has plagued Western culture ever since.

"People do not 'spring up like mushrooms,'" declares Rothman. "We are conceived inside of bodies, we come forth after months of hearing voices, feeling the rhythm of the human body, cradled in the pelvic rock of our mothers' walk. . . . We spend years in intimate physical contact with other bodies, being cradled, held, rocked, carried, suckled. That is who we are and how we got to be who we are, not separate beings that must learn to cope with others, but attached beings. . . . Our connectedness is the reality; the separation is the illusion" (17). It is very hard to imagine how replacing these elements of generational intimacy and love with a cold petri dish could possibly contribute to an improvement in the level of cooperation and understanding between people, whether genetically identical, whether biologically twinned, or not. (There is a similar misunderstanding of the nature of human relations in the currently fashionable emphasis on chemical treatment of painful psychological states that derive from inadequately nurtured social relations; treatment that can never do more than mask the symptoms of hurt and thereby confuse the political issues underlying such relations.) On the other hand, emulating the empathy and cooperation often observed among twins as a model for social interaction, based on the observation of their experiential intimacy, could be very useful in enhancing social interactions generally. This is not, however, the role that twins typically occupy in our literature.

When I set out to write this essay, I imagined surveying contemporary Canadian literature for interesting examples of twin stories. I found very few, a depressing conclusion for a twin like me, an estranged one at that, searching for existential literary validation! Twins typically do not occupy the role of protagonists; they are usually portrayed as either identical and inseparable and self-sufficient, if not inscrutable, as in Marian Engel's *Lunatic Villas* and Margaret Atwood's *Cat's Eye*. Or, worse, they are treated as freaks, as in Atwood's short story, "Kat," where the character Kat has what the doctors believed to be a tumour removed, and discovers that it was in fact a hairy ball of tissue, including brain tissue, which is theorized to be her undeveloped twin, swallowed up somewhere in the gestation process (*Wilderness Tips*, 41-56). When twins do assume a central role, they are usually depicted as opposites, illustrating some binary or bipolar pairing of traits, as in Marilyn Bowering's *Visible Worlds*, where the narrating twin is "short and brown-haired," and the other twin "tall and straight . . . a combination of snow, ice, and sun," and mostly absent (17), or Bill Gaston's *Tall Lives*, where one twin is frustrated and respectable and the other flamboyantly outlaw. The most engaging and important fictional account of twins in Canadian literature to date is Lori Lansens' recent novel, *The Girls*, which combines elements of identicalness, oppositeness and freakishness in a poetic portrait of conjoined twin girls, who share foreheads and intensely intimate lives, and yet manage to fashion separate identities despite their proximity. Lansens avoids over-emphasis on the twins' freakishness by focusing on their intelligence, and by surrounding them with empathetic characters who love them. Like Baldi, Lansens sees twins as exemplary in the accomplishment of human intimacy; unlike Baldi, she posits proximity, shared life experiences and acts of caring, rather than genetic identicalness, as its ingredients. Significantly, Lansens cites the closeness of mother and child as the model for her depiction of the twins' conjoined intimacy: "That feeling of intimacy that you get with nursing—[my babies were attached to me] and I was attached to them. I was nursing, co-sleeping. I was never for a second alone" (interview with Susan Cole, 92). This is the commonly available, primal level of intimacy Baldi would eliminate with his petri dishes. It is not clear that cloned babies without the primal intimacy of the womb would be able to replicate such tender caring between them.

Lansens' novel does not, of course, avoid the conundrum of freakishness altogether, and perhaps too much of the story is taken up with the mechanics of how to live in conjoined bodies, and what it's like for separate identities to be so closely entwined and still have separate sexual experiences, and so on. Living in conjoined bodies for these twins means, among other things, that the narrator Rose carries a syringe of Tatranax, a poison, with her throughout her adolescence and twenties, so she can kill herself quickly when her sister, Ruby, who is biologically weaker and diagnosed with an imminent fatal aneurysm, dies. Extraordinary intimacy, this novel suggests, comes at a very high price, though Lansens takes great pains to show how strong and generously available, on the other hand, the love that has nurtured and sustained the conjoined twins is all around them.

The notion of freakishness as exemplary of human experience rather than its outer limit was made popular in literary criticism in the late '70s by Leslie Fiedler, who published a literary survey of deviants under the title *Freaks*. Fiedler, never one to shy away from controversy, lamented the loss of the public display of abnormal human beings such as giants, dwarfs, conjoined twins, hermaphrodites, fat ladies and living skeletons in circuses under the guise of political correctness, and applauded its return in the celebration of freakishness in '60s counter-culture. Fiedler interpreted the significance of the freak psychoanalytically, as representative of the universal human fear of our own monstrosity. Conjoined twins, for Fiedler, exemplified psychic immaturity, the lack of proper individuation. His catalogue of conjoined twins includes numerous horrific images of "One-and-a-Halfs," culled from historical records predating modern surgical methods, which prevent their occurrence nowadays. These are humans with incomplete "parasitic" bodies attached to their own, such as Frank Letini, who was famous in the American circus in the early twentieth century, billed as the "Three-legged Wonder." Letini's third leg belonged to a "rudimentary twin, who weighed only twenty-five pounds but possessed a pelvis and an imperfect penis" (219).

Lansens' twins are not quite One-and-a-Halfs, but they do have a parasitic relationship, as well as experiencing extraordinary emotional intimacy. Ruby doesn't have feet, and Rose must therefore carry her around and respond to her needs and wishes, even though they have separate personalities and inner lives. By insisting on the twins' loveliness and even happiness, Lansens avoids over-emphasis on their freakishness. But by normalizing their shared emotional life as somehow exemplary in its capacity for intimacy and empathy, she risks something equally disturbing. If the parasitic relationship of Ruby and Rose is somehow analogous to the relationship of a mother (or parent) and child, does that mean maternal subjectivity and intimacy are terminally tied to child dependency, i.e., expendable once the labour of childrearing is done? If the precarious and cumbersome physicality of conjoined twins is emblematic of exemplary emotional intimacy between individual human beings, does that suggest that intimacy itself is outside the norm, very hard to get, and even pathological?

Lansens' novel aside, the spectacle of infinitely repeating selves represented by identical twins seems much more prevalent and tantalizing to the contemporary imagination than freakishness. If the freak represented, at least in its '60s incarnation, youthful free-spiritedness and the desire for individual self-expression, the contemporary clone surely represents its opposite, the fantasy of intimacy through identicalness and homogeneity. For Hillel Schwartz, identical twins represent the "culture of the copy," in which the increasing ease of duplication of images and objects surrounds us with facsimiles and doubles, to such an extent that the very notion of authenticity and originality is seriously undermined. Schwartz worries that our contemporary obsession with identicalness will result in the loss of "discernment" between authenticity and duplicity, generativity and diversity, and virtual reality. "Are we little else but futile reenactments," laments Schwartz, "or is reenactment the little enough that we can be truly about?" (387-378). Jean Baudrillard expresses a similar concern: "When the body . . . ceases to be conceived as anything but a message, as a stockpile of information and of messages, as fodder for data processing. . . . then it is the end of the body, of its history, and of its vicissitudes" (99-100). The spectre of the loss of human subjectivity and cultural identity in precisely these terms is the driving image of Atwood's haunting dystopia, *Oryx and Crake*. Along with these authors, I am worried that the emphasis on identicalness and infinite duplication of ourselves implies a significant loss of diversity and tradition in every realm—biological, linguistic and cultural. More ominously, it points to a loss of human values such as tolerance, appreciation of otherness, nurturance of difference, and respect for the intrinsic self-determination of living beings, which are the cornerstones of healthy human relations, and surely hold the key to healthy ecosystemic relations as well.

How is it that twins have come to represent something so diametrically opposite to what they represented in ancient times in creation myths around the world, where they happily enacted and symbolized the magnetic polarity and paradoxical image of intimate difference, or contrast in unity, needed to create and sustain life (Ward 57-79)? Twins were traditionally understood to provide the model for our symmetrical body shape, which enables us to practise left/right distinctions without losing our innate sense of unity (Narby 88-90); they also provided the mythological basis for contrasting systems of exchange, as Elaine Jahner points out, by implying the underlying twinness of disparate cultures (173). A beautiful example of an ancient and still extant creation myth featuring magical twins can be found in Paula Gunn Allen's retelling of Navajo creation stories in her collection of indigenous *Grandmothers of the Light*, where the all-powerful Thinking Woman, S's'tsi'naku, also known as Spider Grandmother, weaves the dancing multiverse into being with the power and beauty of her thinking, her heartsong. The first beings to appear in the newly created space-time are the twins Ic'sts'ity and Nau'ts'ity, who continue the song of creation with their chanting and singing, until around them,

> swirling, whirling globes of light began to form. They began pushing outward in a great whirling spiral, a great wheeling multitude of stars, all singing as they circled and wheeled like great geese upon the void. As they spiraled outward, they grew larger and brighter. Around and around the still, invisible center where Spider, Ic'sts'ity and Nau'ts'ity sang. They whirled, the outer ones flinging themselves farther and farther from the center, great arms forming in the spiral dance, following the lines of the song, the lines of the power, reaching out farther and farther into the mystery, carrying the song in their light, in their fingers, making both the darkness and the light as they danced, finding the power coming to them from the darkness, flinging it out from them in the light. The power danced in the void, in the light, in the midnight reaches of the gleaming dark. It sang. (36)

It seems, notes Schwartz, that while images of duplication and identicalness have proliferated in our time, "the companionate, faithful, heavenly twins have become clashing antagonists," evidenced in such alarming symptoms as bipolar and dissociative disorders, and gothic-style narratives of the evil twin or double (83). There seems to have been an intermediate stage between these two modalities, historically, where heroically clashing twins became the basis for religious and national founding myths, including Cain and Abel and Jacob and Esau in Judaism, Romulus and Remus in Rome, and Asha and Drug in the Zoroastrian tradition (Bianchi 104). In many cultures, as we know, the appearance of twins came to be seen as a calamity, the children put to death and the mothers punished (Ward 57-79).

It is reasonable to assume that the image of dueling twins is connected psychically, and perhaps archetypally, to the prenatal battle for physical space in the womb, which has been documented visually through ultrasound imaging (Louis Keith, cited in Wright 52). Recently researchers have been reporting widespread twin conceptions resulting in singleton births. The astonishingly high incidence of the "vanishing twin," first professionally documented in 1980, has been variously interpreted. Perhaps we are all conceived as twins and, in most cases, only one of us survived the hazards of gestation and birth. Perhaps the stronger vanquished the weaker, or even cannibalized it, as instances of chimeras and cysts with teeth and hair in them suggest. Or is it the weaker that preys on the stronger, as historic examples of autosites with attached parasitic limbs or extra heads seem to illustrate (see Fiedler's catalogue of such instances, 219-225)? However, to interpret twinship as a predominantly warring condition, as the valorization of warring twins in traditional heroic literature and the survival-of-the-fittest slant of genetic science implies, is erroneous for many reasons. Even if the statistics are correct in the global sense (in Charles Boklage's landmark 1989 study, only 61 out of 325 early twin pregnancies resulted in the birth of twins), the phenomenon is not as remarkable as it seems, given that most pregnancies, whether multiple or single, fail anyway, so hazardous is the gestation and life process (Wright 52). The minority pairs of twins who make it to birth and adulthood are remarkable precisely for their cooperation and togetherness, despite primeval territorial disputes—it is their extraordinary capacity for companionship in cramped quarters, that enabled them, after all, to survive as twins! While twin fetuses have been observed fighting, they have also been observed kissing, and there is widespread written and photographic documentation of their extraordinary empathetic awareness of one another even in the moments immediately following birth (Keith, cited in Wright 52). If it is cooperativeness and intimacy and empathy we seek, we should look for it here, in the exemplary case of twins who do make it alive from the womb to the outside world, despite their differences and disputes, aware of each other's presence from their first waking minute onwards, not in vain hopes

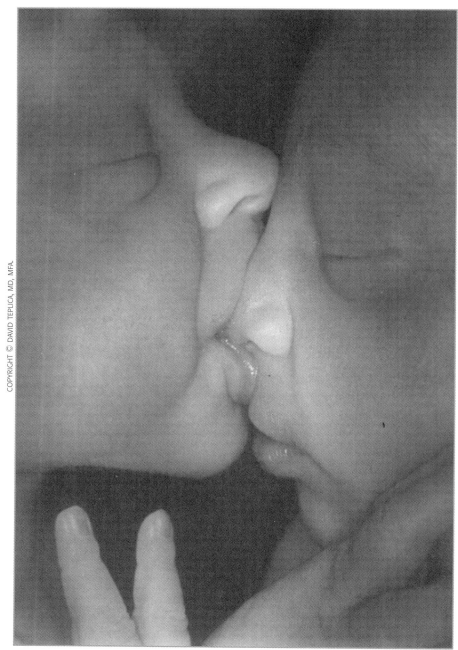

COPYRIGHT © DAVID TEPLICA, MD, MFA.

Fig. 11 David Teplica, "Reunion (The MacCumber Twins)," 1999.

of erasing differences of various kinds through genetic engineering, with its frightening homogeneous and fascist implications.

And what about the twins themselves? Let me speak as a twin for a moment, speaking for all twins, and say that yes, we did experience an extraordinary level of togetherness coming into the world, and thereafter if we were lucky enough to survive and be raised together. Most of us have suffered some version of misunderstanding, or envy, or even outright hostility, for our unique intimacy, and perhaps due to vestiges of old superstitions about the magicalness and/or unluckiness of twins, unless we were born and raised in a culture like that of Yoruba, where twins are openly worshipped as a divine gift, with attendant blessings for the family (Leroy et al, 132-6, see also Pemberton and Picton, ed. 2003). Yet none of us, including the most "identical," would disclaim individuality and difference from the other, a point that was publicly demonstrated in the US in the early 1800s by the example of Chang and Eng, the original "Siamese twins," who lived separate lives though they were joined together, and exhibited many differing personality traits and characteristics (Fiedler ch 8, "Siamese Twins," 197-226). Is it true that all of us are conceived as twins but most of us born single, mourning our vanished twin, much the way Plato imagined in his myth of the originally double human being split in two by Zeus, each half condemned to search for the other throughout their lives? Was Freud right in identifying the uncanniness of the double in fantasy and literature with a primal sense of originary difference in unity, perhaps harking back to that same conceived and lost twin, even if later the double was portrayed more often as a dark shadowy alter ego (Schwartz 83)? Is it true that twins have extrasensory powers and are possessed of magical languages, as is commonly thought, even in the contemporary rationalist West, though we lack rituals of acknowledgement or homage for them? It is not farfetched, I think, to claim that some scientists' eagerness to separate twins for the purposes of research smacks of envy of their initial togetherness. There is certainly a striking lack of admission in such studies of the role the scientists may have played in creating the sense of alienation felt by the twins as they grew up alone, but intently observed by adult figures withholding crucial information about their identities from them (see, for example, Peter Neubauer's pioneering study of the twins Amy and Beth, as reviewed by Wright, 46).

In the midst of contemporary ecological anxieties and fantasies of cyborgs and clones, it is uplifting to see the image of companionate twinship re-emerging in our literature with its promise of togetherness in difference, and in dynamic polarity, where inherent tensions and potential hostilities are held in creative check by a sense of affection and understanding, vibrant with as yet unseen possibilities. After a century of medical expertise admonishing parents to treat their twins as individuals, not as a unit, there are now childrearing manuals with titles like *The Joy of Twins* (1988) and *Make Room for Twins* (1987). It was Phyllis Graham who pioneered this trend in 1955 with her then cross-grain study, *The Care and Feeding of Twins*, wherein she boldly observed that "Twins who develop the same tastes and interests do not always have special social problems, and all twins may realize a happiness available to no one else" (148). Is it relevant to note that she was herself a mother of twins, not a disinterested male "expert" coming into the domestic realm with externally derived questions and methods?

Whatever our cultural affiliations and loyalties, twinship undeniably touches a deep desire for intimate lifelong companionship in everyone, and perhaps great grief in those many of us who have not experienced such closeness in our lives. In this way, the phenomenon of twins raises the possibility of fear and envy and rage in those of us, the majority of humans, who are not in twin relationships. Is this the reason medical researchers seem blithe about the unreasonably huge burden put on parents of multiple births, whose incidence has increased so dramatically in the last few decades due to the new reproductive technologies, and perhaps also due to overchemicalization of our environments, as Alberta veterinarian and poet Nora Gould speculates (in an unpublished manuscript, 2006)? Looked at another way, the encounter with twinship, however closely it touches us, holds out a beautiful challenge, as well as a promise, of closeness, empathy, and understanding between disparate beings who nevertheless find themselves kin at a primordial level— a model that applies after all to everyone, and everything.

& then everything goes bee: A poet's journal

How do you write for bees?

*

"Aganetha, you have re-invented what it means to make art."

This is what I wrote in Aganetha Dyck's guest book at the Winnipeg Art Gallery, in 1995.

She had just opened her spectacular multimedia installation, *The Extended Wedding Party*, created over several years in collaboration with honeybees.

The exhibition gave her instant international fame and invitations to show worldwide.

Little did I know that my excited brief comment would lead to my own involvement in Aganetha's bee project a few years later.

*

Aganetha Dyck began collaborating with bees in 1991. She had been working with beeswax for a few years, and gradually became interested in the bees themselves, their amazing complex labour, and ritually complicated lives.

Aganetha initiated the collaboration by asking the bees which materials they liked to work with. She asked them this by placing twenty-three found and made objects into seventeen hives.

The bees answered back: they didn't much like styrofoam or cardboard. They shredded these materials in short order and spit them out of the hive.

Fig. 12 Aganetha Dyck, "Hive Blanket: Ancient Text." Photo: William Eakin, 1992.

But, the bees said, they loved working with woven cotton, porcelain and glass. These they decorated with mysterious tracks and lavish waves of honeycomb.

*

The tracks resemble ancient hieroglyphic text markings. Or perhaps they are more like the tracks made by wind, or the sea, on sand. Sometimes they look like the fossil remains of small skeletons. In their more extravagant modes, the honeycombs appear regal, like frothy ocean waves. Or like beautiful handwoven lace.

Perhaps, these bee markings suggest, in their utter and simple beauty, we all write in the same languages, live in the same world, animals, humans, the elements, feel the same sun, the same wind at our backs, understand the same joys, despite our profound species differences.

What, after all, is text? "The stratigraphy of rocks, layers of pollen in a swamp, the outward expanding circles in the trunk of a tree," writes Gary Snyder, "can be seen as texts. The calligraphy of rivers winding back and forth over the land leaving layer upon layer of traces of previous riverbeds is text." (66)

*

The Extended Wedding Party featured a room full of beautiful hive garments suspended between wax decorated screens. The installation included food for the wedding feast, gifts, and a multitude of shoes, all molded with beeswax.

The centrepiece was "Lady in Waiting," a spectacular four-foot glass dress, filled with honeycomb, and decorated with exquisite bee lace. It took the bees several summers and dozens of bee generations to decorate the dress.

"Lady in Waiting" was exhibited as a work-in-progress, with thousands of honeybees still swarming over it, intently sculpting its bridal lace. The bees were separated from the viewers by a plexiglass case with a tunnel to the roof of the gallery, so the bees could fly in and out. The bees quickly discovered where the best sources of nectar and pollen were in their new urban location. They were particularly attracted to the manicured gardens of the Manitoba Legislative Building nearby, which coincidentally happens to be a popular cruising ground for rubbies during the day and the Winnipeg gay underground at night.

A few dozen bees were lying at the hem of the bridal skirt, their brief lives already over, dead.

The presence of the bees created an eerie, magical effect in the gallery. The gallery space became mystical, even sacred, redolent with the heady scent of honey. There was a deep sense of waiting, of reverence for the bride. Or perhaps of mourning, a shiver at the mysterious absence of the wedding guests.

Had we missed the wedding, or was it about to begin?

The gallery visitors were hushed, listening to the bees humming intently over the sculpture, completely absorbed in their work. Perhaps it was we who were the wedding guests, about to assume our designated roles as friends and relatives, paying homage to the archetypal presence of the bride and her ardent worshippers, the bees.

The large gallery space was filled with the droning, humming, buzzing song of the bees.

*

The Extended Wedding Party called up a range of responses in people. Many of these responses were about the live, startling presence of the bees themselves.

Novelist Sandra Birdsell called the work "macabre" (cited in Dahle 23).

Fig. 13 Aganetha Dyck, "Lady in Waiting." Photo: Sheila Spence, 1995.

Sigrid Dahle, reflecting on the dark side of hive life in an interview with Aganetha Dyck, called it a "dystopia," a menacing social arrangement.

She was thinking, she said, of the way unproductive bees are shoved out of the hive at the end of the summer without ceremony, to die, and the way the bees sometimes have to defend themselves to the death against rivals and outsiders—as do we all.

Tennyson's nature with its dark underside, "red in tooth and claw," Darwin's relentless reproductive process, the "survival of the fittest," spectres of a natural order ruthlessly devoid of spirit that haunted our nineteenth-century forebears and still haunt us today, nakedly displayed.

Aganetha herself, talking with Sigrid, compared the queen bee, hidden, trapped at the centre of the hive, to the young mothers in *The Handmaid's Tale*, Margaret Atwood's dark futuristic novel, in which single fertile women are held in bondage by a powerful but infertile married ruling class, to produce heirs for it (Dahle 23).

Curator Joan Borsa observed in the exhibition catalogue, "Aganetha Dyck's work seems to follow bees to the limits of human understanding. A place where death and decay, sensory cognition and the necessity of externalizing the troubling interior realms that the body has concealed are acknowledged" (58).

The bees as a site of the coming apart of human consciousness, its unravelling, into the knowledge of mortality, of our physical limits as humans, despite our fantasies and ceremonies of transcendence and cultural or spiritual immortality.

The edge of the human, that is, understood first of all as the site of decay, of death.

*

I was struck by the sense of fear and sometimes horror that people were experiencing in their encounter with the bees.

This sense was confirmed for me in a description of one of Aganetha's collaborative pieces in a 1996 internet web page, entitled "Hive Bodice," featuring a sculptured wax exhibit in a wooden box.

"Hive Bodice," read the caption next to the photograph of the piece, "is about cells, fragile cells containing sensuous, mysterious substances. Cells that are shaped, reshaped, filled, drained, cleansed, painted, prodded, invaded and monitored. Powerful and sexual, they are filled with nurture and desire. Mutant and diseased, they brim with death." (www.HSIMS.com, April 16, 1996).

Aganetha sent me a print-out of this web page during the time we began corresponding about my possible participation in her bee project, with a handwritten note underneath that said, "I did not write this."

She had bracketed and underlined the words, "Mutant and diseased, they brim with death," with the comment, "The words in brackets were written by the curator, I think."

∗

I was relieved to know that Aganetha did not altogether share these negative valuations of the bees or their work.

I remembered the way she described her first encounter with the bees, her admiration and awe in their presence:

> "Being able to open the hive and stand there was such a rush, such an adventure. I thought I had climbed the tallest mountain! Just to be able to stand there . . . in my regular clothes and know I wouldn't get attacked! What really amazed me once I knew this was possible, was the power of something so small . . . We always talk about brute force; but the bees are so small and yet they have more power than a whole football team" (Dahle 22).

I remembered other tender descriptions of the bees by Aganetha:

> "Part of working with the bees is just playing. It's just the most amazing thing to have this connection to this warm creature that massages your hands and makes you feel alive. Especially if you are in the sun and it's very beautiful and the flowers are blooming and you think the world's OK . . .

> "Those bees have a lot of fun. They don't work all of the time . . . You know that saying, 'busy as a bee'? Well, you find the workers sitting around, talking, and their life of seven weeks might be like ours of 79 years. So I'm sure they have a lot of fun. I love the bees" (Dahle 26).

*

I found out that "Hive Bodice" was commissioned for the exhibition *Survivors in Search of a Voice*, curated by Barbara Amesbury in dialogue with eight women survivors of breast cancer. After spending a day listening to the stories of cancer survivors, Aganetha Dyck and Wanda Koop, another artist working on the project, were "in tears" and for weeks, Aganetha recalled later, "we could not work in the studio, so horrific were some of the tales of a struggle to survive in what seemed like a hopeless situation" (email to Di Brandt, Spring 1999).

"Hive Bodice" was Aganetha Dyck's and the bees' response to the deep suffering of women, whose bodies are registering the ravages of environmental pollution in ever greater numbers. In twenty-four hours, the bees had filled the glass bodice with "perfect honeycomb cells." The bees' labour was a message of beauty, courage and hope, and gave the survivors a powerful public voice of protest, and of healing.

*

So this was one of the questions I asked myself when I began thinking about writing for the bees:

Why are people reminded of disease and deformity when they encounter the bees? Why would they describe this incredibly successful and intricate social arrangement, dating back to at least the time of the dinosaurs, and considered essential to global vegetation cycles and human food sources, as dystopian, a world gone wrong?

A question made all the more striking when you reflect that bees were worshipped by many ancient cultures as incarnations of the divine, whose artworks, both beeswax and honey, are prized around the world for their beauty, sensuousness and marvellous healing properties.

What exactly is it, I asked myself, that has gone wrong? Why would Aganetha or the curator have described the bees' work in such strikingly clinical, industrial, even military terms? Filled, drained, cleansed, painted, prodded, invaded, monitored.

And why would people think of the limits of the human, that edge, that interface between humans and other, the animal, the natural, first as a place of decay, of death?

Aren't there other ways of thinking about the edges of the human? I asked. Isn't the place where we encounter the other, where we meet the face of the stranger who is not us, the not human, isn't this the place of adventure, engagement? The place of risk, of danger, yes, but also, surely, the place of nurturing, where we are reflected back to ourselves, where we are fed.

Isn't this place, I reflected, this edge, where *I* ends and the rest of the world begins? Isn't this where we are born? Isn't this where we give ourselves to the other? Isn't this, as Emmanuel Levinas and Hélène Cixous and others have said, supremely, the place of love?

*

Of course Aganetha Dyck wasn't the first person in the world to collaborate with bees. The whole history of bee-farming, you might say, is a collaboration between humans and bees.

The ancient Druids revered bees as the bringers of honeymead, which they considered a divine solar drink, and for their ideal community centred on their Mother Queen. Six times a year celebrants gathered at Tech Midchuarta, the House of Mead Circling, a hive-shaped assembly hall, to pay homage to the Goddess, imitating the bees' divinely inspired sun dance, and drinking potent golden intoxicating honeymead, which they passed around in a circle until every drop was consumed (Carr-Gom 110-113).

Plato, Mohammed and Porphyry all included bees in their portraits of heaven, considering them the bearers of souls (Simons 26).

Many of Bernini's sculptures included images of bees. The tomb of Pope Urban the VIII, Bernini's patron, in St. Peter's in Rome, is decorated with an ornate sculpture featuring, among its figurines, bronze bees, the size of pigeons.

A Mayan community fighting military occupation in Chiapas, Mexico, calls itself Las Abejas, or The Bees. Unlike its armed counterpart, the Zapatistas, Las Abejas believes in non-violent resistance to exploitation and displacement. "We are a multitude," explains one of its members, "and we want to build our house like the honeycomb where we all work collectively . . . producing honey for everyone . . . We all march together with our queen, who is the reign of God" (Lehman 9).

*

In medieval Europe, it was customary to include the bees in funeral and wedding rites. Here is a description of the age-old folk custom of "telling the bees":

> If a member of the family marries, the bees should be told,
> or they will leave the hive and not return. If a member of
> the family dies, the bees in their hives must be told, or they

will die. The procedure is that as soon as the master or mistress has breathed his or her last, a younger member of the household, often a child, is told to visit the hives and rattling a chain of small keys taps on the hive and whispers three times:

Little Brownies, little brownies, your mistress is dead
Little Brownies, little brownies, your mistress is dead
Little Brownies, little brownies, your mistress is dead

Silence is then observed for a few moments. If the bees begin to hum, they have consented to continue living. A piece of funeral crepe is then tied to the hive and later sweet drink or a piece of funeral cake is brought to the hives for the bees to feed upon. In addition the bees are often invited to the funeral. The letter to them is written in the same hand and terms as that to relatives of the deceased: "*You are invited to the funeral of—which is to take place at—, &c, &c.*" (Simons 25)

✳

It breaks your heart when you think about what it is we tell the bees nowadays. Standard North American farming practice, for example, for the past few decades has been to gas the entire hive at the end of the summer, and send for a new shipment, complete with queen, the next spring. Cheaper than figuring out how to winter the bees after taking all their honey. (I am happy to say that Aganetha's bees, including the queen, are kept safe and warm in the hive through the long harsh Manitoba winter.)

The drastic increase in the use of toxic pesticides in industrialized countries has also taken their terrible toll on bees. According to a recent estimate, 95 per cent of the wild bees in North America have died in the last few years due to lowered resistance to mites, and farmed honeybees are being kept alive, as Aganetha puts it, by "all sorts of trial and error and tons of medication" (email to Di Brandt, Spring 1999). And now there is the new worry that genetically modified crops will kill or mutate butterflies and perhaps other insects in disastrous numbers.

What does it do to the bees' sense of history to kill their great queen, keeper of hive memory, after only one summer, when she should live for a good three, threading her great ancestral presence through the honeybees' brief lives of seven weeks? Does it break the bees' hearts to be treated with such cruelty, such rudeness, by their human collaborators? What does it do to the bees' delicate complex inner workings (and to the rest of the world) to absorb and pass on chemically modified, transgenic, herbicide-resistant genes?

Margot Leigh Butler eloquently documents the concerns of beekeepers and environmentalists around the world who are tracking the alarming effect of transgenic mutations caused by GMOs (genetically modified organisms) on the world of bees and everything they touch, in her poetic essay, "Swarms in Bee Space" (in *West Coast Line* 35/2, 2001). "When poisoned by insecticide," writes Butler, bees "do their 'Alarm Dance,' running in spirals or zigzags and vigorously shaking their abdomens sideways; neighbouring bees also start dancing & stop flying; poisoned bees may die in 1-2 hours" (82).

Butler also documents shocking tactics used by multinational companies like Monsanto to stop public criticism of, and even just information about, their profit-based takeover of agricultural methods and territories around the world. More dangerous than the chemicals themselves, Butler suggests, is the corporate structure that enables such takeovers against the democratic wishes of people and even nations. "BEELINES" is her compilaton of contemporary "research, reports, recommendations, representations" on contemporary biotechnology and its impact on bees and trees and animals and people, and includes hard to get resources like the British journal *The Ecologist*'s special issue on Monsanto, which was pulped by the printer "who was worried that Monsanto might take them to court," but has been reprinted and can be ordered from www.theecologist.org/archive.asp (114-5).

And after you've seen the bees' lavish, dreamy sculptures, you can't help thinking how frustrating it must be to work in the standard boxed beehive, with its fixed trays of honeycomb starters. Every time they fill the trays with their industrious nectar gathering, honeycomb building and honeymaking, just before they get to that moment of extravagant artistic expression, not to mention drunken honeymead celebration afterward, it gets snatched from under their noses, and they have to begin all over again.

Do they worry, the elders of the hive, watching the progress of history around them, about losing their ancient arts, their lavish folk customs, so carefully preserved over time? Do the bees know how threatened their ancient livelihood is in the toxic environment of contemporary farming practices? Do they understand their ancient lineage, their royal stature, their pivotal role as pollinators of the green world, that if they go down, the green world goes down?

Does all this human destructiveness make the bees sad, despairing, angry? No wonder they come zinging at us sometimes when we approach them, stinging mad!

*

How do you write for bees?

This was the intriguing question Aganetha posed for me when she decided to extend her multimedia cross-species collaboration to include human-written text. I was thrilled to be invited to write a poem for her bees.

To tell the truth I was terrified.

*

There is, in the mysterious and ritualized space of *The Extended Wedding Party*, a gesturing toward the ancient ritual of homage to the Great Mother, the earth goddess, along with a celebration and interrogation of modern women's elaborate rituals of fashion and food preparation, for what remains one of the most highly regarded ceremonies in our time, the wedding.

Shirley Madill, curator for the exhibition, traces the genealogy of the bride as follows:

> In the Western tradition the bride has many guises, from the ancient goddess, Isis and Asherah, the bride of Baal and classical mythology's multiplicity of heavenly marriages, though the Shehinah, or God's consort in the Jerusalem Temple of the Biblical Hebrews to the Virgin Bride, the Mother of God, Mary. These Brides follow a common narrative in their histories. The story is of a continual diminishment of the place of the Bride, from Mother of God, our feminine Creator to the present almost non-existent role in a time when the need for compassion and the salvation of Mother Earth are so great (13).

Let me add to this list the names given to her by North American Aboriginal peoples, Grandmother Spider, Grandmother Moon, White Buffalo Maiden, names that celebrate a profound relationship to the natural world (Allen 1991).

"We say truly," declares Kateri Damm, Anishinabe Canadian poet, "that the land is our mother, Mother Earth. Our connection to the land, our role as protectors of the earth, and our willingness to stand our ground in protecting what is sacred to us all make us a threat to the colonizers, with their deeply inculcated ideas of their exclusive 'dominion' over nature and all other beings" (22).

*

Sylvia Plath wrote a famous poetic sequence about bees:

> The white hive is snug as a virgin,
> Sealing off her brood cells, her honey, and quietly humming.

> Smoke rolls and scarves in the grove.
> The mind of the hive thinks this is the end of everything.

Here they come, the outriders, on their hysterical elastics.
If I stand very still, they will think I am cow-parsley,
A gullible head untouched by their animosity,

Not even nodding, a personage in a hedgerow.
The villagers open the chambers,
    they are hunting the queen.
Is she hiding, is she eating honey? She is very clever.
She is old, old, old, she must live another year,
    and she knows it . . ."

("The Bee Meeting," *Ariel*, 57)

Marianne Boruch comments: "A poem, Plath insisted, 'excludes and stuns.' And the precise strangeness of the imagery here—the hive 'quietly humming,' the bees' confused flight as 'hysterical elastics' and later, in the final stanza, the mob of them rising as 'a blackout of knives'—does stun. The significance of this passage can be understood if by *excludes* she means that our witness has ruined us, at least briefly, for polite conversation, that we are outside, abruptly hypnotized by beauty that, as Rilke put it, is terror, or rather that partofterrorthatwecan—butbarely—endure." (52)

*

According to European folklore, bees issuing from the mouths of sleeping persons could take their spirits on enlightening journeys while they slept. In one such story, repeated by folklorist Sarah Simons,

"The sleeping person was moved by a companion. A few moments later, a bee returned to the spot and scurried hither and thither in terror looking for the sleeping form, but failed to know it. When the sleeper was nudged in her new resting place, she was found to be dead.

"This belief that the bee is a soul of one departed," Simons' storyteller concludes, *"is the origin of the belief of 'Telling the bees,' for souls of the departed, are they not in communion with God?"* (26)

*

I was terrified to meet the face of the bees, the face of God, perhaps, because I was ashamed of my own human face. Imagining myself ambassador to the bees, I could feel only shame, guilt, terror, at the way we're living on the earth now, our massive human egoism and runaway selfishness, the way we're treating the bees and everything else now with such relentless cruelty, such unthinking barbarity, such unwitting, dead-ended despair.

How did we come to forget all our ancient wisdom about how to be in the world, how to make room for each other, how to talk, laugh, play together, how to honour the lands we share with so many other creatures, the earth that is our mother, how to invest in a long slow future that spans many many generations after us?

My human shame made me speechless.

I thought the bees must surely want to kill me, if they could get their stingers on me. What message could I possibly want to give to them, that they could possibly want to hear?

*

I was staying at the St. Norbert Arts Centre (SNAC) just outside Winnipeg, which is situated in a renovated Trappist monastery. The grounds include a beautiful flower and herb garden, and scenic cathedral ruins looking out onto the prairie, which are used all summer as an outdoor performance space for visiting artists.

Running through the grounds is the sluggish Le Salle River, named for its coppery colour, flanked by the remains of an old forest. A few years ago this forest was threatened by a golf course project, which was happily defeated by a group of concerned St. Norbert residents led by the SNAC community under the leadership of its visionary founding director, Louise May.

Everywhere at SNAC you can hear the sounds of Celtic harps carried on the wind, and glimpse the swaying forms of dancers through the trees. The serene spirit of the departed monks, for whom this location proved too close to encroaching urbanization a scant fifty years ago, is palpable in the air.

And if you put your ear to the ground, you can hear, just beyond the edge of consciousness, the faint echo of drumming buffalo hooves, horses, sharp hunters' cries, the thud of bodies hitting earth, thirty thousand years of Indian life surging through the long rooted prairie grass, the century old memory of Métis rebels falling on this very site flashing in the sun.

The bees lived just down the road, in a little grassy clearing next to the forest, surrounded by what on the prairies is called bush, small Manitoba maples and birch and trembling aspen, and varieties of scrub brush.

My first glimpse of the bees was there, above the hives, small swarms of them playing in the sun, as the occasional small wind rustled through the surrounding branches and wafted through the grass.

Nothing prepared me, not Aganetha's words, not all the books I'd read, for the dark rush of the opened hive, its powerful current of energy, its aliveness, the overwhelming intensity of the bees, crawling around, completely absorbed in their work.

*

"To be invisible," writes Marianne Boruch, trying to get hold of the fiery magical process by which Sylvia Plath wrote her poems about bees. "To be observer."

"'How shall I describe it?' Plath wrote that last year about poetry itself, 'a door opens, a door shuts. In between you have had a glimpse: a garden, a person, a rainstorm, a dragonfly, a heart, a city . . . So a poem takes place.'

"But nothing is as brief or as happenstance," comments Boruch, "nothing so unasked for. It starts stubbornly in the body, and beyond—father and mother, even back of that. Which is to say, it starts in memory; we want to repeat. 'What do I remember/that was shaped/as this thing is shaped?' Williams keeps insisting in 'Asphodel, That Greeny Flower.' A door opens and shuts, a glimpse. And it begins—the long unfolding into image, specific image culled from a life, two lives or more. Faced without sentiment or nostalgia, such images *release*." (48-49)

Not just images, I want to add, but also sound, line, breath, spacing, *curvature* (to use Phyllis Webb's haunting term), *synactivity*, intertext with its infinitely resonating outward reach, rhythm with its primal pull.

*

I spent the summer watching Aganetha's bees, trying to see the world as they saw it, trying to shrink myself to bee size, to become "invisible."

*

It is perhaps an indication of the shortsightedness of modern thinking that *The Feminine Monarchie*, Charles Butler's treatise on honeybees, published in 1609, should have created an intellectual stir. Butler's investigations had led him to the controversial discovery that the hive was run by women, not by men, and was ruled by a mother queen, not by a king.

But surely, we ask ourselves from this distance of four centuries, concealing a smile, didn't the ancients know this already? Did the newly invented scientific method, with its venerable spirit of open enquiry and narrow focus on controlled evidence, help or hinder in acquiring this startling new knowledge?

Reading about certain contemporary scientific research practices, I can't help wondering this same thing.

American entomologist Thomas Seeley, for example, quick-freezes his bees in the deep freezer so he can number each one with paint, for future observation. He then thaws and releases them back into the hive.

Seeley has built a meticulously attentive professional practice on his method of observing the bees, enabling him to document what he calls their "social physiology" in impressive detail. I can't help thinking, though, there must be a whole lot of missing information in this method.

How can you find out anything about the bees' spirit, their intimate lives, this way? How will they ever reveal themselves with this kind of treatment?

*

Jovette Marchessault writes that the reason we're all getting sick these days is because the air is polluted with the cries of the billions of deliberately tortured animals, whose immense suffering has gone into the construction of what we call knowledge (Marchessault 88).

What kind of knowledge is that?

*

Barbara Shipman, combining the disciplines of mathematics and biology, theorizes that the bees' famous waggle dance is a form of quantum behaviour.

After observing the complexity of the dance code in relation to the relatively simple brain structure of the bees, Shipman turned her attention to the mathematical dimensions of the dance. She noticed that the shape of the dance corresponds exactly to the curves of a *manifold*, or six-dimensional space.

Shipman claims that the bees are able to interact with quantum fields, and use not only nuclear magnetic resonance, but also quarks, or potential particles, as a script for their dance.

If this is so, then the honeybees are able to do something remarkable that no other living being we know of can do, that is, "touch" the quantum field without breaking it.

Shipman's groundbreaking discovery makes her, as Adam Frank observes, a modern-day Kepler, offering a single framework to explain what until now have existed as discrete disciplines and perceived phenomena. In Shipman's own words, she has discovered "a mathematics that takes all the different forms of the dance and embraces them in a single coherent geometric structure" (84).

In fact, her work outreaches Kepler's in its creative marriage of mathematics and biology, reversing the fatal mind/body, right brain/left brain split that marked the beginning of modern philosophy and science, on the one hand, and art and religion, on the other, putting them back into creative, dare I say erotic, conversation with one another.

*

Aganetha explained to me her plans for the poem. I will have it transcribed into Braille, she said, a language of dots the bees will surely know how to read, because they too make dots on surfaces every time they begin a new honeycomb, and touch them over and over in the darkness of the hive with their hands/feet. Who knows, we thought, what the bees will do with the poem after they've read it? Or what they will want to say or write back to us?

Or, as Aganetha put it, "What transformations and transmutations . . . will occur in this translation and transcription process," this "Working in the Dark" (1998, 1)?

*

Rupert Sheldrake began his career as a biologist in the conventional manner, torturing, then gassing and incinerating animals for the sake of experimentation. Eventually he rejected this method in favour of studying live animals in a more empathetic manner.

Sheldrake is currently trying to develop a theory of "morphic fields" to explain the highly intuitive and seemingly precognitive connection that he has observed between certain animals, for example, mothers and their young, but also cross-species, for example, between dogs and their owners. He has collected thousands of stories from around the world of dogs who saved their owners' lives by warning them in advance of impending dangers, such as fires, car accidents, and even earthquakes, and who know when their owners are coming home even when there is no physical evidence for it.

Sheldrake suggests that members of social groups, whether or not they belong to a single species, are "parts of the same system. They share food, breathe the same air, are interlinked through their minds and senses, and interact continually. When they are separated, the parts of the social system may retain a nonlocal or nonseparable connectedness comparable to that observed in quantum physics. "If this is the case," writes Sheldrake, "then morphic fields could be reinterpreted in terms of quantum theory. This would involve an enormous extension of quantum theory to cover biological and social organization" (307).

Sheldrake's inquiry has taken him to the margins of institutional science, but he likes it there. He believes that scientific inquiry should be widely democratic instead of hierarchically and institutionally controlled, and heavily biased toward technology and profit, as it is at present. He is interested in opening the conversation to people of any persuasion or discipline around the world, and invites anyone who's interested to participate in his experiments through his website: www.sheldrake.org.

*

I saw at once that for the bees, there could not be the same distinction between flowers and weeds we humans make:

Marigolds, delphiniums, pansies, daisies, petunias, amaranth, starflowers, borage, comfrey, oregano, chives, angel's trumpets, scarlet runner, alyssum, dill, sunflowers, goatsbeard, lamb's ears, yarrow, waterlilies, tigerlilies, motherwort, gallardia, mint, irises, anise, hyssop, echinacea, evening primrose, beans, snapdragons, pumpkin, kale, swiss chard, creeping thyme, forget-me-not, verbena, purslane, black-eyed Susan, showy milkweed, swamp milkweed, wild mustard, goldenrod, shepherd's purse, horsetail, pigweed. All these would appear together in the bees' eye, despite our careful culling of one from another.

Of course the bees would have their own preferences among them, would zero in on calendula and goldenrod more often than pigweed, culling for nectar.

I rather liked the calendula myself, after finding out that its blossoms were edible to humans. I spent long hours sitting in the sun, sipping delicious calendula blossoms, thinking about bees, letting traces of my colonialist farm upbringing, our immigrant settler project to break the wild prairie into agricultural submission with mechanical efficiency and violence, seep out of me into the serene summer air.

Sometimes, on our visits to the hive, Aganetha gave me chunks of dripping honeycomb. The fresh honey tasted, as the Druids would have said, divine. After a few mouthfuls, the poison ivy on my legs, a recurring malady I have taken many harmful drugs to control in the past, miraculously vanished.

*

Every poet, it seems, has some sort of imaginative connection with bees, and has written at least one poem about them.

Here is performance poet Penn Kemp's:

> List

> List
> List ten
> List ten too
> List ten to tooth
> List ten to thumb
> List ten to the hum

List ten to the humph
List ten to the hum off
List ten to the hum of the
List ten to the hum of the Bee
List ten to the hum of the Bee, love
List ten to the hum of the Bee, love Ed
List ten to the hum of the Beloved

win
wing
win gong
winging a
winging a cross
winging across a
winging across a crow
winging across a crow dead
winging across a crow dead rue
winging across a crowded room
winging across a crowded rumour

her
herd
heard oh
heard own
heard on lea
heard only by
heard only by spear
heard only by spear it
heard only by spirit tear
heard only by spirit ears

Listen to the hum of the Beloved winging across a crowded
rumour heard only
by spirit ears

(119)

Lakota poet and critic Paula Gunn Allen observes that poetry is the only professional Western discourse that has preserved, along with nonverbal artistic media such as painting and music and dance, the multi-layered, spiritually informed, feminine-centred sense of reality that once came naturally to all people, and is still practised in shamanic cultures around the world (lecture, University of Alberta, 1996).

American quantum physicist Fred Alan Wolf agrees. He has recently turned to shamanism as a more adequate conceptual system than that of conventional science, to explain, for example, the "observer effect," an important aspect of Heisenberg's uncertainty principle. "If you take quantum mechanics as it's presently understood, that's magic. You have a cloud of possibilities that suddenly manifest into one actuality" (cited in Leviton 53).

Add a dimension of spirit, Allen would say, and that's poetry. That's worship. That's art.

*

Leonard Cohen describes the madness of his grandfather, eerily, in a poem entitled "Prayer of My Wild Grandfather," as God singing in his ear—"like a lost bee after pollen/in the brain." It is no wonder, the poet laments, that

> fields and governments
> rotted, for soon you gave him all your range,
> drove all your love through that sting in his brain.

The poem is tender, raging, bittersweet, and draws on the long, ancient association of bees with madness, and poetry, and the divine. Cohen resists absolutely the fashionable atheism of our time, though he is on intimate terms with cynicism and despair—but also hope. The violence of the grandfather toward his own children led to his madness, the poem suggests, thereby demonstrating, by inversion, the inherent sanity and beauty and order of the cosmos. How precise, how empowering a diagnosis this is, the causes of madness understood to be intimately related to psychic habits and actions, "karma," the choices we make. (How different from the ethically blind approach to madness as an incomprehensible biochemical imbalance in the brain, heavily promoted by the psychiatric profession in collusion with the big multinational pharmaceutical industries nowadays, as if our emotional, mental, physical, spiritual lives and health were unrelated to the contexts that sustain them, culturally and environmentally.) The poem is addressed to "God, God, God," who insists on making honey, that is, insists on restoring balance and wholesomeness, sweetness, from the violence inflicted and suffered by psychically damaged humans:

> Nothing can flourish in your absence
> except our faith that you are proved through him
> who had his mind made mad and honey-combed.

("Prayer of my Wild Grandfather" 72)

*

A few summers ago "Lady in Waiting" was damaged in shipping. Aganetha gave the dress back to the bees for the summer.

The accident proved fortuitous. By the beginning of August the bees had not only repaired the dress, they had far surpassed their first attempt at bridal fashion design.

The dress was exquisitely transformed. The lace now billowed grandly, elegantly, where before it had curtsied.

*

Do bees have consciousness? Do they know what they're doing? Do they have feelings and intentions? Do they experience love, and grief, and happiness? Can bees make art?

Ecologist Jim Nollman, citing Donald Griffin's work on "animal thinking," asserts that it is "anthropomorphic absurdity" for entomologists to deny intentionality in insect behaviour.

When ants dance the fighting dance to incite each other to fight, it is absurd to say that it is merely coincidence that the fighting dance prepares the ants for fighting rather than food gathering.

"It seems," observes Nollman, "the same ingrained thinking that leads our nuclear industry to state that it is merely coincidental that the building of nuclear weapons also prepares human beings for nuclear war" (64).

In the case of bees, we know that the waggle dance communicates sun position, a system of measure, direction, and the desirability of the nectar source. The waggle dance can also communicate the location of water to cool an overheated hive, and even the location of materials to repair a damaged hive.

Isn't this, exclaims Nollman, what we humans call art, language, astronomy, mathematics, navigation, adjectives and adverbs, and even thermodynamic engineering and architecture (66)?

And when the yellow jackets in Nollman's yard came to carry away their dead who had been accidentally hit by his woodsaw, it is willfully blind—is it not—for us to assume, as the entomologists Nollman talked to insisted, that they were led by instinct alone, without any grief or compassion or love whatsoever for their fallen kin.

*

Anthropologist Jeremy Narby dramatically extends the notion of consciousness in nonhuman species to include the very heart of matter itself, as inscribed in the newly discovered DNA code. "To transmit information," Narby points out, "the genetic code uses elements (A, G, C, and T) that are meaningless individually, but that form units of significance when combined, the same way that letters make up words. The genetic code contains 64 three-letter 'words,' all of which have meaning, including two punctuation marks" (135).

Narby cites linguist Roman Jakobson's observation that "such coding systems were considered up until the discovery of the genetic code as 'exclusively human phenomena'—that is, phenomena that require the presence of an intelligence to exist" (135).

All living beings, Narby writes, contain this same alphabetic code, suggesting a commonality among species that is far greater than what Western thinking has assumed, but that is synchronous with shamanic theories of the nature of the universe in traditionalist cultures around the world. It is exciting to see the radically differing epistemologies and ontologies of traditional and contemporary cultures coming together, meeting each other. This is the challenge and beauty of the "post-postmodern," the present moment.

*

Reading prairie writer Tim Lilburn's philosophical essays on the knowability of the world, I can't help being struck by the deep sense of alienation running through them, his lament for the way we humans have lost our sense of community with animals and the land:

> Contemplative knowing of the deer and the hill must gather
> about the conviction that neither can be known. It is the
> resolute taking of a stance before the world, a positioning
> of oneself in desire-filled unknowing before the hill and deer,
> that refuses all consolation (18-19).

By contrast, indigenous prairie poet Louise Halfe, whose Cree name is Sky Dancer, moves easily in and out of realms of consciousness which span dream, ancestral voices, and animal spirits, amid a spirited retelling of family stories. Her poems protest eloquently the colonizing efforts of white settlers on her Aboriginal community, with its close ties to the land:

> Still in my walks, the mountains beneath my feet, I picked
> feathers as I climbed, the wolves gentle in their following.
> Soon the mountain too had feet. I swam down her clear water

and stood naked beneath her falls. Nearby, wind-burned fences enclosed crosses, their hinged grey arms dangled. I heard screams and gunshot in the early dawn. After the fierce weeping of thunder and mad dash of lightning, the robins danced with the drumming of the Little People. I woke as the brilliant ribbon of Northern Lights melted into a sunrise. (1)

And later,

She came in a Vision, flipped many faces. Stone-aged wrinkled, creased like a stretch drum, thin flesh, sharp nose. When the Sun sleeps she takes faded rays, dresses her gown. She's the burnt rose of autumn, a blue-winged warbler. The awakened river flanked in every woman, rolling pebbles over and over till stone eggs are left. I travel with her youth, this Night Mistress. Hair fresh, sweet grass braided in perfection. Long ago Grandmother danced in glades, women crushed chokecherries, saved the blood, cleaned porcupine quills, wove them into birch baskets, chewed sinew. They drummed, danced, lifted their dreams. Ribboned the Sky. Raw-boned, they left their blood. In these moccasin gardens I pick my medicines. (89)

＊

My poem for the bees, when it comes, catches me by surprise.

I am walking through the forest at Quetico Park, in Ontario, along an old explorers' trail, surrounded by the rushing sound of trees, rustling their branches above me, delighting in the smell of moss and jackpine, accompanied by the clear startling notes of jays and woodthrush.

The first line throws me off guard. No, I whisper, no, I didn't intend it to be like this. I meant to remain discreet, human, humble, invisible.

And then it takes hold of me, the knowledge of the bees rushing into me, their plenitude, their grace, their message of hope and beauty and terror. I try to stay with it as it wings through me, this glimpse, this fleeting vision, lifting me airborne through the trees.

Back at the camp, I take out pen and paper and try to write down this too brief illumination, follow its particular nuances and rhythms, go where the words take me, try to make a poem of it.

*

& then everything goes bee
sun exploding into green
the mad sky dive
thru shards of diamond light
earth veering left then right
then left sweet scented
the honing in
the buzz
the yes no dance
the quantum leap into
open swoon of calendula
yellow orange delphinium starflower
ultraviolet milkweed forget-me-not
caress of corolla carpel calyx
sharp tongue flick into nectar
delicious rub of belly against silk
shudder of pollenheavy thighs
the long slow sip of honeymead
sigh of sated petals in the wind
the drunken stagger hiveward
confused weave thru
chlorpyrifos malathion
ribboned corridors of poisoned
insectless late afternoon air

drumbee doombledore hummabee
the familiar brush swarm crawl
of bee on bee on bee on bee
sentries
warriors
scouts
promiscuous
architects
sculptors
whimsical
perfectionist
singers
nurses
studs
this honeyed home
Tech Midchuarta
this droning harem
this feminine monarchie
the mother deep in her dark cell
quivering licked & adored
O mother bride
O queen of earth & sky
O goddess
at the end of this dark century
of human destruction
& despair
as always of joyful delirious
magick flowered
honey love

Fig. 14 Aganetha Dyck, "The bees at work." Photo: Di Brandt, 1999.

So this is the world & here I am in it:
Orality and the Book

I grew up in a house without books, other than the Book, which was more of a talisman than book in the way we think of books nowadays, surrounded by paper, texts, as we are in this culture, centuries, aeons, away from the village of my childhood. My dad read to us from the Book every morning at breakfast, in German. He was a traditionalist Mennonite prairie peasant, with thick fingers and sunbrowned leathery skin. He loved farming. He leaped out of bed every morning, eager and energetic, to tend to his beloved farm, the cows in the barn waiting to be milked, the pigs snuffling to be fed, the crops in the fields waiting to be tended, the machinery in the sheds needing oiling and polishing, the granaries bursting with grain, or standing empty, waiting for the new summer crops. He was a brilliant farmer. He grew up in a large poor family and didn't inherit land, as most Mennonite children did. My mother was given twenty acres and a cow as a wedding gift, and he pieced the rest together, bit by bit, a dozen acres at a time, stroking, cajoling, seducing the neighbouring farmers into selling him a field here, a field there, when someone died, over the course of his lifetime. It was high risk, back breaking labour. He was in his element. He scoffed at "city people" who sat tamely at desks in little offices all day, with predictable little paycheques waiting for them at the end of the week. He felt sorry for people who got their exercise in gyms, futilely punching rubber bags or running treadmills, instead of wrestling fiercely, robustly, with the sensuous earth, animals, weeds, weather, daily, seasonally, as he did. He would come in from the fields rimed with dirt, his white teeth gleaming against the redbrown blackened leather of his face. Joyful, is how I remember him, then, sizzling with energy. He never read operating manuals. He figured out how everything worked with his hands. He built his own barns and sheds and granaries and even our new house himself, with help from relatives and neighbours. By the time I left home at age seventeen, my parents owned a flourishing thousand-acre debt-free farm, fully modernized, with gigantic brand new tractors and combines and harrows resting in the sheds, the barns filled with silver gleaming milking machines. His literacy level was approximately grade two. He followed the words across the page with his thick sunbrowned finger as he read, slowly, in a language he understood but didn't speak. We would sit, sullenly eyeing the porridge steaming in our bowls, waiting for the reading to be over. My mother was restless during the readings, fussing with the coffee pot, the toaster, the grapefruit, the sugar bowl. He was displeased. He wanted reverent attention. Reading was a sacred act to him.

Once every six months or so, my dad would reach the Book ceremonially across the table and say, Mary, why don't you read today. We were reading our way through the Book, from Creation to the Apocalypse, and then all over again, a chapter a day. None of the extravagant stories in the Book seemed very relevant to our rambunctious sweaty village lives, told in a language we heard in church but never spoke. Many of them didn't seem at all credible, though our salvation from eternal damnation apparently hinged on believing in their facticity. My mother would reach for the Book with a small flourish, and begin to read. My mom had completed grade nine before she was called home to work on the farm. She was the eldest daughter in a family of ten children, and my grandmother badly needed her to help with the cooking and cleaning and looking after the children. She was a formidably talented farmwoman, a whiz at elaborate Mennonite cooking, gardening, canning, baking, sewing, embroidering, crocheting, quilting, entertaining, looking after children. In this way my parents were an excellent match. She also had the gift of an extraordinary memory, and for this reason served as the keeper of stories in our large extended family; whenever someone wanted to remember something, they'd ask Mary. Her oral archive included a large repertoire of folk tales, nursery rhymes, sayings of all kinds, in Plautdietsch, our mother tongue, and also in German and English, which she liberally sprinkled into ordinary conversation, with wit and panache. I didn't realize then how special that was, to receive so much delightful literary education so casually, while kneading the dough or weeding the carrots or mending men's trousers. She loved reading poetry and novels, though it was hard to come by books, or the time to read them. Tante Jay, my mother's youngest sister, a schoolteacher who lived in "the city," in another world, an hour and a half away by car, had read all kinds of interesting books and seen Hollywood movies, which she recited to us in great detail in the kitchen over my mom's fresh baked apple pie. Sometimes she brought novels for my mom to read. My mom and I were fascinated by her stories and shared a secret yearning to travel and see the exotic world beyond our peasant villages, thus tantalizingly glimpsed. My sister wasn't there, she was usually outside playing with the boys or tagging along with the men. My dad definitely wasn't there—Tante Jay certainly wouldn't have told her lively stories of city life if he had been. I was a clumsy kid, prone to breaking dishes and cutting myself accidentally with kitchen knives. This made my mom impatient. On the other hand, I was good at school, bringing home high grades and prizes, which made my parents proud. For these reasons I was the only kid in the village allowed, and even encouraged, to read books even during the busy spring or summer or fall seasons. I consumed Tante Jay's novels with ravenous hunger and curiosity and lustful pleasure. I knew I wasn't staying in the village when I grew up, and this was a great way to begin to find out about the world outside our village community. My mother's readings from the Book at the breakfast table were dramatic and elegant, and quick. Suddenly we were in Egypt, or Palestine, or Babylon, among shepherds and sheep and treacherous kings and magic mountains and devious beautiful women. My mother would hand the Book back to my dad across the table with a small smile. This exchange, we knew, wouldn't happen again for awhile.

When I was fifteen, my Uncle Henry, who was also a schoolteacher and had attended university, gave me a book of stories by Anton Chekhov, with an introduction in which the editor cited the Russian writer as saying, "I had to wrestle with the serf in every cell of my body in order to become a writer." This statement was like a bucket of clear ice water poured over my head. It startled me into awareness, identification, dreaming. I wasn't the only person with an illiterate lowly heritage foolish enough to want to become, of all arrogant, unachievable things, a writer. Who did I think I was. But still. It hadn't stopped him, why should it stop me. There were many years between that event and the volatile moment of my stepping off the cliff of my life into print. But that was the moment perhaps when it began, my underground writerly aspiration, though, if I think about it, it was there from the beginning, from my earliest memories, the fascination with language, words, images, cadence, rhythm, intonation, as was also the determination to get away, to leave the narrow enclave of my ancestral culture with its strict separatist rules against the mainstream. I'm thinking now that both of these things were hatched to a great extent by the style, intelligence and simmering restlessness of my mother, for whom village life was not large enough, not stimulating enough, though it's taken me most of my life to recognize her as an ally, so divided was she in her loyalties, encouraging her daughters to break away, on one side, and chastising, even actively betraying us for it, on the other.

I loved school. I loved the spectacular imaginative explosion that happened in my head entering grade one. I loved having my own desk, my own space, in our little village school. I adored my beautiful teacher, Rita Klassen, who wore pretty dresses and read poetry to us and drew marvellous pictures for us on the chalkboard with coloured chalk, to illustrate her stories. I didn't mind sitting still for hours on end, as many of the village children did. Indeed, I was happy for it, to get away from the rough and tumble of farm life. I bruised easily, I was always getting hurt in one way or another, at home. Mennonite childrearing practices at that time included violent beatings in early childhood to instill passive obedience in us, and I had received large doses of extreme violence in my early years which have haunted me ever since. I was mentally and imaginatively robust, though, endlessly curious about everything bookish. School opened me to the world. There were books, not many, but some, a tiny library in the corner of the room, to read. Six months after entering the classroom, I could read and write and speak both English and German, and soon read my way through the entire library. Some of our relatives moved to Mexico and Paraguay in the 1920s, to establish pioneer farms all over again in inhospitable landscapes in the Mexican desert and the Chaco, "the Green Hell," in protest against the enforcement of English curricula in Manitoba schools. They were worried about the effects of an English school education on their children, the loss of tradition and culture that would result. They were quite right. I'm sad now to see the enormous losses that did occur in my generation, which I enthusiastically helped to enact, but then, I just couldn't wait to get away, to throw it all away. I embraced the otherness of English culture eagerly and joyously, though it didn't always make sense. I remember in grade four we were taught how to introduce people to each other in an English school text: Mr. Smith, this is Mrs. Jones. Mrs. Jones, this is Mr. Smith. Mrs. Smith, this is Mr. Jones, Mr. Jones, this is Mrs. Smith. Such conversations seemed astonishingly nonsensical to us, who knew everyone in our village and the neighbouring villages intimately, where introductions were made in advance, elaborately, contextually, obliquely, so that by the time you met someone face to face, you already knew their name, their immediate and extended family and their specific place in it, where they lived, their purpose in being here, their relation to you, their current business. Our lives were nested, protected, ritualized, in a way the lives of *de Englische* apparently were not. I have sometimes reflected on the way our humble peasant lives offered many of the privileges only the rich or famous, or somehow ethnically identified, can afford in modern urban life, a wide community, a rich storehouse of ritual and musical performance, a thousand people at your funeral. On the other hand, *de Englische* wrote books, gorgeous amazing books, and I was hooked on literature, stories, essays, poetry. Books offered the possibility of a whole other world, a richly inspiring, poetically inflected one, a grand getaway. Only children poised between cultures, with access to art and literature, can imagine the future filled with so much freedom and promise and hope.

I'm remembering the precise moment I became aware of myself as an individual conscious being. I was sitting at my desk in grade five, writing answers to History questions in my notebook, enjoying the sun coming in through the window, and suddenly I thought, I am sitting here, in this desk, writing in this notebook, and all these other people are sitting in their desks, and they are not me, they have their own inner lives and plans, they are thinking about completely different things than I am. The philosopher Rudolf Steiner believed that the moment of coming into individual consciousness was a more significant growing up moment than puberty; perhaps he was right. I remember it as a breathtaking moment, filled with awe and loneliness, and a deeply felt, if dimly understood, sense of responsibility. People don't talk about "vocation" much anymore, but if there is a "calling" involved in one's life choices, that is when it came to me, writing in my notebook, knowing that what I was thinking was somehow relevant, important beyond myself. Grade five was special in many ways. Our Second Room teacher, Valentine Thiessen, loved literature and taught it eloquently to the grade sevens and eights on the other side of the classroom, while I eavesdropped, guiltily but mesmerized. *Julius Caesar*, *Jean Val Jean* (in Solomon Cleaver's retelling of Victor Hugo's *Les Miserables*), and *A Midsummer Night's Dream* filled my mind with grand recognitions of treachery, and heroism, and desire. In order to preserve Mennonite customs, we received supplementary courses in the village schools, German, catechism, Mennonite history, and of course choral singing. The German course in grade five consisted entirely of memorizing German poetry, reciting it out loud, and writing it out for the final exam. Many children and parents complained about the course, finding the poems hard to memorize and perhaps hard to stomach, and the course was changed to something more colloquial and superficial a few years later. But for me it was a feast of imaginative pleasure. And terror. No one thought to explain any of the poems to us, it was straight mainlining into the blood. Goethe, Schiller, Hölderlin, Heine, the rich vein of German Sturm und Drang, and full-bodied expressionism, palpable in the poems, fed my Germanic spirit in a way that English writing, with its streak of Puritanism (with the brilliant exception of Chaucer and Shakespeare) could not.

And then everything broke open. One of our teachers decided I should skip a grade, so I finished the curriculum in our little village school, grade eight, a year earlier than my twin sister. Few village kids went on to high school after grade eight. Those that did were either sent off to boarding school somewhere, or enrolled in correspondence courses, with occasional tutoring from the school principal in a little room in the back of the school. The year I hit grade nine, high school instruction in the village schools became consolidated, and widely encouraged. I found myself on an hour-and-a-half-long bus ride every morning and evening to attend Garden Valley Collegiate in Winkler, only twelve miles away, but with many villages to stop in, without my friends, and most importantly, without my twin, from whom I had never ever been apart, for even an hour. I was mesmerized by the new world of town life, so radically different from life in our villages, and considerably more cosmopolitan. My sister felt left behind and did not want to hear about my exciting experiences in grade nine. The town kids and teachers discriminated against the village kids with our unsophisticated *Darp* ways, both subtly and blatantly. My parents were alarmed by my blossoming sense of independence and disapproved of everything I said and did. I felt deeply bereft, in shock, as if my arms and legs had been cut off. Perhaps it was my sense of exile, coinciding so exactly with the moment of adolescence, that propelled me into an intellectual life and took me, unwaveringly, as far away as possible from the world of my childhood, my people, my homeland, though I have spent much of it mourning for the deep loss of them. I spent two years at Garden Valley Collegiate, then transferred to Mennonite Collegiate Institute in Gretna, Manitoba. This was a boarding school with a rich music and sports curriculum, and strict rules. We were locked in our little rooms for four hours every evening for study period. We were not allowed to cross the campus to talk with boys. We wore uniforms with strict hemline requirements. Miniskirts were just coming into fashion then, and blue jeans and sandals for everday wear. Our mothers had carefully measured our hemlines, while we kneeled upright, to reach just below our knees, touching the floor. When we got to the school, we shortened these carefully sewn hems several inches with safety pins, or Scotch tape or staples. They would often come undone walking from math period to music, a minor embarrassment that was mostly a joke. We experimented with makeup, which we wore all week and washed off before visiting our families at home on the weekend. It was a strictly controlled environment, but I loved every minute of it. My sister was there then too, and we shared a room in the student residence, but we were no longer twins. Our deep childhood connection had been severed; we knew we were headed in different directions.

My parents somehow didn't see it coming, they didn't see that having encouraged me to excel at school, and discouraged me from being involved with the farm, would mean I'd want to leave the village community and life after high school and not come back. Everyone "leaves home" nowadays, so my parents' irrevocable grief over my departure is perhaps incomprehensible now. I arrived in urban Canada in the heydey of the '60s counter culture, and leaped enthusiastically from the Middle Ages into the psychedelic world of peace marches and sit-ins and folk festivals and experimental European films and hippie communes and free love, all of which suited my lurking anarchist rebel genes just fine. I am after all a descendant of Anabaptists, who were reviled and hunted all over Europe in the sixteenth century for their sectarian exuberantly utopian views.

I don't think my dad ever really got over it. He had failed, he thought, to preserve the traditionalism he so cherished, though he had done his utmost to distill the old ways in his children. My mother was of two minds about it, as was typical of her. Her internal dividedness contained a certain treachery to us, most of all to me, who alarmed her so with my independence of spirit. I see it now as one of her greatest gifts to us, her children: she was a dreamer, a revolutionary, without allies or strategies to enact what she wished to become, and fed our spirits, our creativity, our imaginations with the underground river of her unhappiness. I was not the only one to leave the village; my twin sister, and eventually my other siblings, and most of the village children of our generation left, too. But I was the first one to reject Plautdietsch in favour of English, the first to attend university, other than to get an Education or Nursing degree in order to come back to serve the community, the first to leave Manitoba to pursue a graduate degree, in Toronto, the first to stop attending church, the first to go secular, assimilationist, mainstream. The whole edifice of our Mennonite separatism, preserved so carefully at so high a cost through four centuries of exile and migration and hard labour, in harsh, inhospitable landscapes, was coming, as my father rightly perceived it, crashing down. My father held these things darkly against me, though he tolerated them in the others later on. There are certain privileges attached to the difficult role of scapegoat, as I have come to know in detail: you get blamed for everything, but in exchange you're granted a certain precarious outlaw freedom that is much admired and envied, as well as feared and hated and punished.

My father died when I was twenty-seven. I wasn't finished fighting with him yet. We had argued loudly and bitterly about everything since I was about twelve or so. My father was a peasant intellectual, a farmer philosopher, but I was quicker, more articulate than he was, I could talk circles around him. This delighted and astonished and infuriated him. And then he was gone. Virginia Woolf said she was thankful her father died young, otherwise she couldn't have become a writer, he simply took up too much space in her life. I believe that was true for me too, though I say this out of great love for him, and great grief, who was such an inspiration to me, and such a foe. Perhaps he needn't have worried as he did. Even though I ran away from my Mennonite upbringing, as far and fast as I could, I never really left it, it never really left me. Eventually I was shunned by the rest of the family, and by most of the Mennonite community, as I had long feared I would be, for my iconoclastic writing, for breaking the centuries long taboo against print culture, for breaking open their separatism, their stowed secrets, betraying them, as they saw it, to the world. That is another great grief, ongoing. Like James Joyce, who lived his entire adult life in exile from his loved and hated mother country, and wrote about nothing else, like Leonard Cohen, who threw away his noble rabbinic lineage for bohemian excess only to recapture its grandeur in his poetry and contemplative practice, I put myself, precipitously, in their company to claim that I've been faithful, are you listening, daddy, grandma, somewhere up among the stars, I've been true, trying as hard as I can to understand what that idealistic, crazy, stubborn, ecstatic, beautiful, terrible heritage was about, and what it means to me, and to everything, now. *So this is the world, and here I am in it, one of the many lost & found, if you can believe it across all this space, and I think I can say this from so far away, that I love you, I love you.*

Acknowledgements

Thank you to Eunice Scarfe for a long beautiful friendship and for asking the questions that inspired the essays in this book. Thank you to Smaro Kamboureli, editor for the press, par excellence. Thank you to Heidi Harms for inspiration loyalties far beyond what can be said here. Thank you to the many people whose hospitality, collegiality and conversation on several continents sustained me while writing these essays, including Lillian Allen, Marie Anneharte Baker, Pamela Banting, Andrea Bennett, Kathy Bergen, bill bissett, Laurie Block, Lisa and Ali Brandt, melanie brannagan, Mike Cardinal, Klaus Dieter-Ertler, Marta Dvorak, Aganetha Dyck, Jenny Erpenbeck, Paul Friesen, Suzanne Gott, Jeff Gundy, Kristjana Gunnars, Louise Halfe, Ann Hostetler, Lynette Hunter, Alexis Hurtado, Walter Isaac, Maria Jacobs, Mary Janzen, Owain Jones, Sherry Jones, Smaro Kamboureli, Ryan Knighton, Ursula Krechel, Fay Lawn, Dale Lakevold, Myra Laramee, Tang Lee, Johanna Leseho, Maria and Martin Loeschnigg, Roydon Loewen, Daphne Marlatt, Louise May, Lorraine (Brundige) Mayer, Lillian McPherson (in memoriam), Yuichi Midzunoe, Philippe Moser, Emily Munroe, Shirley Neuman, Sandra Paivio, Anna Pellatt (in memoriam), NourbeSe Philip, Martín Prechtel, Darrell Racine, Magdalene Redekop, Douglas Reimer, Constance Rooke, Susan Rudy, Gloria Sawai, Eunice Scarfe, Jacob Scheier, Sherry Simon, Heather Spears, Birk Sproxton, Andris Taskans, Michael Tescher, Janine Tschuncky, Hildi and Paul Tiessen, James Urry, Matthew van der Giessen, Carol Ann Weaver, Françoise Wemensfelder, Rudy Wiebe, Janice Williamson, b.h. Yael, Waldemar Zacharasiewicz and my students at the Universities of Alberta, Windsor and Brandon, who taught me more than they know.

Thank you to the following institutions for generous support through grants, residencies, conferences and bibliographic assistance: ASLE (University of Eugene, Oregon), Arnes House (Manitoba Writers' Guild), Brandon University, The Canada Council for the Arts, The Canada Research Chair Council, Château de Lavigny (Switzerland), Chiba University (Japan), Foreign

Affairs (Canada), Conrad Grebel College (University of Waterloo), Gibraltar Point Centre for the Arts, Karl-Franzens Universität (Graz, Austria), the Manitoba Writers' Guild, Menno Simons College (University of Winnipeg), the Social Sciences and Humanities Research Council of Canada, St. Norbert Arts Centre, University of Alberta, Brandon University, University of Leeds (UK), University of Manitoba and University of Windsor. Thank you to Katherine Melnyk and Alice Moulding at NeWest Press for the detailed conscientious labour of transforming my manuscript into a book.

Thank you to the following journals, programs, galleries and anthologies for commissioning and/or featuring previous versions of essays, stories and poems appearing in this book: *Alberta Anthology* (CBC Radio, 1997); *Border/ Lines: Multiculturalism Issue* 40 (1997), ed. NourBese, ill. Lydia Chiussi (1997); *Canada 2000: Identity and Transformation/Identite et transformation Central European Perspectives on Canada/Le Canada vu a partir de l'Europe centrale* (Frankfurt am Main: Peter Lang, 2001), ed. Klaus-Dieter Ertler and Martin Loeschnigg; *Canada in the Sign of Migration and (Trans)culturalism/ le Canada sous le signe de la migration et du transculturalisme: From Multi- to Trans-Culturalism* (Frankfurt am Main: Peter Lang, 2004), ed. Klaus- Dieter Ertler and Martin Loeschnigg.; *Capilano Review* 32/2 (2000), ed. Ryan Knighton (2000); De Leon White Gallery, as part of Aganetha Dyck's honeybee installation, *Working in the Dark*, cur. Clara Hargittay (1999); *Fresh Tracks: Writing the Western Landscape*, ed. Pamela Banting (Polestar, 1998); *Journal of Mennonite Studies* 20 (2000), ed. Royden Loewen (2000): *Prairie Fire: Winnipeg in Fiction* 20/2 (1999), ed. Birk Sproxton (20.2, 2000); *Prairie Fire: David Arnason* 22/1 (2001), ed. Douglas Reimer (22.1, 2001); *Transient Questions: New Essays on Mavis Gallant*, ed. Kristjana Gunnars (Amsterdam, New York: Rodopi, 2004); *West Coast Line: Women and Texts and Communities* 29/33/2 (1999), ed. Susan Rudy (1999); *Writing Life: Celebrated Canadian and International Authors on Writing and Life*, ed. Constance Rooke (McClelland & Stewart, 2006); and *The Winnipeg Connection: Writing Lives at Mid-Century*, ed. Birk Sproxton (Winnipeg: Prairie Fire Press, 2006).

Thank you to the following people and institutions for letting me copy the following images: Bibliothèque Nationale, Paris, for "Peasants Dancing" by Albrecht Dürer, 1514, and "De anabaptistengemeente" by Solis and Aldegraver, 1536; Lydia Chiussi, for "Euphonia," 1996; Aganetha Dyck, for

"Lady in Waiting," photo Sheila Spence, 1995, and "Hive Blanket: Ancient Text," photo William Eakin, 1992; Louise Jonasson, for "Viking statue at Gimli," 1999; Mennonite Publishing Network, for "Twelve Christians Burned at the Stake," by Jan van Kuykens, 1660; Naturhistorisches Museum, Vienna, Austria, for "Venus von Willendorf, c. 25,000 years old," ; James Reaney, for "When the clouds cross the sky," 1976; Eunice Scarfe and Paul Tétrault (Tétro Design), for "Di with the bears of Berlin," 2003; Heather Spears, for "Newborn twins," 1986; David Teplica, for "Ovum," 1998, and "Reunion (The MacCumber Twins)," 1999.

Thank you to Maddie, my beloved black Labrador (in memoriam), the land, fields, gardens, rivers, and trees of Winnipeg, Brandon, Edmonton, Windsor, Berlin and Lavigny (Switzerland), the bees and flowers of St. Norbert, and the water and shores of Lake Winnipeg, Lake Ontario, Lake Erie and Lake Geneva, for inspiration and sustenance while writing these essays.

Notes

This land that I love, this wide, wide prairie

1. I am grateful to Heidi Harms for this citation.

That crazy wacky Hoda in Winnipeg: A brief anatomy of an honest attempt at a pithy statement about Adele Wiseman's *Crackpot*

1. The mother who gives up the name of the mother in order to be a mother figures frequently in Victorian literature as a woman who abandons her "illegitimate" child to a wealthy benefactor, then hires herself out as a servant to him, accepting social indignity in order to be near and care for her child. Robert Altman's recent film, *Gosford Park* (2001), set in 1932 prewar England, includes a variation on this theme in the figure of Mrs. Wilson, housekeeper to Sir William McCordler, jealously watching over the servant Robert Parks, revealed near the end of the film to be her son.

"Why do you lie there just shaking with laughter?" Revisiting Dorothy Livesay's *The Husband*

1. The University of Manitoba Libraries published a catalogue of the Livesay Archive, *The Papers of Dorothy Livesay*, in 1986. The catalogue includes numerous short descriptive essays by Pamela Banting and Kristjana Gunnars, who organized the Archive in the mid '80s and signed their names to their frequently interpretive comments.

2. Box 95, Folder 1 contains a typewritten manuscript subtitled "First Draft only," with minor handwritten corrections (referred to as First Draft A in this essay). Folder 2 contains two versions of the manuscript. The first is subtitled "first draft only"; this seems to be the original typed version, with numerous passages stroked out and typed over, as well as extensive handwritten corrections (referred to as First Draft B). The second copy is untitled and disordered. Folder 3 holds two copies of the manuscript. The

first appears to be a carbon copy of the manuscript in Folder 1, minus handwritten corrections. The second appears to be a second carbon copy of the same manuscript. Both are subtitled "First Draft."

The happiest reader in the world

1. Many of Arnason's short stories have been published several times, slightly altered, in different collections. The versions of "Mary Yvette," "My Baby and Me," and "Sons and Fathers, Father and Sons" I am citing here appeared in *The Circus Performers' Bar* (1984, 57-61, 31-36, 37-48).

2. See Ann Ferguson, *Sexual Democracy: Women, Oppression, and Revolution* (1991); Dorothy Dinnerstein, *The Mermaid and the Minotaur: Sexual Arrangements and Human Malaise* (1976); and Nancy Chodorow, "The Enemy Outside: Thoughts on the Psychodynamics of Extreme Violence with Special Attention to Men and Masculinity," in *Masculinity Studies and Feminist Theory: New Directions*, ed. Judith Kegan Gardiner (2002, 235-60).

3. The new reproductive technologies pose an alarming new threat to the old problem of protecting maternal agency in the polis. According to science writer Pierre Baldi, removing the locus of conception and gestation from women and their wombs, and giving it to (mostly male) scientists with petri dishes, is one of the aims of technoscience (*The Shattered Self: The End of Natural Evolution*, 2002). For a critique of Baldi's vision, see my essay, "'Twins are not the same baby twice': Twin intimacies and clone fantasies," in this volume (151).

4. See Paula Gunn Allen, *The Sacred Hoop: Recovering the Feminine in American Indian Traditions* (1992); Mary O'Brien, *The Politics of Reproduction* (1986); Luce Irigaray, *Sexes and Genealogies*, trans. Gillian C. Gill (1993), and *je, tu, nous: Toward a Culture of Difference*, trans. Alison Martin (1993).

Je jelieda, je vechieda: Canadian Mennonite (Alter)Identifications

1. R. Po-Chia Hsia's *The German People and the Reformation*, and *Calvinism and Religious Toleration in the Dutch Golden Age*, for an overview of recent scholarship of the period.

2. The full title is *The Bloody Theater or Martyrs Mirror of the Defenseless Christians Who Baptized Only Upon Confession of Faith, and Who Suffered and Died for the Testimony of Jesus, Their Saviour, From the Time of Christ to the Year A.D. 1660, Compiled from Various Authentic Chronicles, Memorials, and Testimonies.*, compiled by T.J. van Braght. The complete edition I am reading, published in 1964 in Scottdale, Pennsylvania, runs to 1157 pages and contains numerous engravings illustrating martyr scenes.

3. Cree writer Tomson Highway has written eloquently about the social dynamics inherent in traditionalist oral languages, particularly in his native Cree, highlighting their ribald, sensuous, spiritual aspects, not unlike the characteristics of Plautdietsch I am describing here ("Why Cree is the Funniest of All Languages," *Me Funny*, ed. Drew Hayden Taylor, 159–168).

4. German Mennonite historian Hans-Jürgen Goertz made a more muted, but related, argument in his 1988 essay, "The Confessional Heritage in its New Mold: What is Mennonite Self-Understanding Today?" (*Mennonite Identity: Historical and Contemporary Perspectives*, ed. Calvin Redekop and Samuel J. Steiner, 1-12). Goertz argues, somewhat coyly, not naming names or events, that Swiss Anabaptism originated "in, with and under" the "revolution of the common man," and occurred in solidarity with "'the common man' in his fight for political, social and religious liberation," (8-9). Goertz is less circumspect about what he sees as the pervasive identity crisis of contemporary Mennonites. The community, he argues, has given up the "religious ethic of fraternity," which the Anabaptists gave their lives in such large numbers to defend against the rise of the modern, rationalist capitalist economy in the 16th century. At present, declares Goertz, the Mennonites "maintain only a toothless, anachronistic nonconformity. The Mennonites have made their accommodation with bourgeois, capitalist society. More than that, they have availed themselves of the opportunity to participate and profit from this system, without noticing the extent to which they have thereby come into contradiction to their confessional heritage" (11). As I argue in my essay here and elsewhere in this volume, the assimilation crisis has been profoundly noticed and extensively suffered, and struggled with, at least by Mennonites of Dutch origin, whose communitarian pioneer settler experience in Canada (and also in Central and South America) is recent and still strongly characterized by traditionalist utopian aspirations.

5. Having just watched Wolfgang Becker's evocative 2003 film dramatizing East Berliner utopianism, *Goodbye, Lenin*, for the second time, I am struck by the similarities between the communist vision of the GDR, as depicted by Becker, with its double edges of inspiring utopianism and naïve optimism gone wrong, and the Münsterite uprising of 1534–35, which happened after all not far from Berlin. Like the Anabaptists, the Berliners got caught between large violent political forces that were for the most part not of their own making. Surely the Ossies are contemporary heirs of Anabaptism, as are Canadian Mennonites, which would make us cousins of sorts. I like to think so.

6. I am grateful to Kathy Bergen for this observation.

7. Métis writer Maria Campbell has composed a poignant vignette, "Kookum Mariah and The Mennonite Mrs.," which describes her childhood memory of her grandmother and her Mennonite neighbour and friend, gathering herbs, grinding up roots, "making medicine," in rural Saskatchewan. The story ends, "In my family the homeland stories are not about a place called Park Valley, rather they are about Nugeewin. . . . Not about Lamire's wheat field, but about Notekew Nipissah, Willow Place of Two Old Women. And among those stories is the story of Kookum Mariah's friend the Mrs., an old Mennonite woman who understood what it was like to be erased and made invisible" (12). Not all Mennonite-Aboriginal relations were as friendly as the grandmotherly one described by Campbell. The *Journal of Mennonite Studies*, Volume 19, 2001, where the story appeared, features several essays by Mennonite scholars wrestling with the thorny issues of the adoption of Native children by Mennonite families, and cultural and land appropriation by Mennonite colonies in a colonialist context.

8. These ideas were first expressed to me in separate conversations by Ann Hostetler, Mennonite poet and Dorothy Friesen, Mennonite novelist and peace activist. It was Eunice Scarfe, award-winning fiction writer, who first pointed out to me the tribal character of Mennonite communities, compared with other Christian groups such as that of the Norwegian Lutherans of the American Midwest, her own heritage, and in pushing me to find an answer to why this was so, inspired the long meditation of which this study is a part. See also Jeanne Achterberg's analysis of the Burning Times as a suppression of traditional European shamanic healing practices in her book, *Imagery in Healing* (1985).

9. Internal contradictions in the community along these lines were highlighted at an international conference on Mennonites and the City, hosted by Roydon Loewen at Menno Simons College, University of Winnipeg, in 2001, where indeed two origins were proposed for Anabaptism, one urban and intellectual, the other rural and peasant. Everyone at the conference seemed to feel strongly allied with one or the other, given their particular family experiences, even if they'd been living in similar village communities for several centuries. Papers from this conference were published in the *Journal of Mennonite Studies*, Vol. 20 (2002), including my keynote address, "The poet and the wild city" (89–104). A revised version of the essay appears in this volume (73-87).

10. Jonathan Bate points out the uncomfortable fact that Hitler was the most "green"-minded political leader of the twentieth century, even if his return to rootedness in German soil turned out to be erroneously connected with fascist dreams of power and racial purity, rather than the celebration of multicultural diversity and wild-minded indigenosities. Bate explains Heidegger's initial attraction to Nazism (before its megalomaniac aspirations became clear) as an answer to "the dehumanization wrought by American technology on the one hand and Soviet mass industrialization on the other" (2000, 268–269).

11. American ecotheorist and activist Joel Kovel likes us too—he cites the Hutterian movement, a branch of Anabaptism that retained the socialist practice of "community of goods" and cultural separatism from the surrounding world more literally than the Mennonites did, as exemplary of the kind of "ecosocialist" organization at the local and international level needed to combat the environmental ravages of multinational capitalism around the world (Kovel 2002). The Hutterites were a model for the organization of the kibbutz in Israel as well.

Souwestoegg on Winnipuzz: James Reaney's Winnipeg

1. Dorothy Livesay famously remarked that living in New Jersey in the 1930s, with its more flamboyant cultural fabric, loosened her from the tame domesticity of Canada and enlarged her poetic vision. Seven decades later this trope seems to have been flipped on its head; writers as disparate as Canadian

novelist Thomas King, in *Green Grass, Running Water*, and American film director Michael Moore, in *Bowling for Columbine*, have recently portrayed Canada—even hyperindustrialized southwestern Ontario, in the case of Moore—as wilder, freer, and more imaginatively minded than relentlessly corporatized, propagandized America.

2. I myself had written the libretto for three-hour opera the previous year, *The Bridge*, with composer Esther Wiebe, a commission from the Mennonite Historical Society to commemorate the 100th anniversary of the Mennonites' arrival in Manitoba in 1872 from Ukraine. It had been produced that summer, 1972, with orchestra, in gymnasiums and church auditoriums across Manitoba, including the Winnipeg Centennial Concert Hall. There was southern Manitoba prairie in it, and references to local Mennonite village life, including folk dancing: details completely absent from any published literature I had encountered until then. It was an insider job, understood by all involved to be for Mennonite audiences only. Multiculturalism hadn't happened yet. There was a radical disjunct in my mind between that event and the study of English literature. I am astonished now to think of it.

3. Tricia Wasney points out in a photo essay on Winnipeg in the '50s, close to the time Reaney would have been conceiving his "Message to Winnipeg," how many catastrophic public fires Winnipeg endured in that decade (15-41). The launch of the anthology, *The Winnipeg Connection: Writing Lives at Mid-Century*, in which her essay appears alongside a version of this essay on Reaney, occurred the night after a catastrophic windstorm blew out downtown hotel windows in Winnipeg in October 2006. Wasney and members of the audience joked about the apocalyptic Reaneyesque weather of our fierce landscape, which also regularly featured large scale prairie fires in pre-industrialized times. It is intriguing to read Reaney's apocalyptic vision as a visitor's alarm at the rigorous conditions of prairie life, which appears in much of our home-grown literature as a big, if formidable, cosmic joke (I am thinking, for example, the bug-infested city in Carol Shields' *The Republic of Love*, and the hot sticky rainy mosquito-overrun streets in Miriam Toews' *Summer of My Amazing Luck*.)

4. I am grateful to b.h. Yael for introducing me to Keller's work, and for pointing out the link between apocalyptic thinking and environmental despair.

"Twins are not the same baby twice":
Twin intimacies and clone fantasies

1. See Lawrence Wright, "Double mystery," *The New Yorker* (7 Aug 1995): 45-62; Nancy L. Segal, "MZ or DZ? Not even their hairdresser knows for sure," *Journal of the Forensic Sciences* 31 (Jan 1986): 10-11; Martin, N.G., et al, "The power of the classical twin study," *Heredity* 40 (1978): 97-116; Charles Boklage, "The embryology of human twinning," *Acta Genet Med Gemellol* (Italy) 28 (1989): 118.

References Cited

Abram, David. *The Spell of the Sensuous: Perception and Language in a More-Than-Human World*. New York: Pantheon Books, 1996.

Achterberg, Jeanne. *Imagery in Healing: Shamanism and Modern Medicine*. Boston: New Science Library, Shambhala, 1985.

Aeschylus. *The Oresteia*, trans. Robert Fagles. Middlesex: Penguin Books, 1977.

Alexander, Terry Pink. *Make Room for Twins*. Toronto: Bantam Books, 1987.

Allen, Paula Gunn. *The Sacred Hoop: Recovering the Feminine in American Indian Traditions*. Boston: Beacon Press, 1992.

———. *Grandmothers of the Light: A Medicine Woman's Sourcebook*. Boston: Beacon Press, 1991.

Allen, Woody, dir. *Crimes and Misdemeanors*. Orion Pictures, 1989. Feature film.

Altman, Robert, dir. *Gosford Park*. Alliance Atlantis, 2001. Feature film.

Angier, Natalie. *Woman: An Intimate Geography*. New York: Anchor Books, 2000.

Amesbury, Barbara, cur. *Survivors In Search of a Voice: The Art of Courage*. Toronto: Woodlawn Arts Foundation, 1995.

Archibald, Elizabeth. "'Worse than Bogery': Incest Stories in Middle English Literature." *Incest and the Literary Imagination*, ed. Elizabeth Barnes. Gainesville, Tallahassee, Tampa, et al: University of Florida Press, 2002. 1-16.

Arnason, David. *Fifty Stories and a Piece of Advice*. Winnipeg: Turnstone Press, 1982.

———. *The Circus Performers' Bar*. Vancouver: Talonbooks, 1984.

———. *The Happiest Man in the World*. Vancouver: Talonbooks, 1989.

Atwood, Margaret. *Cat's Eye*. Toronto: McClelland & Stewart, 1988.

———. "Kat." *Wilderness Tips*. Toronto: McClelland & Stewart, 1991. 41-56.

———. *Oryx and Crake*. Toronto: McClelland & Stewart, 2003.

———. "Reaney Collected." *Canadian Literature* 57 (1973): 113-177.

Baldi, Pierre. *The Shattered Self: The End of Natural Evolution*. Cambridge, Mass. and London, England: MIT Press, 2002.

Banting, Pamela. "Personal and Professional Profile." *The Papers of Dorothy Livesay: A Research Tool*. University of Manitoba Libraries: Department of Archives and Special Collections, 1986. 5-23.ss

Barnes, Elizabeth. "Introduction." *Incest and the Literary Imagination,* ed. Barnes. Gainesville, Tallahassee, Tampa, et al: University of Florida Press, 2002. 1-16.

Bate, Jonathan. *Romantic Ecology: Wordsworth and the Environmental Tradition*. London and New York: Routledge, 1991.

————. *The Song of the Earth*. London: Picador, 2000.

Baudrillard, Jean. "Clone Story." *Simulacra and Simulation*, trans. Sheila Faria Glaser. Ann Arbor, Michigan: University of Michigan Press, 1994. 95-103.

Becker, Wolfgang, dir. *Goodbye, Lenin*. Germany, 2003. Feature film.

Belkin, Roslyn. "The Consciousness of a Jewish Artist: An Interview with Adele Wiseman." *Journal of Canadian Fiction* 31-32 (1981): 148-176.

Berger, John. "The Hour of Poetry." *John Berger: Selected Essays*, ed. Geoff Dyer, New York: Pantheon Books, 2001. 445-452.

Besner, Neil K. *The Light of Imagination: Mavis Gallant's Fiction*. Vancouver: University of British Columbia Press, 1988.

Bianchi, Ugi. "Twins." *Encyclopedia of Religion*, Vol. 15, ed. Mircea Eliade. New York: Macmillan, 1987. 98-107

Bloch, Ernst. *The Spirit of Utopia*. California: Stanford University Press, 2000.

Boklage, Charles. "The embryology of human twinning." *Acta Genet Med Gemellol (Roma)* 28 (1989): 118.

Boose, Lynda E. "The Father's House and the Daughter in It: The Structures of Western Culture's Daughter-Father Relationship." *Daughters and Fathers*, ed. Lynda E. Boose and Betty S. Flowers. Baltimore and London: The Johns Hopkins University Press, 1989. 19-74.

Borsa, Joan. "The Absent Bride: Intimate Acts & Interior Movements." *Aganetha Dyck*. Winnipeg Art Gallery and St. Norbert Arts and Cultural Centre Exhibition Catalogue, 1995. 50-58.

Boruch, Marianne. "Plath's Bees." *Poets Teaching Poets: Self and the World*, ed. Gregory Orr and Ellen Bryant Voigt. Ann Arbor: Universitiy of Michigan Press, 1996. 48-64.

Bowering, George. "Reaney's Region." *Approaches to the Work of James Reaney*, ed. Stan Dragland. Toronto: ECW Press, 1983. 1-14.

Bowering, Marilyn. *Visible Worlds*. London, UK: Flamingo/HarperCollins, 1999.

Braidotti, Rosi. *Nomadic Subjects: Embodiment and Sexual Difference in Contemporary Feminist Theory*. New York: Columbia University Press, 1994.

Brandt, Di. "& then everything goes bee." Broadside. De Leon White Gallery, 1999.

————. *Now You Care*. Toronto: Coach House Books, 2003.

————. *questions i asked my mother*. Winnipeg: Turnstone Press 1987.

————. "Souwestoegg on Winnipuzz: James Reaney's Winnipeg." The Winnipeg Connection: Writing Lives at Mid-Century, ed. Birk Sproxton. Winnipeg: Prairie Fire Press, 2006. 133-148.

————. *The Bridge, or, What's Wrong with Jim McKenzie?* Winnipeg: CMBC Publications, 1973.

Brentano, Clemens and Freiherr Ludwig Achim von Arnim, ed. *Des Knaben Wunderhorn. Alte Deutsche Lieder*. Studienausgabe in neun Bänden, hrsg. von Heinz Rölleke. Stuttgart, 1979.

————. *Freundschaftsbriefe*. Berlin: Eichborn, 1998.

Brundige, Lorraine F. and J. Douglas Rabb. "Phonicating Mother Earth: A Critique of David

Abram's *The Spell of the Sensuous: Perception and Language in a More-Than-Human World." Ayaangwaamizin: International Journal of Indigenous Philosophy* 1/2 (1997): 79-88.

Butler, Charles. *The Feminine Monarchie*. London: Oxford, 1609.

Butler, Margot Leigh. "Swarms in 'Bee Space.'" *West Coast Line* 35/2 (2001): 77-123.

Cairns, Douglas L. *Aidos: The Psychology and Ethics of Honour and Shame in Ancient Greek Literature*. Oxford: Clarendon Press, 1993.

Campbell, Maria. "Kookum Mariah and The Mennonite Mrs." *Journal of Mennonite Studies* 19 (2001): 9-12.

———, and Linda Griffiths. *The Book of Jessica: A Theatrical Transformation*. Toronto: Coach House Press, 1989.

Carr-Gom, Philip and Stephanie. *Druid Animal Oracle*. New York: Simon and Schuster, 1994.

Carson, Anne. *Plainwater*. Toronto: Vintage Canada, 2000.

Chatwin, Bruce. *Song Lines*. London: Vintage, 1982.

Chaunu, Pierre. *De Reformatie: De 16de-eeuwse Revolutie in de Kerk*, transl. into Dutch by S. Groenveld and S.B.J. Zilverberg. Netherlands: Uitgeverij Uniepers, 1986.

Chodorow, Nancy. "The Enemy Outside: Thoughts on the Psychodynamics of Extreme Violence with Special Attention to Men and Masculinity." *Masculinity Studies and Feminist Theory: New Directions*, ed. Judith Kegan Gardiner, New York: Columbia University Press, 2002. 235-60.

———. *The Reproduction of Mothering*. Berkeley: University of California Press, 1978.

Cixous, Hélène. "Castration or Decapitation?" trans. Annette Kuhn. *Signs* 7/1 (1981): 41-55.

———. *Stigmata: Escaping Texts*. New York, London: Routledge, 1998.

———. "The Laugh of the Medusa," trans. Keith and Paula Cohen. *New French Feminisms*, ed. Elaine Marks and Isabelle de Courtivron. Amherst: University of Massachusetts Press, 1980. 245-64.

———. *Three Steps on the Ladder of Writing*, trans. Sarah Cornell and Susan Sellers. New York: Columbia University Press, 1993.

Cixous, Hélène and Catherine Clement. *The Newly Born Woman*, trans. Betsy Wing, intro. Sandra M. Gilbert. Minneapolis: University of Minnesota Press, 1986.

Clasen, Claus-Peter. *Anabaptism: A Social History, 1525-1618. Switzerland, Austria, Moravia, and South and Central Germany*. Ithaca and London: Cornell University Press, 1972.

Cohen, Leonard. "The Genius." *The Spice Box of Earth*. Toronto: McClelland & Stewart, 1961. 78-79.

———. "Prayer of My Wild Grandfather." *Selected Poems 1956-1968*. Toronto: McClelland & Stewart, 1968.

Cole, Susan. "Lori Lansens." *NOW Magazine*, September 22-28, 2005. 92.

Conn, Marie A. *Noble Daughters: Unheralded Women in Western Christianity, 13th to 18th Centuries*. London and Westport, Connecticut: Greenwood Press, 2000.

Dahle, Sigrid. "Talking with Aganetha Dyck: A Ten Year Conversation." *Aganetha Dyck: The Extended Wedding Party*, cur. Shirley Madill. Winnipeg Art Gallery Catalogue, 1995. 8-14.

Damm, Kateri Akiwenzie. "We Belong To This Land: A View of 'Cultural Difference.'" *Journal of Canadian Studies* 31/3 (1996): 21-28.

Davidson, Arnold E. *Coyote Country: Fictions of the Canadian West.* Durham, NC: Duke University Press, 1994.

Delvoye, Wim. *Cloaca.* Antwerp, Belgium: Museum of Contemporary Art (MuHKA), 2000. Installation.

Derluguian, Georgi M. *Bourdieu's Secret Admirer in the Caucasus: A World-System Biography.* Chicago and London: University of Chicago Press, 2005.

Dickens, Charles. *Dombey and Son,* ed. Peter Fairclough, introd. Raymond Williams, illustr. Hablot K. Browne ("Phiz"). London: Penguin Books, 1970.

Dinnerstein, Dorothy. *The Mermaid and the Minotaur: Sexual Arrangements and Human Malaise.* New York: Harper and Row, 1976.

Dragland, Stan. "Afterword: Reaney's Relevance." *Approaches to the Work of James Reaney,* ed. Dragland. Toronto: ECW Press, 1983. 211-35.

Dupont-Bouchat, Marie-Sylvie. *Heksen in de Zuidelijke Nederlanden (16de-17de eeuw).* 1000 Brussel: Algemeen Rijksarchief, 1989.

Dyck, Aganetha. *The Extended Wedding Party.* Winnipeg Art Gallery, cur. Shirley Madill, 1995. Catalogue, ed. Madill, 1995.

———. *Working in the Dark,* cur. Clara Hargittay. Toronto: De Leon White Gallery, 1999.

Eliot, George. *Silas Marner,* with critical and biographical material by G. Robert Strange. New York: Harper's Modern Classics, 1961.

Engel, Marian. *Lunatic Villas.* Toronto: McClelland & Stewart, 1986.

Erpenbeck, Jenny. *Katzen haben sieben Leben.* Berlin: Eichborn, 2000; trans. Di Brandt, *Cats Have Nine Lives,* unpubl., 2004.

Ferguson, Ann. *Sexual Democracy: Women, Oppression, and Revolution.* Boulder, San Francisco, Oxford: Westview Press, 1991.

Ferry, Luc. *The New Ecological Order,* trans. Carol Volk. Chicago: University of Chicago Press, 1995.

Fiedler, Leslie. *Freaks: Myths and Images of the Secret Self.* New York: Anchor Books, 1993.

Frank, Alan. "Quantum Honeybees." *Discover* (1997): 80-87.

Gallant, Mavis. *The Pegnitz Junction.* London: Jonathan Cape, 1974.

Gaston, Bill. *Tall Lives.* Toronto: Macmillan, 1990.

Goertz, Hans-Jürgen. "The Confessional Heritage in its New Mold: What is Mennonite Self-Understanding Today?" *Mennonite Identity: Historical and Contemporary Perspectives.* Ed. Calvin Wall Redekop and Samuel J. Steiner. Institute for Anabaptist and Mennonite Studies. Lanham, New York, London: University Press of America, 1988. 1-12.

Gordon, Ellen Jean. *Myth and Metaphor in Adele Wiseman's Fiction: A Study in the Relationship Between Ancient Texts and Modern Narrative.* MA thesis. Montreal: Concordia University Press, 1992.

Goto, Hiromi. *Chorus of Mushrooms.* Edmonton: NeWest Press, 1994.

Goudeket, Maurice. *Close to Colette.* London: Secker & Warburg, 1957.

Gould, Nora. Unpubl. poetry manuscript, 2006.

Gowdy, Barbara. "Touching letters from a prison or a sanctuary." Review of Dorothy Livesay's *The Husband. The Globe and Mail*, Metro Edition, April 21, 1990. C17.

Grady, Wayne. *Toronto the Wild*. Toronto: McFarlane, Walter and Ross, 1995.

Graham, Phyllis. *The Care and Feeding of Twins*. New York: Harper, 1955.

Grass, Günter and Hélène Grass. Performance, *Des Knaben Wunderhorn*, by Clemens Brentano and Achim von Arnim, Berliner Ensemble, Berlin, September 2003.

Griffin, Donald. *Animal Thinking*. Cambridge, Mass.: Harvard University Press, 1984.

Griggs, Terry. "James Reaney's Giants." *Approaches to the Work of James Reaney*, ed. Dragland. 15-31.

Gunnars, Kristjana. "Personal and Professional Profile." *The Papers of Dorothy Livesay: A Research Tool*. University of Manitoba Libraries: Department of Archives and Special Collections, 1986. 5-23.ss

Halfe, Louise. *Blue Marrow*. Toronto: McClelland & Stewart, 1998.

Hancock, Geoffrey. "An Interview with Mavis Gallant." *Canadian Fiction* 28 (1978): 18-67.

Haraway, Donna J. *Modest_Witness@Second_Millennium. FemaleMan©_Meets_ Oncomouse™: Feminism and Technoscience*. New York, London: Routledge, 1997.

———. *Primate Visions: Gender, Race, and Nature in the World of Modern Science*. New York: Routledge, 1989.

———. *Simians, Cyborgs, and Women: The Reinvention of Nature*. New York: Routledge, 1991.

Harrison, Dick. *Unnamed Country: The Struggle for a Canadian Prairie Fiction*. Edmonton: University of Alberta Press, 1977.

Hatch, Ronald. "The Three Stages of Mavis Gallant's Short Fiction." *Canadian Fiction* 28 (1978): 92-114.

Heilbrun, Carolyn. "Afterword." *Daughters and Fathers*, ed. Boose and Flowers. 418-423.

Highway, Tomson. *Dry Lips Oughta Move to Kapuskasing*. Saskatoon: Fifth House, 1989.

———. *Kiss of the Fur Queen*. Toronto: Doubleday, 1998.

———. "Why Cree is the Funniest of All Languages." *Me Funny: A far-reaching exploration of the humour, wittiness and repartee dominant among the First Nations people of North America, as witnessed, experienced and created directly by themselves, and with the inclusion of outside but reputable sources necessarily familiar with the Indigenous sense of humour as seen from an objective perspective*, ed. Drew Hayden Taylor, Vancouver, Toronto, Berkeley: Douglas & McIntyre, 2005. 159-168.

Hirsch, Marianne. *The Mother/Daughter Plot: Narrative, Psychoanalysis, Feminism*. Bloomington and Indianapolis: Indiana University Press, 1989.

Hofsess, John. "Citations for Gallantry." *Books in Canada* 7 (1978): 21.

Hsia, R. Po-Chia, ed. with Introduction. *The German People and the Reformation*. Ithaca and London: Cornell University Press, 1988.

———, ed. *Calvinism and Religious Toleration in the Dutch Golden Age*. London: Cambridge University Press, 2002.

Huxley, Aldous. *The Doors of Perception and Heaven and Hell*, with foreword by J.G. Ballard; intro. by David Bradshaw. London: Flamingo, 1994.

Hyde, Lewis. *Trickster Makes this World: Mischief, Myth, and Art*. New York: North Point Press, 1998.

Irigaray, Luce. *je, tu, nous: Toward a Culture of Difference*, trans. Alison Martin. New York, London: Routledge, 1993.

———. *Sexes and Genealogies*, trans. Gillian C. Gill. New York: Columbia University Press, 1993.

Irvine, Dean, ed. *Archive for Our Times: Previously Uncollected and Unpublished Poems of Dorothy Livesay*. Vancouver: Arsenal Pulp Press, 1998.

Jahner, Elaine A. "Metalanguages." *Narrative Chance: Postmodern Discourse on Native American Indian Literatures*, ed. Gerald Vizenor. Norman and London: University of Oklahoma Press, 1993.

Jantzen, Grace M. *Foundations of Violence*. New York and London: Routledge, 2004.

Kaplan, Benjamin J. "'Dutch' religious tolerance: Celebration and revision." *Calvinism and Religious Toleration in the Dutch Golden Age*, ed. Hsia, 1988. 8-26.

Kaye, Francis W. "Prairie Witness to the Holocaust: Henry Kreisel, Adele Wiseman, and Rick Salutin." *Alberta* 2/2 (1990): 81-92.

Keefer, Janice Kulyk. *Reading Mavis Gallant*. Toronto: Oxford University Press, 1989.

Keller, Catherine. *Apocalypse Now and Then: A Feminist Guide to the End of the World*. Boston: Beacon Press, 1996.

Kemp, Penn. *Animus*. Caitlin Press (revised), 1999.

Kermode, Frank. *The Sense of an Ending: Studies in the Theory of Fiction*. New York: Oxford University Press, 1967.

King, Thomas. *Green Grass, Running Water*. Toronto: Houghton-Mifflin, 1993.

———. *Medicine River*. New York: Penguin, 1989.

Kleiman, Ed. "Crystal Pillow." *Alphabet* 1 (1960): 59-68.

Koestler, Arthur. *The Thirteenth Tribe: The Khazar Empire and its Heritage*. New York: Random House, 1976.

Kovel, Joel. *The Enemy of Nature: The End of Capitalism or the End of the World?* New York: Fernwood Publishing, 2002.

Kroetsch, Robert. "The Sad Phoenician." *Completed Field Notes*. Toronto: McClelland & Stewart, 1989. 57-72.

———. *The Stone Hammer Poems, 1960-1975*. Lantzville, BC: Oolichan Books, 1976.

Lansens, Lori. *The Girls*. Toronto: Vintage Canada, 2006.

Laurence, Margaret. *The Diviners*. Toronto: McClelland & Stewart, 1974.

Lehman, Wendy. "The Bees of Chiapas on the Path of Peace." *Rhubarb* 1/1 (1998): 9-10.

Leroy, Olaleye-Oruene, et al. "Yoruba Customs and Beliefs Pertaining to Twins." *Twin Research* 5/2 (2002): 132-6.

Lessing, Doris. *The Four-Gated City*. London: MacGibbon and Kee, 1969.

Levinas, Emmanuel. "Ethics as First Philosophy," trans. Sean Hand and Michael Temple. *The Levinas Reader,* ed. Sean Hand. Oxford, UK: Blackwell, 1994. 75-87.

Leviton, Richard. "Through the Shaman's Doorway: Dreaming the Universe with Fred Alan Wolf." *Yoga Journal* 105 (1992): 48-55, 102.

Lilburn, Tim. *Living in the World as if it Were Home: Essays.* Toronto: Cormorant Books, 1999.

Livesay, Dorothy. *The Husband: A Novella.* Charlottetown: Ragweed Press, 1990.

———. *Journey with My Selves: A Memoir 1909-1963.* Toronto/ Vancouver: Douglas & McIntyre, 1991.

———. *The Husband*: Novella Manuscripts: First Draft "A"; First Draft "B"; Draft Pages. The Papers of Dorothy Livesay, University of Manitoba Libraries, Department of Archives and Special Collections. MSS 37, Box 95, Folders 1-3. Quoted by permission of the Livesay Estate.

———. *The Unquiet Bed,* illustrated by Roy Kiyooka. Toronto: Ryerson, 1967.

Livingston, John A. *Rogue Primate: An Exploration of Human Domestication.* Toronto: Key Porter Books, 1994.

Loewen, Roy. *Family, Church and Market: A Mennonite Community in the Old and the New Worlds, 1850-1930.* Urbana and Chicago: University of Illinois Press, 1993.

Lykken, David. *The Antisocial Personalities.* New York: Lawrence Erlbaum Associates, 1995.

Lynes, Adrian, dir. *Fatal Attraction.* Paramount, 1988. Feature Film.

McCallum, Pamela. "'They cut him down': The Discourse of Race in Livesay's 'Day and Night.'" Unpublished essay, presented at the conference/festival, Wider Boundaries of Daring: The Modernist Impulse in Canadian Women's Poetry, co-hosted by Di Brandt and Barbara Godard, University of Windsor, Art Gallery of Windsor, and the Scarab Club, Detroit (as part of Detroit 300), September 2001.

MacLean, Gerald, Donna Landry, and Joseph P. Ward, eds. *The Country and the City Revisited.* London: Cambridge University Press, 1999. Introduction by MacLean, Landry and Ward. 1-23.

MacLean, Marie. *The Name of the Mother.* New York, London: Routledge, 1994.

MacLeod, Alistair. *The Lost Salt Gift of Blood.* Toronto: McClelland & Stewart, 1989 c.1976.

Madill, Shirley. "Introduction: Out of the Home and into the Hive." *Aganetha Dyck*: The Extended Wedding Party. Winnipeg Art Gallery Catalogue, 1995. 1.

Malka, Jeff. "Sephardic Genealogy." www.orthohelp.com/general/names.htm, 2005.

Mandal, Veronique. "River teems with toxins; fish tumours warn of cancer threat." *The Windsor Star*, September 8, 2001, A1.

Marchessault, Jovette. *White Pebbles in the Dark Forests.* Trans. Yvonne Klein. Vancouver: Talonbooks, 1990.

Martin, N.G., et al. "The power of the classical twin study." *Heredity* 40 (1978): 97-116.

Merchant, Carolyn. *The Death of Nature: Women, Ecology, and the Scientific Revolution,* New York: HarperCollins, 1980.

Miller, Alice. *For Your Own Good: Hidden Cruelty in Childrearing and the Roots of Violence,* trans. Hildegarde and Hunter Hannum. 4th ed. New York: Farrar, Straus and Giroux, 1983, 2002.

Mittelstaedt, Martin. "Blinded by Light," *The Globe and Mail*, Saturday, January 12, 2002, F1, F6.

Montgomery, Christina. "Wife's tale intrigues but ultimately disappoints." Review of Dorothy Livesay's *The Husband*. *The Vancouver Sun*, Saturday, June 2, 1990. D20.

Moore, Michael. *Bowling for Columbine*. MGM, 2002, 2003.

Mouré, Erin. *Furious*. Toronto: Anansi, 1988.

Narby, Jeremy. *The Cosmic Serpent: DNA and the Origins of Knowledge*. New York: Jeremy P Tarcher/Putnam, 1998.

Neimark, Jill. "Nature's Clones." *Psychology Today*, 30/4 (August 1997): 36-54, 64, 69: Photographic illustr. Roderick Angle.

Nichol, bp. "Letter re James Reaney." *Open Letter* 2/6 (1973): 5-7.

Nollman, Jim. *Spiritual Ecology: A Guide for Reconnecting with Nature*. New York: Bantam Books, 1990.

Novotny, Pamela Patrick. *The Joy of Twins and Other Multiple Births: Having, Raising, and Loving Babies Who Arrive in Groups*. New York: Crown Books, 1988.

O'Brien, Mary. *The Politics of Reproduction*. Boston: Routledge and Kegan Paul, 1983.

Pacey, Desmond. Commentary on *The Husband*, n.d. The Papers of Dorothy Livesay, MSS 37, Box 95, Folder 1.

Panofsky, Ruth. *Adele Wiseman: An Annotated Bibliography*. ECW Press, 1992.

The Papers of Dorothy Livesay: A Research Tool. Compiled by the Staff of The Department of Archives and Special Collections, University of Manitoba Libraries, 1986.

Pemberton III, John, and John Picton, ed. *Ibeji: The Cult of Yoruba Twins*. Milan: Five Continents Editions, 2003.

Plath, Sylvia. *Ariel*. New York: Harper and Row, 1965.

Popinoe, David. "Modern Marriage: Revising the Cultural Script." *The Gendered Society Reader*, ed. Michael S. Kimmel, with Amy Aronson. Oxford University Press, 2000. 151-166.

Pratt, David. "Consciousness, Causality, and Quantum Physics." *Journal of Scientific Exploration* 11/1 (1997): 69-78.

Prechtel, Martín. *Secrets of the Talking Jaguar: Memoirs from the Living Heart of a Mayan Village*. New York: Putnam, 1999.

———. *The Disobedience of Daughter of the Sun: Ecstasy and Time*. Cambridge, Mass: Yellow Moon Press, 2001.

Pritchard, William H. "*The Pegnitz Junction*." *New York Times Book Review* (24 June 1973): 4.

Read, Donna. *The Burning Times*. Montreal: NFB, 1990. Documentary film.

Reaney, James. *Colours in the Dark*. Vancouver: Talonplays/Macmillan, 1969.

———. "Introduction." *Alphabet* 1 (1960): 1-3.

———. "James Reaney's Canada: The Poetic Rubbings of a Defensive Driver." *Maclean's Magazine*, Dec. 17, 1971. 18, 46, 51.

———. "A Message to Winnipeg." *Selected Longer Poems*, ed. Germaine Warkentin. Erin, Ont: Porcépic, 1977. 30-38.

———. *The Sun and the Moon*, in *The Killdeer and Other Plays*. Toronto: Macmillan, 1962. 93-174.

Redekop, Magdalene. *Mothers and Other Clowns: The Stories of Alice Munro*. London and New York: Routledge, 1992.

Reed, Evelyn. *Women's Evolution: From Matriarchal Clan to Patriarchal Family*. New York, London, Montreal, Sydney: Pathfinder, 1975.

Relke, Diana. *Greenwor(l)ds: Ecological Readings of Canadian Women's Poetry*. Calgary: University of Calgary Press, 1999.

Rich, Adrienne. *Of Woman Born: Motherhood as Experience and Institution*. Tenth Anniversary Edition. New York and London: W.W. Norton. 1986.

Richler, Mordecai. *The Apprenticeship of Duddy Kravitz*. Toronto: Emblem Editions, 2001. c. 1959.

Rooke, Leon. *A Good Baby*. Toronto: McClelland & Stewart, 1989.

Roper, Lyndal. *Oedipus and the Devil: Witchcraft, Sexuality and Religion in Early Modern Europe*. London: Routledge, 1994.

Ross, Ian. *Joe from Winnipeg*. Winnipeg: J. Gordon Shillingford Publishing, 1998.

Rothman, Barbara. *Genetic Maps and Human Imaginations: The Limits of Science in Understanding Who We Are*. New York and London: W.W. Norton, 1998.

Ruddick, Sara. "Maternal Thinking." *Rethinking the Family,* ed. B. Thorne and M. Yalom. New York and London: Longman, 1982.

Rush, Florence. *The Best Kept Secret: Sexual Abuse of Children*. Englewood Cliffs: Prentice, 1980.

Sabatini, Sandra. *Making Babies: Infants in Canadian Fiction*. Waterloo: Wilfrid Laurier Press, 2003.

Scarr, Sandra and Richard A. Weinberg. "IQ Test Performances of Black Children Adopted by White Families." *American Psychologist* 31 (1976): 726-39.

Schoenberg, Shira. "Ashkenazim." *Jewish Virtual Library*, www.us-israel.org/jsource/Judaism/Ashkenazism.html, 2004.

Schroeder, William. *The Bergthal Colony*, revised edition. Winnipeg: **CMBC** Publications, 1986.

Schwarts, Hillel. *The Culture of the Copy: Striking Likenesses, Unreasonable Facsimiles*. New York: Zone Books, 1996.

Scofield, Gregory. "Oskan-Acimowina (Bone Stories)." *Prairie Fire: First Voices, First Words,* ed. Thomas King, 22/3 (2001): 114.

Sedgwick, Eve Kasofsky. "Paranoid Reading and Reparative Reading; or, You're So Paranoid, You Probably Think This Introduction Is about You." *Touching Feeling: Affect, Pedagogy, Performativity*. Durham and London: Duke University Press, 2003. Ch. 4, 123-152.

Seeley, Thomas D. *The Wisdom of the Hive: The Social Physiology of Honey Bee Colonies.* Cambridge, Mass., London: Harvard University Press, 1995.

Segal, Nancy L. "MZ or DZ? Not even their hairdresser knows for sure," *Journal of Forensic Sciences* 31 (1986): 10-11.

Shakespeare, William. *King Lear*, ed. Claire McEachern. New York: Pearson/Longman, 2005.

Shaw, Sylvie. "Reclaiming the Eco-Erotic." Paper. For the Love of Nature? Interdisciplinary Conference, Findhorn, Scotland, hosted by the Centre for Human Ecology, University of Edinburgh, Scotland, July 1998. Published as "Reclaiming the Eco-Erotic: Celebrating the Body and the Earth Ecotheology." *The Journal of Religion, Nature and the Environment* 8/1 (2003): 85-99.

Sheldrake, Rupert. *Dogs That Know When Their Owners Are Coming Home, and Other Unexplained Powers of Animals.* New York & London: Crown Publishers, 1999.

Sheldrake, Rupert. www.sheldrake/org/homepage.html

Shell, Marc. *Children of the Earth: Literature, Politics and Nationhood.* New York and Oxford: Oxford University Press, 1993.

Sherman, Kenneth. "*Crackpot*: A Lurianic Myth." *Waves* 2/1 (1974): 4-11.

Shields, Carol. *The Republic of Love.* Toronto: Viking, 1994.

Siemerling, Winnfried. *Writing Ethnicity: Cross-Cultural Consciousness in Canadian and Quebecois Literature.* Toronto: ECW, 1996.

Simons, Sarah. *Telling the Bees: Belief, Knowledge & Hypersymbolic Cognition.* Los Angeles: Museum of Jurassic Technology Leaflet. n.d.

Snyder, Arnold C. and Linda A. Huebert Hecht, ed. *Profiles of Anabaptist Women: Sixteenth-Century Reforming Pioneers.* Waterloo, Ontario: Canadian Corporation for Studies in Religion, Wilfrid Laurier Press, 1996. Vol. 3.

Snyder, Gary. *The Practice of the Wild.* San Francisco: North Point Press, 1990.

Sollors, Werner. *Beyond Ethnicity: Consent and Dissent in American Culture.* New York: Oxford University Press, 1986.

Stallybrass, Peter and Allon White. *The Politics and Poetics of Transgression.* New York: Cornell University Press. 1993.

Stayer, James. *The German Peasants' War and Anabaptist Community of Goods.* Montreal, Kingston, London, Buffalo: McGill-Queen's University Press, 1991.

Steiner, George. *Martin Heidegger.* Chicago: University of Chicago Press, 1989.

Stern, Daniel. *Diary of a Baby.* 1990. New York: Basic Books, 1998.

Stevens, Peter. *Dorothy Livesay: Patterns in a Poetic Life.* Toronto: ECW Press, 1992.

ten Kortenaar, Neil. "The Trick of Divining a Postcolonial Canadian Identity: Margaret Laurence Between Race and Nation." *Canadian Literature* 149: *Postcolonial Identities* (1996): 11-34.

The Ecologist 01/07/03, available at www.theecologist.org/archive.asp

Toews, Miriam. *A Complicated Kindness.* Toronto: A.A. Knopf, 2004.

———, *Summer of My Amazing Luck.* Winnipeg: Turnstone Press, 1996.

Tostevin, Lola Lemire. "Fred Wah: In Conversation." *Subject to Criticism*. Stratford: Mercury Press, 1995. 51-72.

Urry, James. "Growing up with Cities: The Mennonite Experience in Imperial Russia and the Early Soviet Union." *Journal of Mennonite Studies* 20 (2002): 123-154.

van Braght, Thieleman J. *The Bloody Theater or Martyrs Mirror of the Defenseless Christians Who Baptized Only Upon Confession of Faith, and Who Suffered and Died for the Testimony of Jesus, Their Saviour, From the Time of Christ to the Year A.D. 1660, Compiled from Various Authentic Chronicles, Memorials, and Testimonies*. Illustr. with engravings by Jan van Luykens. Trans. into German by Joseph F. Sohm, 1748-49. Trans. into English from Dutch by Historical Pennsylvania: Mennonite Publishing House, 1964. 7th Ed.

Wah, Fred. *Faking It: Poetics & Hybridity. Critical Writing 1984-1999*. Edmonton: NeWest Press, 2000.

Ward, Donald. *The Divine Twins: An Indo-European Myth in Germanic Tradition*. Berkeley and Los Angeles: University of California Press, 1968.

Wasney, Tricia. "Making Way: Loss and Transformation in Winnipeg's Urban Landscape—A Miscellaneous Photo Album." *The Winnipeg Connection: Writing Lives at Mid-Century*, ed. Birk Sproxton. Winnipeg: Prairie Fire Press, 2006. 15-41.

Weaver, J. Denny. *Becoming Anabaptist: The Origin and Significance of Sixteenth-Century Anabaptism*. Scottdale, Pennsylvania, Kitchener, Ontario: Herald Press, 1987.

Webb, Phyllis. *Water and Light. Ghazals and Antighazals*. Toronto: Coach House, 1984.

Wiebe, Armin. *The Salvation of Yasch Siemens*. Winnipeg: Turnstone Press, 1984.

Wiebe, Rudy. *Sweeter Than All the World*. Toronto: Vintage, 2002.

Willeford, William. *The Fool and His Sceptre: A Study in Clowns and Jesters and Their Audience*. Evanston, IL: Northwestern University Press, 1969.

Wilson, Elizabeth. "Not in This House: Incest, Denial, and Doubt in the White Middle Class Family." *The Yale Journal of Criticism* 8/1 (1995): 35-58.

Winterson, Jeanette. *Lighthousekeeping*. Orlando, FL.: Harcourt, 2004.

Wisechild, Louise M., *She Who Was Lost Is Remembered: Healing from Incest through Creativity*. Seattle, WA: Seal Books, 1991.

Wiseman, Adele. "A Brief Anatomy of an Honest Attempt at a Pithy Statement about the Impact of the Manitoba Environment on my Development as an Artist." *Mosaic* [Manitoba Centennial Issue] 3/3 (1970): 98-106.

———. *Crackpot*, intro. Margaret Laurence. Toronto: McClelland & Stewart, 1978.

Woodcock, George. "Memory, Imagination, Artifice: The Late Short Fiction of Mavis Gallant." *Canadian Fiction* 28 (1978): 74-91.

Wright, Lawrence. "Double mystery," *The New Yorker* (7 Aug 1995): 45-62.

Yoshikawa, Mako. "The New Face of Incest: Race, Class, and the Controversy over Kathryn Harrison's *The Kiss*." *Incest and the Literary Imagination*, ed. Elizabeth Barnes. Gainesville, Tallahassee, Tampa, et al: University of Florida Press, 2002. 358-376.

Zacharias, Peter D. *Reinland: An Experience in Community*. Reinland, Manitoba: Reinland Centennial Committee, Manitoba, 1976.

Index

Russia, 6, 23, 45, 82-83, 109-110, 122-124, 205

Ryerson Press, 40

S

Sabatini, Sandra: *Making Babies*, 62-64

Sacred Hoop, The (Allen), 217

Sad Phoenician, The (Kroetsch), 58, 60

Salutin, Rick, 36

Salvation of Yasch Siemens, The (A. Wiebe), 25

Sara, 91

Sarnia, 145

Scarfe, Eunice, 98, 219

Scarr, Sandra, 161

Schalks, Arnold, 99

Scheier, Libby, 36

Schoenberg, Shira, 122

Schroeder, William, 5-6

Schwartz, Hillel, 165-166, 169

Schwarzenegger, Arnold, 97

Scofield, Gregory: "Oskan-Acimowina (Bone Stories)," 85, 237

Scotland, 9, 81

Scott, Gail, 39

Sedgwick, Eve, 136

Seed Catalogue (Kroetsch), 143

Seeley, Thomas, 188-189

Selected Longer Poems (Reaney), 135, 138, 145-146

Sephardic Genealogy (Malka), 124

Sexes and Genealogies (Irigaray), 217

Shakespeare, William, 55, 58, 68, 113, 134, 208: *Julius Caesar*, 207; *King Lear*, 58-59, 61; *A Midsummer Night's Dream*, 207

Shattered Self, The (Baldi), 151, 154-155, 159, 161, 163, 217

Sheldrake, Rupert, 69, 190-191: *Dogs That Know when their Owners are Coming Home and Other Unexplained Powers of Animals*, 158-159

Shell, Marc: *Children of the Earth*, 131

Sherman, Kenneth, 29, 36

Shields, Carol, 34, 70, 86, 140: *The Republic of Love*, 24-25, 221; *The Stone Diaries*, 25

Shipman, Barbara, 189-190

Siemerling, Winfried: *Writing Ethnicity*, 130

Silas Marner (Eliot), 65

Simons, Sarah, 180-181, 185

Slovenia, 96, 106

Snyder, Arnold: *Profiles of Anabaptist Women*, 117

Snyder, Gary, 173

Solis and Aldegraver: "De Anabaptistengemeente," 120-121

Sollors, Werner: Beyond Ethnicity, 129-130

Song Lines (Chatwin), 127

Sophocles, 129

South America, 218

South Bend, 118

Spain, 115, 122

Spears, Heather: "Newborn twins," 157

Spell of the Sensuous, The (Abram), 126-128

Spence, Sheila, 175

Spengler, Oswald, 128

Spirit of Utopia (Bloch), 128-129

Sproxton, Birk, 24, 141: *The Winnipeg Connection*, 221

Stallybrass, Peter, 33

Stayer, James, 114, 116

Steiner, George, 128-129, 207, 218

Stein, Gertrude, 102

St. Norbert, 186

Stone Diaries, The (Shields), 25

Stone Hammer (Kroetsch), 143

Suit of Nettles, A (Reaney), 140

Summer of My Amazing Luck (Toews), 221

Sun and the Moon, The (Reaney), 133, 135

Survivors in Search of a Voice (Amesbury), 178

Suzanne, 103

"Swarms in Bee Space" (M.L. Butler), 182

Other Works by Di Brandt

Speaking of Power: The Poetry of Di Brandt, ed. Tanis McDonald. Waterloo: Wilfrid Laurier University Press, 2006.

Re:Generations: Canadian Women Poets in Conversation, ed. Di Brandt & Barbara Godard. Windsor: Black Moss Press, 2005.

Now you Care. Toronto: Coach House Books, 2003.

Dancing Naked: Narrative Strategies for Writing Across Centuries. Toronto: Mercury Press, 1996.

Jerusalem, beloved. Winnipeg: Turnstone Press, 1995.

Wild Mother Dancing: Maternal Narrative in Canadian Literature. Winnipeg: University of Manitoba Press, 1993.

mother, not mother. Toronto: Mercury Press, 1992.

Agnes in the sky. Winnipeg: Turnstone Press, 1990.

questions I asked my mother. Winnipeg: Turnstone Press, 1987.

Di Brandt grew up in Reinland, a traditionalist Mennonite farming village in southern Manitoba, and has lived in Winnipeg, Edmonton, Toronto, Windsor and Berlin. Brandt is an accomplished poet and critic, and taught Canadian Literature and Creative Writing at the Universities of Winnipeg, Manitoba, Alberta, Windsor. She has lectured and performed extensively in Europe, the US, Asia, the Middle East and South America. Since 2005, she has held a Canada Research Chair in English at Brandon University. Brandt's poetry has been adapted for television, radio, film, video, installation, and dance, and music. Brandt has received numerous poetry awards, including the CAA National Poetry Prize, the McNally Robinson Book of the Year Award and the Gerald Lampert Award. Her poetry has twice been short-listed for the Governor General's Award for Poetry, as well as the Commonwealth Poetry Prize, the Trillium Ontario Book of the Year Award and the Griffin Poetry Prize. Brandt is a former poetry editor of *Contemporary Verse 2* and *Prairie Fire*. Her website address is www.dibrandt.ca.